WI

HOW TO CHEAT
AT
Organizing

HOW TO CHEAT
AT
Organizing

Quick, Clutter-Clobbering
Ways to Simplify Your Life

JEFF BREDENBERG

The Taunton Press

648.8
BRE

The Taunton Press
Inspiration for hands-on living®

The Taunton Press, Inc., 63 South Main Street,
PO Box 5506, Newtown, CT 06470-5506
e-mail: tp@taunton.com

Editor: Erica Sanders-Foege
Copy editor: Betty Christiansen
Indexer: Lynda Stannard
Jacket/Cover design: Michael Amaditz
Interior design: Amy Griffin, Ralph Fowler / rlf design
Layout: Ralph Fowler / rlf design
Illustrator: Matt Foster

Library of Congress Cataloging-in-Publication Data
Bredenberg, Jeff.
How to cheat at organizing : quick, clutter-clobbering ways to simplify
   your life / Jeff Bredenberg.
      293 p. cm.
   Includes bibliographical references and index.
   ISBN 978-1-56158-940-1 (alk. paper)
   1. Storage in the home. I. Title.

TX309.B74 2008
648'.8--dc22

                    2007031063

Printed in the United States of America
10 9 8 7 6 5 4 3 2 1

The following manufacturers/names appearing in *How to Cheat at Organizing* are trademarks:
AeroBed®, AeroBeds®, Amazon.com℠, American Woodmark™, Barbie®, BlackBerry®, California Closets®,
The Container Store®, Design Yourself Interiors™, Diet Coke®, Eagle Creek®, Ebates.com℠, eBay℠,
Edmunds.com℠, EZcarry™ handles, *Fine Cooking*®, FoodSaver®, Freedom Financial Network℠,
FreshDirect®, Frisbee®, Gerber®, G.I. Joe®, Gmail℠, Google™, GPS®, Hoboken Eddie's®, Holy Cow™,
Honda®, Hotmail℠, Hotspot®, HouseWall®, H&R Block℠, Hummel®, iPod™, Jenny Craig®, Kar's®, KFC®,
Lego®, MapQuest℠, Marie's®, Metro®, Microplane®, Microsoft® myShape™, NorthStar Moving Company℠,
Outlook®, Pendaflex®, Pritikin Longevity Center℠ and Spa, Purell®, Purseket®, Rand McNally®, Rolodex™,
Salvation Army℠, Seal-a-Meal®, Short Message Service℠, Shout®, Silly Putty®, Skippy® Super Chunk®,
Smart Auto Management (SAM)℠, Sonic Solutions®, Starbucks®, Sue Bee®, TiVo®, TurboTax®,
Upromise.com℠, VCR Plus+®, Weber®, WeGo®, Windows® Live Local, Yahoo℠

For Paul Bredenberg,

my dad, who never cheated in his life—

so I had to learn on my own

Acknowledgments

The author is grateful to the following sources for their generous contribution of time and ideas:

Michelle Anton, author of *Weekend Entrepreneur*, based in Los Angeles, California.

Jennifer Armentrout, test kitchen manager and recipe editor for *Fine Cooking* magazine, based in Newtown, Connecticut.

Silvia Bianco, chef and author, based in Ridgefield, Connecticut.

Laurie Borman, editorial director at Rand McNally, Skokie, Illinois.

Dorothy Breininger, professional organizer and coauthor of *The Senior Organizer,* based in Canoga Park, California.

Bobbie Zucker Bryson, coauthor of *Collectibles for the Kitchen, Bath & Beyond,* based in Westchester, New York.

Denise Caron-Quinn, professional organizer, New York, New York.

Lisa Chavis, pharmacist for Medco Health Solutions, Franklin Lakes, New Jersey.

Missy Cohen-Fyffe, proprietor of www.cleanshipper.com, Pelham, New Hampshire.

Raymond Crowel, Ph.D., psychologist, vice president of mental health and substance abuse services at the National Mental Health Association, based in Alexandria, Virginia.

Fred Cyprys, managing partner, Cypress Financial Consultants, based in Rochester, New York.

Michael Dagen, founder and CEO of the HouseWall garage storage systems company, Miami, Florida.

Jessie Danninger, CPA for the Rosen Law Firm, based in Raleigh, North Carolina.

Melody Davidson, cofounder of Design Yourself Interiors in Prairie Village, Kansas.

Connie Edwards, director of design, American Woodmark Corp., based in Winchester, Virginia.

Adam Fingerman, organizing software expert, Sonic Solutions, of Santa Clara, California.

Susan Fletcher, Ph.D., psychologist and author of *Parenting in the Smart Zone,* based in Plano, Texas.

Barb Friedman, professional organizer, Milwaukee, Wisconsin.

Michael Fritsch, a.k.a. "the Gizmo Ph.D.," CEO of Prometheus Performance Systems, based in Austin, Texas.

Pauline Frommer, creator of Pauline Frommer's Travel Guides, New York, New York.

John Gabaldon, home chef and representative for www.cooking.com, based in Los Angeles, California.

Judi Gallagher, chef, based in Sarasota, Florida.

Lynne Glassman, Washington, D.C., image consultant, "closet surgeon," and proprietor of www.doctorofdress.com.

Maria Gracia, professional organizer and author of *Finally Organized, Finally Free,* based in Watertown, Wisconsin.

Guido Groeschel, cofounder of Sherpa Performance Guides, based in San Diego, California.

Elizabeth Hagen, professional organizer and author of the book *Organize with Confidence,* based in Sioux Falls, South Dakota.

Art Jacobsen, Tucson, Arizona–based product manager for Smart Auto Management, Environmental Systems Products Holdings.

Scott James, head chef at the restaurant 115 Midtowne, in Raleigh, North Carolina.

Reecanne Joeckel, partner in advertising and public relations company BrandEra, based in Fort Worth, Texas.

Ingrid Johnson, professor of textiles at the Fashion Institute of Technology, New York, New York.

Ram Katalan, president of NorthStar Moving Company, Chatsworth, California.

Ali Kaufman, professional organizer, Boca Raton, Florida.

Misha Keefe, president of the organizing company Misha K, based in Washington, D.C.

Jackie Keller, nutrition and health coach, based in Los Angeles, California.

Ron Knaus, D.O., sports medicine physician and productivity coach, Clearwater, Florida.

Dana Korey, professional organizer in Del Mar, California.

Linda Kruger, executive director of the Collector's Information Bureau, based in Grundy Center, Iowa.

Michael Laimo, staffer at the sportswear wholesaler Mercury Beach-Maid, New York, New York, and a horror novelist as well.

Laura Leist, organization and productivity consultant, Mill Creek, Washington.

Allyson Lewis, author of *The Seven Minute Difference: Small Steps to Big Changes,* based in Jonesboro, Arkansas.

Janet Luhrs, author and proprietor of www.simpleliving.com, based in Seattle, Washington.

Sharon Mann, Bellmore, New York–based organizational expert for the filing supplies company Pendaflex.

Karol McGuire, public relations professional, Colorado Springs, Colorado.

Tiffany Mock, organizing consultant, San Francisco, California.

Birgit Mueller, Emmy Award–winning costume designer for television, Los Angeles, California.

Michelle Neujahr, speaker and author on families and excellence, Yarmouth, Maine.

Brent Newbold, CFO, Holy Cow cleaning products company, Rocklin, California.

Jeff Novick, director of nutrition for the Pritikin Longevity Center and Spa, Aventura, Florida.

Kurt Owen, senior director of marketing for AeroBeds, Schaumburg, Illinois.

L. Jo Parrish, vice president of institutional advancement for the Society for Women's Health Research, based in Washington, D.C.

Lisa Peck, Minneapolis, Minnesota, interior designer.

Shayla Price, college student from Thibodaux, Louisiana.

Marcia Ramsland, a.k.a. "The Organizing Pro," San Diego, California.

Laura Ray, professional organizer, Atlanta, Georgia.

Philip Reed, senior consumer advice editor for Edmunds.com, Santa Monica, California.

Paul Reyes, pharmacist for Medco Health Solutions, [location].

Eva Rosenberg, a tax expert based in Northridge, California.

Erika Salloux, personal and business organizer, Cambridge, Massachusetts.

Janine Sarna-Jones, professional organizer, New York, New York.

Pat Saso, family therapist, Milpitas, California.

Ginny Snook Scott, vice president and organization expert for California Closets, based in San Rafael, California.

Paul Shrater, vice president and cofounder of www.minimus.biz, Newbury Park, California.

Scott Simmonds, insurance consultant, Saco, Maine.

Patrick Snow, professional speaker and author of *Creating Your Own Destiny*, based in Bainbridge Island, Washington.

Susan Sommers, author and fashion coach, New York, New York.

Rafi Spero, cofounder of NeatReceipts, Philadelphia, Pennsylvania.

Bobette Stott, clothing designer, Los Angeles, California.

Brad Stroh, co-CEO of Freedom Financial Network, based in San Mateo, California.

Lisa Talamini, R.D., chief nutritionist and program director for Jenny Craig, based in Carlsbad, California.

Bill Wagner, author of *The Entrepreneur Next Door*, Westlake Village, California.

Vanessa Wakeman, owner of the Wakeman Agency, an event planning and public relations firm based in New York, New York.

Louise Wannier, CEO of myShape, Inc. (www.myshape.com), based in Altadena, California.

Gillian Wells, professional organizer, New York, New York.

Dali Wiederhoft, public relations executive, based in Reno, Nevada.

Mona Williams, vice president of buying at The Container Store, based in Coppell, Texas.

Stephanie Worrell, public relations executive for Peyron & Associates in Boise, Idaho.

The author is also grateful for the contributions of executive editor Pam Hoenig, editor Erica Sanders-Foege, assistant editor Katie Benoit, the rest of the staff at The Taunton Press, and agent Linda Konner.

Contents

Introduction
Let's Organize Just Enough

If you're a persnickety perfectionist, then you'd better drop this book and run, because some of the ideas here will give you a heart attack. On the other hand, if you're looking for super-easy ways to organize your life, you're in the right place. *How to Cheat at Organizing* is about creating enough order that you'll be happy with your environment—but taking shortcuts every chance you get.

If you have any doubts about this approach, you will want to know this revealing statistic: Organizing experts say that if a task takes you 10 hours to complete, you get 90 percent of it done *in the first 5 hours*. The second 5 hours are devoted to futzing with the spit-and-polish details. Many people fail at organizing their homes because 100 percent perfection is too intimidating a goal. So why not shoot for getting 90 percent organized? Compared to utter chaos, that's still pretty darned good—and you get there in half the time!

How exactly do you cheat at organizing? It means setting aside myths, misconceptions, and unreasonable traditions. It means learning clever tricks and shortcuts. It means being brave enough to walk away from some activities that are no longer relevant to your life. It means snapping up innovative products and technology that save you time and money. And it means getting help from family, friends, and professionals. *How to Cheat at Organizing* is jam-packed with the details you need in order to succeed with these tactics.

In this book, you will learn some radical ways to simplify your life—ignoring supermarket coupons, managing your finances without a budget, and giving up your formal living room, for instance. You'll also find out about the world's simplest—and highly effective—weight-loss diet; how to stock your home with hardworking furniture; how to whip a wanton clothes closet into shape; how to slash your grocery-shopping time and organize your kitchen; how to dig out from under a mountain of e-mail; and how to get your roasting turkey to page you when it's done to perfection. And because we enjoy a good laugh along with good advice, you'll hear about the guy who snacks on baby food, about the company that sends single-serving condiments into space, and about the cure for an Unwanted Gift Headache (UGH).

Cheaters at organizing are big fans of time- and money-saving devices. In these pages, experts will reveal to you what gadgets they pack when they hit the road, how to create instant bedding for overnight guests, the world's greatest food grater, and a clever gizmo that will turn the car maintenance industry on its ear.

Speaking of products, I want to make a few points about the products mentioned in *How to Cheat at Organizing.* I don't believe in buying glitzy new stuff just to show off. If I mention a product, it's because I believe it more than pays for itself. In some cases, it's impossible to give specific advice without mentioning brand names. But there is no influence behind these mentions—I accepted no freebies while researching this book.

As with the companion book *How to Cheat at Cleaning,* you will see that I quote scores of sources in this book. Many are experts, and some are regular folks with great ideas. Now that you are in the "How to Cheat" fold, you might want to share your own cheatin' ideas with readers. So feel free to write to me in care of this publisher, or stop in at www.howtocheatbooks.com or www.jeffbreden berg.com.

In closing, I want to emphasize that I'm not your conscience, and I'm not your mother. You will find tons of advice here that will make your life better—but if you encounter a suggestion that doesn't work for you, pass right on to the next item. The world is full enough of guilt and unreasonable demands, and I don't intend to add to them. I want you to enjoy your new, organized-just-enough life—guilt free!

—*Jeff Bredenberg*

Chapter One

Taking the Leap

Simplify—and Sometimes Let Go

WHEN YOU think about organizing your home, you get dizzy and your eyes roll back into your head. You envision a world of school-marmish rules. An environment where you can't lay a paperback book down on the coffee table without setting off an alarm. A house where robotlike family members reorder the cans in the pantry every hour on the hour. I know you fret about these things—not because I am psychic, but simply because you are reading a book called *How to Cheat at Organizing*. You want to have an orderly home you can be proud of—but you don't want to work too hard for it.

Lucky you. When you cheat at organizing, the physical work is actually minimal. The big challenge is mental. If you shake loose a few ingrained habits and attitudes, the battle is won. In the chapters that follow, we will examine specific shortcuts for organizing your living areas, clothing, kitchen, office, family, finances, automobile, and more. Here, we're going to talk about the broad strokes—some ways of thinking about organizing and some simple techniques that will turn you into a cheater of the highest order, as they say.

Keep it simple. Don't make a new organizational system any more complex than is absolutely necessary. If you have to dive into minutiae every time you use the new system, you're going to dread using it, and things will drift back into disorder. Filing is an example. Start out with one folder marked "Insurance." Later, you can break that folder down into subcategories such as "Insurance—Car," "Insurance—Home," and "Insurance—Medical"—but only if that folder gets so bulky that you can't find the papers you need.

Keep it going. Organization is an ongoing process, not a finite project. Clustering all of the soup cans on one pantry shelf is not enough. When you buy more soup, those new cans have to go in the same spot, and you have to keep those pesky little cans of beans

The 8-Point Storage Master's Credo

1. Orderly, functional storage in the home is the foundation for an orderly, functional home.

2. Making organizational improvements—even small ones—makes my life better, both immediately and long term.

3. The more often I use an item, the handier it should be.

4. Like things should be stored together so they can be found easily.

5. I will always leave a little room for expansion. If I need two containers, I will buy three. If I rearrange the CD shelf, I will leave 20 percent empty space for future acquisitions.

6. If I stick to one brand of containers, they will be compatible and easier to manage.

7. Storing a daily-use item does not mean making it inaccessible. Whatever is out of sight and out of mind will not get used, and I'll end up buying another one.

8. I will quickly review stored items once a year to see that they're still organized and to decide whether they're still worth keeping.

from getting mixed in. So every time you bring order to a part of your home, don't just stand back and admire—envision how you're going to keep it that way.

Memorize the S's. The S4 technique is a simple four-step approach to bringing order to any chaotic corner of your home, whether it's as small as a junk drawer or as big as the garage. This is a strategy you will use again and again, so memorize the four S's, write them in ink on the tips of your sneakers, or laminate the License to Cheat (found on p. 8) and stick it in your wallet. You need the S4 technique mentally at your fingertips just the way you need your car keys and cell phone. Here's how it works:

STRIP: Start by stripping every object out of the space. While you have that drawer, shelf, or room empty, give it a quick cleaning. It will be years before you see it free and clear again.

SCRAP: Throw away everything that's out of date, in poor repair, or otherwise nonfunctional.

SORT: Cluster like things together so they will be easy to find in the future. In the bathroom, for instance, extra toothbrushes, toothpaste, and dental floss are a natural grouping.

STORE: Find a container that's the right size for each group of objects and find the right home for that container, keeping in mind how often you need to use the stuff inside.

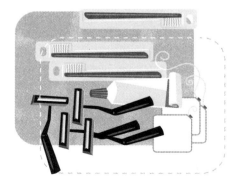

Consider proximity. Store things in your home close to the spot where they are used. The CD rack should be right next to your stereo, for instance, and the magazine holder goes beside the easy chair where you do most of your reading. This way, objects are more likely to be put away after they have been used.

A Memo to Annoying Marketing Folks

Hi, it's me—the fellow you keep calling when he's busy cooking dinner. Sorry if I was rude the first time. The other 20,000 times, you deserved it. You see, I have this theory that part of being organized means removing distractions and annoyances from my life. At the moment, I am working on intrusive or deceptive marketing. Just so you'll know, I have adopted the points below. I'm hoping you'll get the message and treat the public with respect for a change.

- Whenever I pick up the telephone and hear a recorded message, I will hang up the phone.

- Doesn't matter if it's a company or candidate I care about.

- Just because I have done business with you in the past, that's not permission to call me at home. If you call, you'll get an earful.

- If you do call me at home, you have 5 seconds to get to the bottom line. If you don't, I will hang up.

- I am not fooled by "surveys" I'm asked to fill out when they arrive in the mail. This is marketing meant to make me feel like I am joining a cause. It's junk.

- If you send me junk mail that's trying to masquerade as a bill or a check, I will never do business with your company.

- And quit sending those e-mails. I don't know about you, but none of my body parts needs to be enlarged.

—JB

P.S. I'm sharing this with a couple of close friends, hoping they follow suit.

Celebrate letting go. In industrialized countries, we put way too much emphasis on acquiring things and way too little emphasis on getting rid of things and resisting the temptation to buy, buy, buy. Why? Because we are assaulted hundreds of times a day by marketing messages encouraging us to spend our money. For the sake of your sanity and the order of your home, embrace a culture

License to Cheat
Photocopy, clip, sign, and laminate

[BACK OF CARD]

The Cheat Sheet
How to Cheat at Organizing principles:

S4 technique: To declutter, Strip, Scrap, Sort, and Store

HIRE: If a task is Hard, Important, Rarely done, and Elaborate, pay a pro.

One In, One Out rule: When you acquire a new thing, toss the old one.

The SHOK Diet: Salad Helping OverKill.

For more: Visit www.HowToCheatBooks.com

shift. Celebrate getting rid of stuff instead of acquiring. The fewer possessions you have, the easier it is to create order. When you stuff more and more things into your house, keeping them organized becomes impossible.

Embrace innovations. Become a big fan of product innovations. At first glance, this may seem to run counter to the item above called "Celebrate letting go," but it doesn't. You're not going to spend willy-nilly on every new gizmo that comes along. Just keep your eyes—and your mind—open for the new devices that will truly save you time and effort. Run a quick mental check: Is the added expense worth the convenience you gain? If you're accustomed to digging in your heels and resisting change, get over it.

Know when to pick up the phone. Everyone has limits—limits in knowledge, limits in physical ability, and limits in time. When you're accomplishing tasks around the house, send up a red flag when you're about to surpass those limits. Don't make a mess of things by doing a bad job. Hire people who know what they're doing to handle the task, whether it's changing a light switch or debugging the home computer. Use the HIRE criteria: If a task is Hard, Important, Rarely done, and Elaborate, pay a professional to do it. When you find professionals who do a great job, treat them well—be friendly, be fair, and pay promptly.

Keep memories, not objects. If you're a collector, seriously reevaluate what you're doing every year. Life situations and personal priorities change, so have the courage to dispose of or seriously reduce a collection that is no longer relevant. Don't let sentimentality turn your home into a mess. In middle age, for instance, it may no longer make sense to keep every rock 'n' roll T-shirt you ever bought. Find a way to honor the memory of that collection without holding on to every object. Frame the most unusual T-shirt and record the rest with snapshots. This is called the Keep One rule.

Buy the good stuff. Invest your money in quality, not quantity. In respect to clothing, one exquisite, versatile suit is far better than three cheap suits. A professional-grade screwdriver will last you longer than five bargain-bin screwdrivers. A collection of seven porcelain figurines in pristine condition is more satisfying—and far more manageable—than 32 of them that are chipped and cracked.

Buy duplicates. Be willing to store identical products at multiple "stations." For example, keep toothpaste and deodorant not only in the bathroom, but also in your gym bag and in your travel kit. This way, you won't have to remember to grab up those bathroom items every time you hit the road. Keeping scissors in the kitchen, in the laundry room, and at your workbench will save you lots of steps, too.

Eliminate distractions. Don't passively submit to annoying or distracting elements that impose on your life. Proactively eliminate them. Ask your colleague to take you off his circulation list for those chain e-mails he just has to share with 150 of his best friends. Remind telemarketers that you are on the national "Do not call" list and then hang up immediately. Use TiVo®, a DVR, or other recording techniques to skip television ads. Call that catalog company's 800 number and ask to be taken off their mailing list. And toss out junk mail without giving it a second thought (shred the credit card solicitations).

Chapter Two

Make Your Living Areas Work Harder

HAVE SOME very sad news for you: The Queen of England has declined your invitation to drop by for tea. Sorry to throw you into a funk, but you have to admit that this sorry situation begs the question: Who the heck are you maintaining that formal living room or dining room for anyway? I would wager that every single person in your social circle is more comfortable in a casual and friendly room than in a stiff and spotless room. What's more, a museum-quality living area—the kind where no pets are allowed and kids have to tiptoe through quickly—is totally dysfunctional in a modern home. If you have "perfect" furniture that is rarely used, you're going to be really, really tired of it years before it wears out. There are much better uses for the space. For instance, Laura Leist, an organization and productivity consultant in Mill Creek, Washington, recently converted a family's formal living room into a music room. She has turned more than one formal dining room into home offices.

So conduct a quick mental audit of each room of your house. Ask yourself:

- How is this space actually used?
- What are the priorities of this household?
- And do the two match up?

When you convert a minimally used room into a frequently used room, you essentially have built an addition onto your home for zero cost. You will not only be changing the look and feel of one room, but the adjustment will affect the entire dynamic of your household—the way that all family members approach life under your roof. Converting such rooms to friendly and functional spaces is an opportunity you can't afford to miss. If you feel like this is a betrayal of the values you grew up with, so be it—that's why we call it cheating.

Now let's get down to some cheat-at-organizing particulars for the living spaces in your home.

Furnishing and Using Your Rooms

When you organize your living spaces the hard way, you spend an absurd amount of your day trying to impose order on all of your stuff. When you organize your living spaces the cheatin' way, your furniture and possessions do 98 percent of the organizing work for you.

SLEIGHT OF HAND

Give Your Bed a Raise

Here's an easy way to create 20 cubic feet of extra storage space instantly: Drop by a bed-and-bath store and buy a set of sturdy, rubberized posts that are designed for elevating your bed 6 inches. The bed will feel a tad high the first time you use it, but you will have opened up scads of room underneath the bed for storage bins and boxes.

Does Your Furniture Work Hard Enough?

Start stocking your home with furniture that works harder for you. No, not a spinning wheel. I'm talking about furniture that has multiple uses and provides extra storage that you don't find with conventional designs. Ali Kaufman, a professional organizer in Boca Raton, Florida, is particularly fond of a "farmhouse" dining table that comes with benches. The benches can be used not only to hold up people's bottoms, but they're high enough to use as mini serving tables when you're entertaining. When not in use, the benches slide out of the way under the table. Other examples of hardworking furniture include:

- a coffee table that comes with extra storage drawers
- a recliner that has side pockets for holding magazines and reading glasses
- a bed with built-in drawers underneath
- a sofa with a fold-down table built into it
- a breakfast banquette with space underneath for the dog's bed, out from underfoot

Now, I'm not suggesting that you haul all of your current living-room furniture out to the curb and buy all-new furniture that's designed for multiple purposes. The only sane way to approach the acquisition of your double-duty furniture is to follow the MOP philosophy. That is, Materials On a Program. This means that you identify an improvement that needs to be made, and you move

Easy on the Eyes, Hard on the Body

One of the first things that designers learn in school is that "form follows function." And sometimes a designer gets a refresher course on that.

Interior designer Melody Davidson installed a new slipcover on a sofa loveseat in her living room, and then she went shopping for pillows to go with it. She found some beauties that had interesting beading and fringe. They also were in the perfect colors. She threw them onto the newly covered loveseat and told herself, "Oh, these look so great!"

Her husband went into the living room, sat down, and exclaimed, "Ouch!" As it turns out, leaning against the beading was painful enough that they decided to return the pillows to the store.

It's a common mistake in homes everywhere, Davidson says: "The eye candy is what draws our attention, and we make decisions based on that."

toward that goal with gradual acquisitions, all made at the right time. For instance, when your old ottoman finally wears out, that's the time to buy one that works harder in your home. It may have storage space inside, or it may conveniently slide under your coffee table when it's not in use.

Size it up correctly. Finding furniture that's the right fit for your home has become trickier than ever in recent years. The new oversize homes that are built with 15- or 20-foot ceilings require equally oversize furniture to make the rooms look like they're in proportion. So if you're buying furniture for a modestly sized home, beware the pieces designed for McMansions, says Melody Davidson, cofounder of Design Yourself Interiors™ in Prairie Village, Kansas. Furniture that looks great in the showroom might be too big for your living room. For instance, while your old couch may be a conventional 36 inches deep, some of the new ones are as much as 48 inches deep. Even if you could cram it into your living room, you'd need 15 pillows behind you just to sit on it comfortably. So make sure you take these two steps before you give a furniture salesperson your credit card:

SIT ON IT. Make sure you don't need added pillows behind you to feel comfortable. You need back support, and not every couch is right for every person.

MEASURE YOUR SPACE. Take a tape measure to the furniture you already have to get an idea of what's in proportion for your home. Also measure the overall size of the room and note the measurements and position of such features as walkways, vents, windows, and sills.

Dining tables turn over a new leaf. The old-style expandable dining-room table always left the homeowner with a quandary. When there's no company visiting and you have the table knocked down to its smaller size, what do you do with the removable leaf? Wrapping it in a blanket and sliding it under the bed was one typical solution. (No, you couldn't just lean it against a wall in the closet—it would warp unless it was stored flat.) Some modern expandable dining tables have solved this problem, notes Davidson. The middle leaf is self-storing, under the tabletop.

Make accessories work, too. Just as your furniture pulls double duty, make sure the accessories in each room are not only attractive but functional, says Davidson. Beautiful boxes and baskets contribute to the décor and keep small items organized at the same time, for instance. A nice vase will be eye-catching with or without flowers in it. A nice set of candlesticks will add charm to a room as well as illumination when needed.

Get the Best Use of Your Space

Have you surrendered an entire room of your house to stacks of cardboard boxes that you haven't opened since you moved in—seven years ago? That's too bad, because that room could become extra living space: a den, a guest room, a craft room, or even an enormous walk-in closet. Sure, sorting through 27 boxes of personal possessions is a daunting task. After all, who has a spare day to get a project like that done?

Here's the solution, says Dorothy Breininger, a professional organizer and author based in Canoga Park, California: Hire the sorting out to some bright but low-cost college kids. Drop by a couple of the nearest colleges and put up a notice that you have a short-term job. You will typically have to pay around $10 an hour. Give your assistants specific instructions on how you want the sorting done. For instance, if you have been saving cartons of sewing magazines that you couldn't bear to throw out, tell them to tear

Reconfiguring Made Easy

Have you ever repositioned the furniture in a new house five times as you tried to get the right configuration? (Whew!) Or tried to make a decision about what furniture to buy, or where to place it, based on architect's renderings? Save yourself the hassle and heavy lifting. Furniture templates will get you through the decision-making process, and you don't have to lift anything heavier than a sheet of paper.

Interior designer Melody Davidson created templates out of sturdy craft paper. The templates show the "footprint" of typical pieces of furniture, although they can be folded or cut to represent atypical furniture, too. The system works best in an empty room—for instance, when you're moving into a new home or you've sent the furniture out to be recovered. You lay the templates out on the floor so you can consider such issues as fit of the furniture, lighting, location of doors, and traffic flow through the room. When you have the placement just right, you can leave the templates on the floor until the movers arrive. They'll see at a glance where each piece of furniture goes.

Davidson offers kits for four different rooms for about $30 apiece. Check her web site at www.designyourselfinteriors.com.

out all of the cross-stitch articles, since that's why you kept the magazines, and bag up the rest for recycling. Trust your short-term hires to do a decent job, and don't drive them crazy by trying to closely supervise. If something slips through the cracks, so what? As it was, that material was just rotting away in boxes. Cheating at organizing means you have to be willing to let go of the little stuff sometimes. In exchange, you're going to get an entire new room in your house for less than $100. Now, compare that to the cost of a home addition!

Divide rooms by function. Interior designer Melody Davidson is a big fan of room dividers, which can break up a large room into separate areas with different functions—say, a sewing nook on one side and an office area on the other. A free-standing shelf, the kind that is finished and open on both sides, makes a great room divider. The separated areas are distinct, yet not totally cut off from one another.

Take storage to new heights. "Go vertical" is one of the prime rallying cries of organizing experts. In your living room or dining room, this means making optimum use of those walls. Examples: Install shelves that run the entire width—and the entire height—of a wall. Or install a display shelf around the entire perimeter of the room, 10 inches below the ceiling. Also, vertical tower-style CD holders hold scores of disks while only taking up a few square inches of floor space.

Leave your dishes out. The typical dining-room table centerpiece is nonfunctional. To heck with that. Instead, dress your table up by setting your dishes in a stack in the center of the table, says Davidson. This looks great if you buy dishes in two different solid colors and you alternate them in the stack. You can do the same with bowls and saucers. Wrap silverware for each place setting in a colorful napkin, and place each bundle in a drinking glass. With this arrangement, the dishes can go straight back and forth from dishwasher to tabletop and rarely need to be stored in cabinets.

You'll use the same few dishes over and over again. You may have to modify this approach, however, if your display would be endangered by marauding pets or children.

Put your tools where you need them. Be willing to place functional items where they're most often needed—even if you've never seen it done before in other homes. Shredders are an example. While you commonly find them in the home office, they're often needed at the spot where mail is actually opened. This way, you don't have to open your mail in one spot and then schlep an armload of credit card solicitations and other junk mail to the office for shredding. I know of one woman who has a shredder parked by the kitchen table and another who has one in the living room, stationed right between the his-and-hers easy chairs.

Toss out your cabinet. In a room where you have lots of small items to keep organized—the bathroom, for instance—interior designer Melody Davidson uses a clever trick. She had the conventional cabinet removed from a small bathroom in her house and replaced it with a shelf that holds four boxes. The boxes are used for storing such paraphernalia as makeup, skin care products, and toothbrushing items. The box approach is inherently less messy than a cabinet because the boxes force you to compartmentalize your possessions. When the lids are on the boxes, everything's out of sight, creating a clean and uncluttered look. Within those boxes or in drawers, use silverware trays or other compartmentalized trays to keep smaller items organized.

Upgrade your trash cans. If you have dinky little trash baskets scattered about the house, trade them in for larger receptacles wherever space and décor allow. This is a subtle way of ushering more clutter out the door. There's a saying among organizing experts, says Atlanta professional organizer Laura Ray: "The bigger your trash can, the more you'll throw out."

Establish "out" baskets. Supply each of your major living areas with a "go somewhere" basket, says professional organizer Ali

Kaufman. This would typically be an attractive container about half the size of a laundry basket. When you find an out-of-place object in a room, drop it into the "go somewhere" basket. (An example: a dish that a youngster took into the den while eating a snack.) When you pass a "go somewhere" basket and can return the object inside to its home, do so. This is a system intended for all members of the family—not just one or two adults. Some family members may need a little training, but in the long run it will bring order to your living areas and save everyone some steps.

Go mobile. For flexibility, put some of your furniture on wheels. For instance, if you had a wheeled office cart, you would be able to roll it into the same room where your kids are playing and do your work there temporarily.

Media Overload

It's relatively cheap and it's addictive. I'm not talking about your favorite soap opera. I'm talking about the river of magazines, catalogs, books, CDs, DVDs, and other entertainment or informational materials that flood your living spaces. As with other organizational challenges, your first step is to make sure that these possessions are working hard for you. Make some radical cutbacks if they aren't. In this digital age, physically owning this stuff is becoming less and less necessary.

Magazines and Catalogs: The Paper Mountain

Let me guess. You subscribe to 11 different magazines, and reading just a 10th of that material would add up to more leisure time

Code Your Towels

In any bathroom used by more than one person, there's a classic quandary: Who is using which towel? Towels get used and then returned to different racks or hooks—or even tossed onto the floor. So the next time you step out of the shower, you have to hold your breath and take a guess in order to dry off.

Pat Saso, a family therapist in Milpitas, California, has the solution: Color-code your towels. Assign a different color of towel to each member of the family. Buy a minimum of two towels in each color, so a fresh one is available when the other one needs laundering. Color-coding is also a big help to youngsters who are learning to wash their own clothing—they know exactly which towel to pull out of the bathroom. No more guessing games.

than you have in a week—and that's assuming you forgo working, cooking, and washing the kids' clothes. Do a quick audit of your subscriptions. How many have you not read in the last 2 months? How many hark back to some former identity? (Maybe you still receive *Window Designer Monthly* even though you became an accountant 5 years ago.) If you cancel six of your subscriptions right now, you'll probably never miss them. You'll also save hundreds of dollars a year and prevent a large paper mess from ever piling up in your den. Somewhere in the first several pages of each magazine you will find a toll-free number for the subscription department. Punch up those numbers and say, "Cancel me!"

Take magazines on one-way trips. When you're leaving the house and you know you will have a little reading time while you're out, take along one of your I-can't-get-to-it magazines. Read it during your spare moments, and then just leave it for someone else to enjoy. You will have given the magazine all of the attention you'll ever be able to afford, and you will have recycled it in the best possible way—by handing it off to another reader. Misha Keefe, a professional organizer in Washington, D.C., likes to do this at the gym, but it also works with the doctor's office, the hair salon, or your train commute. Tear the mailing label off the magazine so you're not leaving personal information behind.

Let 'er rip. The primary reason you're holding on to that Pike's Peak of magazines is that you know there's gold in them thar hills—an ingenious decorating idea you saw while flipping through one magazine and a yummy recipe in another. You need the rip-and-read habit, says organization and productivity consultant Laura Leist. Whenever you are flipping through a magazine and you find an item you want for future use, tear it out of the magazine on the spot and slide that page into a folder marked "Décor" or "Recipes." Then, after your first session with the magazine, you can drop the remainder into recycling. If you really must hold on to certain whole magazines short term, cluster them in one magazine rack that's near your primary reading spot. If you must hold on to certain magazines long term—say, for professional reference—store them in upright magazine holders, available at office supply stores.

Move without notice. I'll bet every time you move, you go to the post office and obediently fill out a change-of-address form. You know what happens to that information? It quickly lands in the hands of the junk-mail industry, which redirects that river of unwanted paper right onto your new doorstep. With just a small amount of extra effort, you can do your own mailing (or e-mailing) to your most important contacts, alerting them to your new digs. First, send a mass e-mail to as many of those contacts as you can. (To keep those e-mail addresses private, use the "blind carbon copy," or BCC, function.) For the handful of contacts you can't reach by e-mail, visit a stationery store (or find one online) and have moving-announcement cards printed with your new contact information. Then print a sheet of address labels for your friends and colleagues, slap a label on each card, and drop them off at the post office. The junk mailers will wonder how you managed to vanish.

Create a catalog routine. Establish a method for processing your catalogs, says Barb Friedman, a professional organizer in Milwaukee, Wisconsin. Just make sure your final step is dropping the thing into the recycle bin. First of all, when a new catalog comes through your door, toss out the old edition. Assign a specific time for flipping through your catalogs—say, during the downtime while you're cooking, or in the 15 minutes before you go to bed. If you find an item you want to order, tear that page out, rip off the back page (which has the ordering information you will need), and staple them together. When you make the order, write the order number on the catalog page and drop it all into a folder called "Catalog Orders." Toss the rest of the catalog. Also, if you scan a catalog and didn't spot anything you just gotta buy, throw the whole catalog away immediately.

Bullied by Books? Show Some Spine

What shape are your bookshelves in? Got paperbacks crammed onto your shelves in double rows, one in front of the other? Got cookbooks stacked against the wall of the dining room because your kitchen shelf is overloaded? Got an entire shelf in your office devoted to textbooks from your college days? If this sounds like your house, it's time to have a serious talk with yourself about letting go of possessions that aren't pulling their weight in your here-and-now life. Sure, you might have good reasons to hold on to some books. For instance:

- **Books that are genuine antiques.** If you do have books that are collector's items, that's still not permission to let them spill off the shelves. Establish a special spot for these prized items and follow the guidelines for managing—and limiting—your collections, described in Chapter 10.

- **Reference books.** These include dictionaries, cookbooks, health encyclopedias, almanacs, and work-related texts. For each book, ask yourself: Is the information up to date? Have

System Failure

Laura Leist, an organization and productivity consultant, had a client with a software problem. No, not a recurring error message on her screen—she had a gigantic collection of old software and software manuals. You see, the client had worked for decades in the software industry. This bulky collection was a physical representation of all of her hard work. It felt like her personal history, and she could not bear to throw it away.

Leist's response: "Let them go—none of that software is in use anymore." She persuaded the client to tear the covers off of the manuals, save them, and then toss the rest away—an enormous saving of space. Preserve the memory, Leist advises, not the entire object.

I used this book in the last 2 years? If the answer to either question is "No," then the book belongs in a box marked "Yard Sale" or "Recycling."

- **Books you're intending to read.** Okay, an avid reader could easily have 10 or 20 books in a "read these soon" section of a bookshelf. But make sure you're not clinging to unread books that you will never really get around to—for instance, gifts that you don't really want to read.

- **Books you're sentimental about.** Careful with this—not every book can represent some deep connection to your past. Perhaps *The Illustrated Man* was your first introduction to science fiction, and you've been an avid reader of the genre ever since. Fine. Keep that one book, and let the other 532 sci-fi novels go.

Unless someone else in the family has precisely the same reading preferences you do, get rid of books the moment you finish them. Pass them along to friends, drop them off at a used bookstore, or sell them for next to nothing at a yard sale. Just make sure they get out of the house.

And if you have a shelf full of your old college textbooks, there's only one thing to do: Drop them into recycling. Admit it: You never look at them. "I guarantee you the information is outdated," says Leist.

Divide them, and divide them again. Once you have the volume of books under control, split them up by category and shelve them in appropriate places around the house. Kids' books go in the play-room, cookbooks in or near the kitchen, coffee-table books in the

SLEIGHT OF HAND

Save Bucketloads by Clustering Repairs

The cost of a plumbing repair is not simply the dollar figure that appears on the Pipe Professor's bill. There's also the inconvenience—arranging to be at home when the fix is made. To make your life easier, save up those little plumbing jobs. Many of the minor ones can be delayed for weeks or months, so have your plumber repair them all at once. These tasks might include fixing the drippy faucet in the kitchen, the finicky flush handle on the toilet, and the broken shower knob in the upstairs bathroom.

Keep a running list of your little plumbing jobs on the refrigerator, right beside the grocery list, so you won't forget anything on Plumbing Fix-It Day. When you have accumulated three or more small jobs, give the plumber a call and provide a rundown of all of them in advance. Of course, if you have a true plumbing emergency—say, a broken pipe gushing water in the basement—you can have your list of minor problems taken care of during the same call. When you cluster your repairs this way, you'll save time because you don't have to be at the house for multiple appointments, and you'll save money because you're only paying for one trip by the plumber. Use this same strategy for other workers you hire for help around the house, too—your electrician and your handyman, for instance.

living room, and work-related books in the office. At each location, split the books up by broad subcategory and label each section of the shelf so anyone can find the book they're looking for with just a few seconds of browsing. For instance, the children's book categories might be science, games and puzzles, humor, reference, general fiction, and science fiction.

Check out the library for a change. To cut back on the number of books that you buy, develop a serious library habit. When you hear of a book you want to read or a new author you want to explore, make the library your first stop rather than the bookstore. Also, ask the librarian how you can sign up to get first dibs when your favorite authors release new books. Reading library books is free and easy, and you don't have ownership and storage issues when you're done reading them.

Video and Audio: Curing Sensory Overload

You can now liberate your living room from that tyrannical entertainment center. As televisions grew and grew in size over recent decades, homeowners were forced to buy elaborate entertainment centers to house those TVs and all of the other entertainment paraphernalia. As a result, living rooms became dominated by enormous cabinets the size and shape of the Arc de Triomphe. Technology is changing that radically, notes interior designer Melody Davidson. Now you can buy large flat-screen televisions that are only a few inches thick. When you mount one on the wall or a simple stand, you no longer need an entertainment center that dictates the entire look of the room. This opens a wide variety of alternatives for managing your music and game systems on shelving or in less obtrusive cabinets. So think about this when your current television finally gives up the ghost: You have an opportunity to change the entire dynamic of your living space.

Here's an example: Davidson had a client who bought all-new audio and video equipment, including a flat-screen TV that was mounted over the fireplace. Rather than crowding the room with furniture for housing the video and audio components, they rewired the room so that they could station this hardware in the kitchen pantry, 20 feet away. The equipment is controlled by remotes in the living room, while all of the hardware resides in another room. "Technology is making it nice—so you don't have to have all of the components out," Davidson says.

If that sounds overly ambitious, just buy a modestly sized cabinet to position near your wall-mounted TV—one that's just enough to house such components as a DVD player and game system.

Keep the sound to yourself. Wireless headphones for your stereo or television can be a relationship saver, says Eva Rosenberg, a personal finances expert in Northridge, California. If one spouse wants to sleep and the other wants to watch television, the headphones will come to the rescue. In an apartment building, your neighbors will love you for using headphones. If you have a neighbor who turns up the volume because he's hard of hearing, buy him a set—or get all of the neighbors to pitch in. It will be the best $40 you ever spent. Wireless headphones have a particular advantage over the conventional type because you have more freedom of movement. You don't have to worry about tripping your spouse or pulling a floor lamp over as you move around the room.

Movie overload: Yell, "Cut!" If you own more than a dozen tapes or DVDs of commercial movies, stop and ask yourself why. Many consumers have a compulsion to own movies because they feel an emotional connection to a certain flick, or just because they have the financial wherewithal. Stop that. Think about where the movie and communications industries are headed. Minute by minute, it's getting easier to get quick access to any movie ever made, whether you're using the corner video store, a rent-by-mail business, or video on demand over cable or satellite. Rest assured that for the rest of your life, *Casablanca* will be at your fingertips. You don't have to own it, and you don't have to fret about the fact that the format you own it on will be obsolete within a few years.

I know what you're thinking. Yes, there are a few conceivable situations where it's advantageous to own a movie rather than to rent it. Perhaps your toddler has to watch *The Land Before Time* 10 times a month, or a group of teenagers can't gather at your house without throwing *Spaceballs* into the DVD machine. But otherwise, how many times can a human watch the same movie? Box up those movies you never watch, tell them, "Here's looking at you, kid," and donate them to the library.

Label your categories. Don't be afraid to label your CD shelves by music genre, says professional organizer Ali Kaufman. A lot of homeowners believe that labels look cheap or idiotic. Get over it, she says: "Everything is label-able." Arranging your CDs by genre (rock, hip-hop, country, jazz, blues, and classical) is more flexible and less labor-intensive than filing alphabetically. The labels will ensure that your system doesn't fall by the wayside. You can create simple and elegant labels on your PC, or browse the scrapbooking section of an arts and crafts store for attractive options.

There, now—your living spaces, furniture, and possessions are working harder to enforce order on your home so you don't have to. And in your heart, I know you're relieved to be dispensing with your formal living and dining rooms. You can't compete with Buckingham Palace anyway, so you might as well quit trying.

Focusing on Your Wardrobe

Less Is More

YES, I AM ADVOCATING wearing less clothing. Before you start taking it off, however, let me explain. I'm talking about having less clothing in your life in general—a few carefully selected, hardworking garments that you wear frequently. As opposed to all of those lazy, rarely used "hangers-on" that gobble up the airspace in your closet.

When you cheat at organization, you always take the simplest route. With clothing, this will mean resisting all of those marketing messages that tell you to buy-buy-buy garments like a monkey chomping down grapes. Also, delight in getting rid of clothing that is no longer playing a role in your daily life. The result will be a lean and functional closet.

So in this chapter, we will first go through an exercise that will help you focus on what kind of clothing is truly important to you— garments that help you fulfill your goals in daily life. That will help you with the decision making we encounter in the middle of the chapter—revamping your closet. Finally, we will address situations where doing with less is even more powerful: when you're away from home.

For a ton of advice on selecting, caring for, and cleaning clothing, pick up a copy of the companion book *How to Cheat at Cleaning*.

Dressing with a Purpose

If you have trouble eating a tortilla chip without dribbling salsa down your front, you don't want to walk out the door without a good stain-prevention plan in place. If you need your dress shirt to look ironing-board fresh even at a 4 p.m. presentation, then wrinkle prevention is a priority for you. Want to look 10 pounds lighter than you actually are? Want to attract attention? Whatever your goals may be when you go into the world, your clothing choices will play a role in whether you succeed or fail. Remember, effective cheating requires a laser focus on your priorities and a willingness to remove distractions from your life.

So here we're going to examine dressing with a purpose in mind. Whenever one of the following scenarios becomes important to you—and just about all of them will at one time or another—you're going to open up the doors to your bedroom closet in search of solutions. Well, don't wait and get caught off-guard. This evening, figure out how well-prepared your wardrobe is to meet each of these common life situations.

As a first step, assess the strengths and weaknesses of your wardrobe with a list. Write down each of the common priorities listed below—at least, the ones you care about—and jot down the garments you have that meet each need. Not only shirts, skirts, trousers, and sweaters, but undies and socks as well. Then ask yourself: What's missing? You will come away with one of the most practical, powerful clothes-shopping lists you have ever scribbled down. And you will be better prepared, more confident, and more successful in everything you do. You will rule the world, all because you spent a few minutes at list keeping. That's why we call it cheating at organization.

Priority: Looking Slimmer

You do your part to trim down—you watch what you eat and you exercise. However, now and then the special occasion arises when you want to drop an extra few pounds immediately—for that special date, for instance, or for your class reunion. Since no amount of exercising or crash dieting will accomplish the job the night before the big event, we're going to cheat. This time, with a bit of sartorial illusion.

Wear black. "The little black dress is one of the most important items that you can have in your wardrobe," says Birgit Mueller, an Emmy Award–winning television costume designer in Los Angeles. Not only is black naturally slimming, as you've heard many times, but it's also easy to find jewelry, a handbag, and shoes that work well with it, making dressing in the morning much simpler. Also,

SLEIGHT OF HAND

Win a Free Outfit!

Want to play a game? The prize is a free new outfit—no kidding. Here's how clothing entrepreneur Louise Wannier plays the game: She opens up her closet doors and challenges herself. Using only the existing clothing in the closet, without buying a single new item, assemble an interesting outfit that has never been put together before.

The game may take you 5 minutes, or it may take you an hour. But on the next workday, you're going to be sporting a fresh new look. And your charge card never saw the light of day.

a black dress will serve you well from morning into the evening. Make sure your jacket falls at least 5 inches below the hips. The longer it is, the more slimming it is.

Stick to one color. Wear a top and bottom in the same color, says Ingrid Johnson, professor of textiles at the Fashion Institute of Technology in New York City. Wear red from head to toe, for instance, not a red shirt with white pants. "One continuous line of color makes you look taller and slimmer than if you cut up the visual line," she says. One caveat: Very tall women might want to mix and match a little—otherwise you'll end up looking like a red hot chili pepper.

Keep it vertical. Avoid horizontal stripes. Stripes running side to side emphasize your width. For the same reason, avoid plaids.

Just say "no" to nap. Don't wear corduroy, velvet, or any other material with a nap (raised fibers). Fabrics with a nap add bulk to your shape and make you look wider.

Not a time for reflection. Avoid wearing satin or any other shiny clothes. They accentuate bulges.

Skip the spandex. A desire to look slimmer implies that you do not have a perfectly rail-thin, muscular body. Which means that you are outright prohibited from wearing skin-tight clothing of any kind in public.

Hang loose. Wear loose, dark fabrics that hang well. Silk and high-quality rayon are good choices.

Priority: Staying Cool

Never let 'em see you sweat, the saying goes. If that's your policy, here's your wardrobe checklist.

Loosen up. Wear loose clothing, which allows air to circulate over your skin and cool you off. Tight clothing will let your body heat build up, says fashion professor Johnson.

Release the moisture. Cotton and linen clothing draw moisture away from your body, keeping you cooler. Coarse weaves allow your body to breathe. Polyester, being a plastic, won't let air circulate. In athletic wear, however, polyester can cool you down if it's a component of one of the new high-tech fabrics that are designed to draw moisture off even more readily than the natural fibers. These materials will wick your sweat away and help it evaporate quickly (rather than just absorbing the moisture and holding it against your skin). Look for such clothing in the athletic wear section of your retailer.

Lighten up. Wear lighter colors, which reflect sunlight. Darker colors absorb sunlight and hold the heat against your body.

Priority: Attracting Attention

There are a lot of reasons that you might want to attract attention, and the technique you use is going to depend a lot on the scenario. Attracting attention in a nightclub is done one way, and attracting attention in the boardroom is done quite another way. Here are four effective approaches—just use your discretion.

Loud approach. Wear bright colors or wild prints. Tread carefully, however. There's a difference between appearing admirably bold and looking like a clown.

Classy approach. Pick a highlight. Dress simply, recommends costume designer Mueller, but wear one detail that's interesting or offbeat. For a woman, this might be unusual earrings, a necklace, or a great pair of stockings in a subtle, sexy pattern. Don't show too much cleavage—just a hint, leaving more to the imagination. For a man, a fine watch and high-quality shoes would do the trick.

Try on a trend. Look at the magazines and tabloids in the supermarket checkout line to see what the stars your age are wearing, and follow their lead, says Los Angeles clothing designer Bobette

Desert-Tested Travel Trousers

Summer travelers cherish clothing that is cool, lightweight, and practical when they're out and about. I road-tested a pair of super-light nylon trousers recently during 10 summer days in the desert areas of the southwestern United States. These trousers have ample cargo pockets for all of the nifty little things a traveler needs to carry. They have legs you can zip off when the temperature is really cooking. They're no fashion statement, but with the legs zipped on, they'll get you through a restaurant dinner. The fabric dries quickly, is very tough, and doesn't seem to pick up dirt, either. These trousers are extremely compact and add less than 12 ounces to your suitcase.

Pick up a pair of travel-friendly pants like these at a sporting goods store, a camping supply outlet, or an online retailer such as www.duluth trading.com.

Stott. "Trend is more about following what's happening with the stars," she says, "rather than what the designers say."

Master grooming and posture. Basic grooming means a lot if you want people to notice you—in a favorable way. Make sure your clothes and body are clean, your hair is neat, your fingernails are trimmed, and, if you're a man, that you are clean-shaven. "Stand up straight, look people in the eye, and act confident," says fashion professor Johnson. "It's pretty much as easy as that, and a lot of people don't do it."

Priority: Preventing Stains

Nobody wants stained clothes. There are situations in your life, though, when you want to take *extra* measures to keep the spots and splotches at bay—or at the very least, make them easy to remove when you do get clothing stains. Perhaps you're spill-prone and you're going to a nice dinner. Maybe you're traveling and you want the few clothes you have to last for several days. Perhaps you'd like to outfit your kids in some low-maintenance duds. Whatever your reason for making stain prevention a top priority, here are easy ways to go about it.

Go high-tech. This is just a matter of checking the tags when you purchase clothing. High-tech stain-resistant garments are becoming easier and easier to find in stores. Some varieties work by preventing the fabric from absorbing the staining liquid. The liquid will pill up, and you can simply brush that fluid right off your clothes—a particular asset in the travel or nice-dinner scenarios. Other stain-resistant garments have fibers that release stains in the clothes washer more readily than the conventional fabrics do, making your laundry day a breeze.

"I think we're going to see the day when all the fabrics we buy will have the ability to repel or release stains—just as we have now with carpet," says Johnson.

There are a few downsides to stain-resistant garments. Until stain resistance becomes commonplace, such clothing will cost a little more. Stain-resistant treatments often limit the breathability of the fabric, meaning that it feels warmer against your body. Also, the stain resistance can fade after you've washed the garment several times. At this writing, manufacturers are on the

fourth generation of stain-resistant technology, Johnson says, and the science is improving steadily. They're working hard to get it to the point where consumers can't tell the difference between stain-resistant garments and conventional ones. So even if you find this technology lacking at the moment, don't give up on it.

Pick the right fabric. If you don't have clothing that has built-in stain resistance, be aware that it's generally harder to stain petroleum-based fibers such as nylon and polyester, so those would be good choices when staying stain-free is important. One caveat: Unfortunately, petroleum-based fibers are attracted to oily stains, so don't go dripping movie-popcorn butter on that polyester shirt.

If you simply want to make washday go a little easier, cotton, linen, and tencel (a relatively new wood-pulp-based fabric) are generally easier to clean than most other conventional fabrics. Avoid rayon and silk, which get persistent stains.

Pick the right color. When avoiding stains is a priority, just wear black, says Mueller. Stains don't show up as well on black clothing.

Priority: Preventing Wrinkles

You could leave your hair uncombed. You could belch frequently in public. But if you really want to telegraph to the world that you have an unkempt life, all you have to do is walk around in wrinkled clothing. You might whine that wrinkled clothes can still be *clean* clothes, and you might protest that you've been living out of a suitcase for the last week. Too bad. If you step outside in a blouse that has more ripples than the Pacific Ocean, you're going to be branded instantly as a disorganized slob.

Now, you know I am no fan of ironing. So we're going to do some *How to Cheat at Organizing* corner cutting that will keep your clothes wrinkle-free with a minimum of effort.

Once again, go high-tech. Wrinkle resistance is another quality that clothing manufacturers are improving year to year. Launder the garment as directed, pull it immediately out of the dryer, smooth it out with your hands, and hang it up—it's ready for action. Don't expect perfection. Wrinkle-resistant trousers rarely keep a sharp crease, for instance. But you'll hold your head up high, confident that you're passing wrinkle inspection with flying colors. Buy wrinkle-resistant garments for those "workhorse" positions in your wardrobe—the basic pants, skirts, and shirts that you wear frequently.

Load up on knits. Knit clothing just doesn't hold wrinkles the way broadcloth does. This holds true in both the laundry room and when you're pulling clothes out of the suitcase. You can just hold the garment up and give it a shake to release the wrinkles. So work knits into your wardrobe at every opportunity, too.

Pick poly. Among more conventional fabrics, look for garments that are part polyester and part natural fiber—cotton in particular. Fabrics with a touch of polyester in them wrinkle less readily. The newer microfiber polyester garments are intrepid wrinkle-fighters as well.

Banish linen. If avoiding wrinkles is your priority, forget about linen garments. "You look like an accordion when you sit down," says costume designer Mueller.

Find the right weave. When you're buying dress shirts, look for a satin weave rather than plain weave, says professor Johnson of the Fashion Institute of Technology. The satin weave is looser—the fabric relaxes and carries less tension. Now, finding satin-weave garments can be a trick, because you typically won't find it mentioned on clothing labels. You'll have to go by feel: Satin weave feels smoother to the touch than regular weave. If you're not sure, ask a salesperson. You also can conduct this simple test: Take a corner of a shirttail and squeeze your hand around the fabric. When you release it, watch whether the material retains its wrinkles. This is an indicator of what the shirt will look like when you pull it out of the dryer. If it releases its wrinkles, it's probably a satin weave. Satin weave is easier to find in women's clothing than in men's.

True-Blue Trousers

Styles for denim pants go in and out of fashion almost as rapidly as months on the calendar. But there's one cut of jeans that will never go out of style, says Michael Laimo, New York City sportswear wholesaler: the classic five-pocket model like those made by Levi's, Lee, and other manufacturers. These jeans will always be a good investment and a stalwart in the casual section of your closet. You'll never have to ask yourself that anxious question, "Are people still wearing these?"

Priority: Saving Money

Sales and discount stores? I'm sure you're on the case. But those aren't the only ways to save money when you purchase clothing. Make these approaches a permanent part of your shopping routine.

Buy a few good things. Forget about buying lots of clothes in an attempt to keep up with every fad and trend. Instead, buy fewer items, but make sure they're high quality, even if you have to pay more for these select pieces. A pair of high-quality shoes, for instance, can make all the difference in an outfit. Or a great blouse, jacket, or sweater. "Europeans have always done this. They invest in their apparel and accessories," Johnson says.

Fight for the fit. Try on a score of different styles and brands of jeans until you find one that's the perfect, most flattering fit. Pay whatever the jeans cost, and then save money by pairing them with several cute but inexpensive tops. The number one fitting mistake that people make is not being diligent enough about trying garments on. "A consumer may need a size 10 from one designer, a 12 from another, and yet an 8 from a third," says Johnson. "We love

Core Clothing

Ever get the feeling that your wardrobe is adrift—that no matter how many garments you add to it, your closet is directionless and unfocused? Maybe that's because you aren't building your wardrobe on a solid foundation. Here's a checklist, from Los Angeles clothing designer Bobette Stott, of core basics for men and women. When you blend these with more trendy clothing, you'll have a wardrobe that will last forever.

Women

- Suit jacket. Dark and not trendy. Navy is the best choice, but black is okay, too.
- A cardigan sweater, with no beading or embroidery. Wear it over a dress or jeans year-round.
- Classic jeans. No logo on the pocket. No distressed or washed look. Straight-leg cut. Medium to dark in color.
- A great white blouse, no ruffles. Goes equally well with jeans or a suit.
- A classic dress or skirt. Knee to mid-calf in length, not short and trendy.

Men

- A good, classic suit. Dark navy. Moderately sized lapel, nothing trendy, plain straight-leg pants, no stripes. For use at job interviews, funerals, and possibly the office.
- A classic polo shirt.
- Dark khakis. No trendy cuts, just straight legs.
- Medium to dark jeans. No trendy fading, bleaching, or sanding.
- Lightweight sweater. Find one you feel comfortable in. A basic color—navy, brown, or black. Use it like a long-sleeved T-shirt.

to pretend we are truly an 8, but the number is no more relevant than is the number 12 or 10. It is the fit that matters."

Catch them on the rebound. Find a consignment shop that attracts high-quality clothing, and stop by at least once a month. Dry cleaners often donate clothing that is never picked up, says Brent Newbold, CFO of the Holy Cow™ cleaning products company and a laundry owner for 22 years. Consignment shops also benefit from wealthy people who might wear a garment once and discard it. You never know when you might be able to pick up a classic, high-quality designer jacket or gown for a fraction of its original cost.

Taming the Wild Closet

Fashions come and go. Garments show their wear. You change jobs, so your clothing needs change. Your body size changes. Your taste evolves. And you buy more clothes. All of these are excellent reasons to get certain clothing items out of your life. When you have too many clothes, you can't find what you need. Your clothes get musty because they can't breathe, and they get wrinkled because they're mashed together. Quit letting them clog up your closet.

We're going to lean heavily on a couple of core *How to Cheat at Organizing* concepts that you swore to uphold when you read Chapter 1:

- a modified version of the good ol' S4 technique (Strip, Scrap, Sort, and Store)
- and celebrating getting rid of stuff

Stripping and Scrapping

Give your wardrobe a ruthless weeding-out at least twice a year—at the same time you rotate seasonal garments into and out of remote storage (maybe you use the guest-room closet for this, or hanging garment bags in the basement). Sure, this weeding-out sounds like a chore added to your to-do list. However, if you aren't following this practice now, I've got news for you: Purging and sorting your closet is actually an enormous relief. Suddenly your closet makes sense; it's humming like a well-tuned machine.

We'll break down your closet purge into two stages. If you like, do them on two different days—but don't wait more than a day or two between stages.

Stage 1. Set aside 30 minutes every spring and fall to transfer out-of-season clothing out of your bedroom closet for the next 6 months. But first, scrutinize every garment:

- Is it really a keeper?
- Is it out of style?
- Is it worn or losing its shape?
- Has it been ironed to death?
- Is it flattering?
- And the big reality check: Does it still fit?

If a garment misses one of these hurdles, then don't award it any kind of closet space—donate it, throw it away, or tear it up for cleaning rags. Make sure that any garment that you do keep is clean before you put it into storage.

Stage 2. You have a fair amount of clothing that remains in your closet year-round, the stuff that's not season-sensitive. These garments need to be purged, too. It's most convenient to do this at the same time that you swap the seasonal clothes into and out of remote storage. When you're organizing a closet, there's no sense in hanging, arranging, and folding clothes that have become useless to you.

So ask yourself all of the above questions about the perennial, nonseasonal items in your closet, too. And add one more question: Have I worn this in the last year? Again, if any item fails any of these tests, out it goes. There's one caveat: If you're clinging to a garment purely for deep sentimental reasons, that's okay—but don't let it crowd your closet. Store it elsewhere. Otherwise, having an unusable garment hanging in your closet will give you a false sense of your wardrobe.

What if you have diligently rotated your out-of-season clothes and you've done a meticulous purge—and you still don't have enough closet space? Well, first let me observe that you have more clothes than any one human needs. For the sake of your own sanity, pare down your wardrobe and quit buying so much. Knowing that's not what you wanted to hear, I have two backup plans:

1. Rotate your clothing into and out of remote storage four times a year—yup, once for each season.

2. Analyze how well your lifestyle and the clothing in your closet match up. If you wear casual clothes at least 5 days of the week, don't store your fine clothes (suits and sport coats, for instance) in your closet. Put them in the remote location, along with the out-of-season clothing. Reserve your bedroom closet for day-in, day-out duds.

So there—in keeping with the S4 technique, you have *stripped* the clothing out of your closet and evaluated each piece, and you have *scrapped* the items that are no longer relevant to your life. Now let's take a look at the *sorting* and *storing* part of the S4 technique as it pertains to closets.

Sorting and Storing

When you enlisted in the *How to Cheat at Organizing* legion, you probably didn't think of yourself as someone who would merrily sort your clothes closet according to the color of the garments. Now, bear with me a moment. This is not mindless regimentation. Switching the hangers around in your closet will take no more than 3 minutes, and the change will have a big payoff. Rather that rooting through your closet endlessly, hoping to find a garment in the right color, you will be able to tell at a glance whether it's there or not. This will help to focus your shopping expeditions as well. You will be able to identify the gaps in your wardrobe in just seconds. What, no classic navy trousers? Onto the shopping list they go.

So create a flow from the darkest clothing on one end of the closet rod to the lightest clothing on the other. Cluster all of the blacks, browns, blues, reds, greens, and tans separately. Then, within each color, cluster the articles by kind of garment—pants, skirts, and shirts.

GREAT GEAR

Spare the Rod, Spoil the Closet

A slide-out "valet" hanging rod is a simple-but-ingenious addition to any closet, says Washington, D.C., image consultant Lynne Glassman. When extended, the 1-foot-long rod is long enough to hold several garments—an asset when you're packing for travel. Also, just before you go to bed at night, you can zip out the rod and hang the next day's clothing choices on it so you won't have to fumble around in your closet while you're wiping the sleep out of your eyes. Because the rod folds flush with your closet shelf or wall when not in use, it takes up zero space. You will no longer need that valet stand taking up space in your bedroom.

Slide-out closet rods are available at The Container Store® for about $10.

Here are some more closet tricks that will help you get the most out of your wardrobe. It's all in how you hang 'em!

Up the wattage. Most closets have abysmal lighting in them, says Washington, D.C., image consultant Lynne Glassman, proprietor of www.doctorofdress.com. Under such conditions, you can't make good decisions about what to wear. You'll have a tough time identifying colors and getting a sense of which garments work well with each other. You'll also do a lousy job of spotting stains and rips in your clothing. So switch that dim old single-bulb fixture with a light fixture with multiple heads that will illuminate all parts of the closet. "Not expensive, not fancy, just good lighting," Glassman says. Install "natural light" bulbs so you will get an accurate read on clothing colors.

Get the full view. Don't wait for a colleague at the office to tell you that you have missed a belt loop or that there's a store tag still dangling from the jacket that you're wearing. "Everybody should have a full-length mirror," says Glassman. Station it near the spot where you dress so you will check it every time. Do these clothes still fit? Are they in good condition? Do they look good together? Did I forget to put my pants on?

Toss the plastic. Don't store your clothes in those plastic bags that you bring home from the dry cleaner, says former laundry owner Newbold. Your clothes need to breathe, and moisture trapped inside the bag could damage your clothes. Instead, buy a breathable cotton garment bag at a discount store. If you want extra protection from moths, ask your dry cleaner to sell you special mothproof garment bags. These are made of a pillowy blue fabric that you draw over your clothing and tie at the bottom.

Give them air. Make sure your clothes have room to hang freely and are not smashed up against each other. They need air circulation.

Clamp down on pants. If space in your closet is at a premium, hang all of your pants from hangers with clasps. They'll take up less width that way. There's a side benefit to this approach, says Susan Sommers, an author and fashion coach in New York City: You can tell more quickly what kind of pants they are when you're deciding what to wear.

Shelve those knits. Stack your sweaters and other knits on shelves or in drawers. If you hang them up, they will get stretched out of shape. Group them by color so you will be able to find the one you need quickly. If you're using a shelf for your sweaters, buy shelf dividers to keep them neat. Shelf dividers latch on to a shelf and create a vertical barrier between your stacks of sweaters to keep them from sliding to and fro. These dividers are available at discount stores and organizing stores.

An alternative, if you really want to hang your knits: Fold them and drape them over the thick (not wire) horizontal bar of a hanger. Never hang a sweater by the shoulders in the way that you would hang a broadcloth shirt, says Johnson, the Fashion Institute of Technology professor.

Break up your suits. Ladies, don't hang suit pieces together. Hang each piece of your suit on a separate hanger, and mix these pieces in with your other clothes. Why separate a suit? It's a mental trick, says Sommers. If you keep the suit pieces together, you'll never wear them any other way. When they're separated, you'll be more creative with your wardrobe. "In fashion now, the mismatched suit is as acceptable as the matched suit for women," she says.

Guys, ignore this advice. Keep your suits intact at all times. Nobody wants to see you mixing and matching suit pieces—chalk it up to gender differences.

Preselect your outfits. Assemble entire outfits on one hanger in your closet, says image consultant Glassman. Include everything— skirt or pants, shirt, jacket, scarf, and even jewelry. This will make those bleary-eyed early-morning dressing decisions easy. It also will accelerate tenfold your packing for a trip.

Make Your Closet Hang Together

This is purely a cosmetic measure, but if you want to create the *appearance* of having an organized closet, throw out all of your old hangers and replace them with new ones that are identical in color and design. Boom—your closet suddenly looks regimented rather than slapdash. Don't use wire hangers (they damage clothes). Buy wooden ones or thick plastic hangers in a neutral color. Avoid hangers in bright colors—you need to focus on the clothes in your closet, not the hangers themselves.

Once you have assembled your favorite outfits, buy a few shoulder covers to keep dust off so they'll always be in ready-to-go condition. The see-through kind makes it easier to select your clothing. Typically, you can fit two or three outfits under one shoulder cover.

The All-Important Extras

Accessories—your shoes, scarves, belts, and such—are often an afterthought when it comes to closet organization. They lie in heaps in the darkness at the bottom of the closet or jumbled in cubbies and on shelves. Here are some easy ways to keep accessories in good shape, under control, and easy to find when you need them.

Put those shoes on the rack. Once you have more than a dozen pairs of shoes, they take on a mind of their own, and they scatter. (Footloose, we call it.) To keep your leather lovelies matched up and ready for service, says fashion coach Sommers, hang a shoe rack on the back of your closet door or bedroom door—the kind that can accommodate 20 or 30 pairs. Don't put every pair on the rack, however—only the in-season ones.

Off season, shine them up. Spend an evening in front of the television polishing every one of your out-of-season shoes, and then tuck them away into labeled boxes. Why shine them up before storage? Because when you want them again, you're going to be in the midst of dressing, and you will want them ready to hit the bricks. So do it while you have the leisure time.

Treat them to a tree. When leather shoes aren't wrapped around your feet, make sure there's a shoetree inserted inside to keep them in good shape. They'll last years longer that way.

Are your boots a flop? Knee-high boots can't be left to their own devices. Once you take your legs out of them, they're prone to flopping over. If you leave them for long in this relaxed state, they will become creased and misshapen. So if you want to keep them in "made for walking" condition, invest in a boot-shaper to keep them upright in your closet. A reasonable backup plan, says image consultant Glassman: Roll up a thick magazine and slide it down into your boot to hold the leg of the boot erect.

Freshen up your tootsies. Whenever Glassman takes her shoes off in the summer, she likes to slip a dryer sheet into the toe of each shoe to keep them smelling fresh.

Say good-bye to old ties. When you wear a tie frequently, dry-clean it at least every quarter, says Johnson, the fashion-school professor. Otherwise, oils and drips and sneezes will get permanently embedded in the fabric. And quit holding on to your old ties. Wearing one of those old, grimy, frayed rags around your neck just sends the message, "I hate having to wear a tie." A new, crisp tie says, "I'm on top of things."

Get the hang of belt storage. You probably already know that a huge ring dangling from your closet rod is the most space-conserving way to store your belts. But there's one caveat to that, says Glassman: If you have a special belt that goes with one outfit, hang it with the outfit rather than with the other belts. There's no sense in having to search for elements of a tried-and-true outfit.

Get your scarves in the open. Do you store your scarves in a drawer? If so, when's the last time you used one of them? Glassman says women typically forget to incorporate scarves into their outfits when they're tucked away out of sight. Instead, hang them in your closet, where you'll be reminded of the little darlings every day. Pick up one of the special hangers that have multiple holes for drawing a scarf through.

Get hooked on hooks. Mount good ol' peg board on the inside of your closet door, says Sommers, the New York City fashion coach, and paint it to match your décor. You can use scores of little hooks to arrange your belts, handbags, and necklaces in an easy-to-grab fashion.

A sampling of other clever closet hardware:

- hanging shoe bags
- tie hangers, which accommodate dozens of neckties while taking up only 2 inches of rod space
- accessory hangers, with a dozen transparent pockets for holding hosiery, socks, and other small items
- "shepherd's hooks" for reaching clothing hangers on a high rod
- closet rod dividers—disks that slide over your rod to separate categories of clothing
- friction strips that will keep silky garments from sliding off plastic hangers

Taking It with You

The rules change when you walk out the door. We've all seen people with suitcases bursting at the seams, 35-pound purses, and wallets that are thicker than the phone book. Maybe you've been there yourself. The truth is, the accessories that help you get along in the outside world are much friendlier as traveling companions when they're only lightly stocked, slim, and trim. They're easier to carry, and it's easier to find in them the things that you need. The cheating, then, lies in getting a whole lot more out of what little you put into your suitcase, purse, and wallet.

Suitcase Strategies

It would be pretty nice to have eight or 10 outfits folded into your suitcase every time you traveled. However, that would mean taking two or three suitcases—unless you use this technique from image consultant Lynne Glassman. She packs in what she calls capsules, and here's how you do it: Select a top and trousers, both in the same flattering color. Now add to those two base garments several extras that go with them—for a woman, a sweater, a blouse, a

The Store Where Everything Fits

Imagine walking into a clothing store where every garment is carefully selected just for you—your size, your body shape, and your best colors. That would certainly streamline your shopping, wouldn't it? No more frustrating dressing-room sessions, no more weeding through rack after rack of irrelevant garments.

That's the experience that Louise Wannier is offering over the Internet. As the inventor of those VCR Plus+° codes you use to record your favorite TV shows, Wannier knows a thing or two about employing technology to give customers specifically what they want. She describes her new venture, myShape™, (www.myshape.com), as "a personal store where everything fits you and flatters you." The store was just debuting at this writing.

When you first register on the web site, you provide 21 body measurements and answer 10 questions about style preferences. From that point on, your work is done. The site's unique, sophisticated technology matches up your specs with precise data about every garment, gleaned directly from the manufacturers.

At the outset, Wannier's goal is to appeal to busy working women, so the site will emphasize professional wear. Other audiences will eventually follow, including men and teens.

T-shirt, a scarf, and a necklace, for instance. Add a skirt that you can substitute for the trousers. Now, by mixing and matching these items that all work together—the "capsule"—you can create several different combinations, all with a different look. "It's getting multiple uses out of the fewest items, and each combination still looks like it's a new outfit," she says. All neatly transported in a single suitcase.

This same capsule approach will work for men, too. Start with a sport-coat-and-trousers combo as your base garments. Mix in casual shirts, dress shirts, a tie, and a sweater—all in complementary colors so they will work in any combination.

Here are other ways to get more out of your suitcase.

Pack by the formula. How many garments do you need on a trip? Here's how fashion coach Sommers figures it: If you're going to be gone for four days, you need two bottoms, six tops, undies, shoes, sleepwear, and accessories like jewelry for women and ties for men. For every four additional days, add one more bottom and two more tops. You'll also want any location-specific items, of course, such as swimsuits.

Pack by the envelope. Packing envelopes are a handy suitcase accessory that compress your clothes—even jackets and dresses—while keeping them wrinkle-free. These nylon containers typically include a stiff folding board inside. Glassman says packing envelopes allow her to squeeze 30 percent more into a suitcase when she hits the road. Eagle Creek® is one brand.

Roll from town to town. When Sommers travels, she's on a roll. That's how she compacts her clothing and prevents wrinkles at the same time—by rolling them up. When you select a pair of pants to pack, for instance, lay them out on the bed. Start from the bottom and roll them up into a firm little package, compressing the fabric as you go. When you're done, slide the garment into a 1- or 2-gallon zip-closing plastic bag. This will hold the roll together and protect it from spills and inside-the-suitcase leaks. When you reach your

destination, all you have to do to unpack is lift your plastic-covered rolls out of the suitcase and drop them, still intact, into a dresser drawer. Because there are no edges or folds, all of your clothing will come out creaseless. The plastic bags can help you keep your clothing organized as you travel—all of your lingerie in one bag, for instance, and all of your socks in another. Select each bag so that it's just big enough to contain the assigned clothing.

Lighten up with layers. If you're packing for a cold-weather destination, says Sommers, resist the temptation to carry along that 26-pound knit sweater. Instead, take multiple thin layers that can be mixed and matched. Layers will keep you warm, and the multiple pieces will give you lots of wardrobe flexibility. For instance, Sommers likes to pack a camisole, a light sweater to go over it, and a cardigan that goes over everything.

Set up a packing center. Lisa Peck, a Minneapolis interior designer, recommends that frequent travelers establish a packing center right in their clothes closets. Find a spot to store your suitcase in the closet. Install a pull-out valet rod in your closet—it's handy for hanging clothes on when you're assembling outfits (both for travel and for everyday use). Store toiletries and other travel-related incidentals in a small bin in your closet. If possible, set aside a surface for packing, too—perhaps an open shelf or island. With everything you need for packing right at your fingertips, packing your suitcase will be a snap.

Raid the laundry room—or your underwear drawer. Tuck a couple of nice, flat dryer sheets or a sachet from your dresser into the bottom of your suitcase when you travel. They will share their perky fragrance with your entire traveling wardrobe.

Switch shoes every day. When you're traveling for multiple days, here's a strategy for keeping your poor overused feet in the best possible shape from Louise Wannier, proprietor of women's clothing retailer www.myshape.com: Take with you three comfortable pairs of shoes, all of which fit with the clothing color you have packed. If you alternate the shoes you wear each day, she says, your feet won't get sore. Why? Because each model of shoe has its own set of stress points that press against your foot. Varying the kind of pressure that your feet experience from one day to the next "makes a huge difference," she says.

Streamlining Your Purse and Wallet

Here's how to get your purse organized in less than 60 seconds with a nod of thanks to Washington, D.C., professional organizer Misha Keefe for her input. Sit at a desk or table and pull a trash basket up beside you. Now use the S4 technique. (C'mon, you've just about memorized them: Strip, Scrap, Sort, Store.) Dump everything out of your purse and empty all of the purse's pockets as well. Now, bite your lip and take an oath of austerity. Since your purse is a mobile container—and not a strength-training device—keeping it lightweight and uncluttered is important.

Pick out the handful of items that absolutely must hitch a ride in your purse. Select just one lipstick. Packing the cell phone is fine, but leave the address book at home. (Next time you're spending an evening in front of the television, enter all important contact information into your cell phone, so you won't need the added paper.) If you carry a credit card or debit card, you will get along nicely without your checkbook. Depending on the individual, you'll probably also want your wallet, mini makeup bag, sunglasses, one pen, keys, a comb, and another item or two. Return these items to your purse, clustering related items in separate compartments if possible. You're done. Give your purse the S4 treatment at least every other week. Organization, after all, is an ongoing process—not a onetime project.

What about the 25 slips of paper—business cards, notes, receipts, and such? At least half belongs in the trash. Throw the rest into a file or record the info on your computer or cell phone. Toss out the 8-month-old chewing gum, too.

"Whoa," you're saying by now, "I have nine very worthy items left on the table. What about my backup pantyhose? Surely you aren't telling me to forgo sunscreen or skin lotion?" Settle down. There's a very easy way to keep such items at your fingertips without weighing down your purse. During 99 percent of the time you spend away from home, there's a handy storage area nearby—your

SLEIGHT OF HAND

License Reminder

Right now, open up your wallet and look at your driver's license. When does it expire? Go immediately to your computerized calendar and enter a reminder to yourself at least a month in advance of the expiration date. When you get your new license, enter the expiration date immediately, even if it's years away. Renewing your license is easy to forget—and not doing it can bring you a lot of trouble if you get stopped by the police or have an accident.

glove compartment in the car, a drawer at work, and your gym bag, for instance. Keep a small zippered bag at each location to contain the items you've decided not to burden your shoulders with day in and day out. You may end up buying a tube of lotion for each location, but so what? It will all get used eventually. Quit breaking your back.

Your wallet needs the S4 treatment as well. After all, paring an inch out of the thickness of your wallet, whether you carry it in your purse or hip pocket, makes a heck of a lot of difference in your daily comfort. First, consider whether you need a new wallet—is your current one frayed and ugly, and are the plastic card sleeves falling apart? If you buy a new one, pick out a model with two money slots, one to hold your bills and the other to keep receipts and other odd bits of paper.

Pull everything out of your wallet and spread it out on the tabletop. If you're carrying a lot of extra cash because you hate to go to the automatic teller more than once a week, drop half of the extra bills into a dresser drawer and retrieve them during the week as needed. If you've collected business cards from contacts, set those aside and enter the information into your computer or cell phone in your spare time. Throw away any "customer loyalty" cards unless you use them at least once a month (the cards from your bookstore or sub shop, for instance). If you have customer cards that you use less than once a week—say, from your drugstore—drop them into your dresser drawer. You can usually reap any store discounts by providing your phone number anyway. Throw away any expired cards (insurance, auto club, health club).

Throw away old receipts and set aside any relevant ones for filing. Keep one or two credit cards, plus an ATM card. Cancel the rest of your credit cards or keep one or two specific store cards in a drawer and pull them out only for special shopping trips. Put your Social Security card in a secure file in your office (thieves could wreak havoc with your personal finances if they got ahold of that). Photocopy your health insurance card and file the original. If your insurance card has your Social Security number on it, snip the last

Pockets for Your Purse

If you're going for your master's degree in *How to Cheat at Organizing* purse management, you're gonna have to pick up this simple-but-ingenious gizmo: a purse organizer consisting of several pockets side-by-side in a flexible strip. (Purseket® is one brand.) These pocket strips can fold and slide right into your purse. They hold all of your purse's contents—pen, sunglasses, cell phone, keys, and business cards—upright, visible, and easy to grab. Conduct an Internet search for "purse organizer."

four digits off the photocopy, then slide the oh-so-slim copy into your wallet. You will be able to supply the complete number from memory if anyone really needs it. (Thanks go out to Washington, D.C., professional organizer Misha Keefe for her purse and wallet streamlining ideas.)

Now return everything that's left to your wallet. The contents should be no more than a few cards, cash, and your driver's license.

Feels good, doesn't it—being master of your wardrobe for a change? No more overflowing closet. No more shame from wrinkled, stained, or out-of-style clothing. No more fretting for hours just to assemble one outfit that looks classy and together. No more 35-pound purse or bulging wallet. You're a regular garment guru now—a "fashion victim" no more!

Chapter Four

Food

Finding It, Storing It, Fixing It

BUYING, STORING, and preparing food is one of the most complex and time-consuming household activities. Which means it's also a leading source of clutter, confusion, inefficiency, and waste. Well, you know what they say about kitchens: If you can't stand the heat—cheat.

Easy-as-Pie Food Shopping

There's a good chance that your supermarket shopping list system goes like this: A piece of paper is affixed to your refrigerator with a magnet. Whenever you run out of peanut butter, you write "peanut butter" on the list. By shopping day, there are 23 items on the list. You whip the list into your pocket and go. In your mind, you also have a list of the absolute essentials your family needs every week—eggs, milk, bread, and Diet Coke®, for instance. As you shop, you cross each item off the list when you place it into the cart.

Sure, that approach will get you through the store. But there are a few flaws that are slowing you down:

- Every time you enter a new aisle or department in the store, you have to review your entire shopping list (plus your auxiliary mental list) to figure out whether any of the items you need are in that area.

- Once you get through the entire store, there's inevitably an item you missed lurking two-thirds of the way down your list. Now you have to cross the store again to find it.

- You totally forgot to buy juice boxes for the kids' lunches, because you informally relegated that to your "buy every week" mental list but it slipped your mind.

- You're forever asking yourself questions like, "Is honey in the bakery section or with the condiments?" and "Where the heck are the lightbulbs?"

So we're going to fix all of these problems here and now. It will cost you just a minuscule amount of work up front, but the payoff will be enormous: no more forgotten items, no more crisscrossing the store. You'll shave your shopping time by 30 percent. (Thanks go out to psychologist and author Susan Fletcher, Ph.D., based in Plano, Texas, for inspiring this technique, with input from several other experts.)

1. **Save and mark your lists.** For three weeks, save your shopping lists. When you buy each item in the store, don't cross that item off—make a single-character notation beside each item indicating where you bought it. Beside broccoli write "P," for produce. Beside canned black olives write "1," for aisle 1. Beside yogurt write "D," for dairy.

2. **Compile the lists.** With three lists saved and marked, you now have in hand a good representation of the items your family buys regularly. Fire up your home computer, go to the word-processing program, and write out in capital letters all of the departments of your store—in the order

that you encounter them while shopping. The list will read something like, "PRODUCE," "MEAT COUNTER," "AISLE 1," "AISLE 2," and so on. Under each heading, write the items that you buy regularly in that department. Leave extra space under each department for items that you will write in by hand later. Using small type and the column-wrapping feature of your word-processing program (ask a 10-year-old if you don't know how), you can probably fit all of your items on a vertical half sheet of paper. To keep the list under control, use fairly generic entries. Use the broad entry "jam," for instance, and you can always pencil in beside that "blackberry" if you wish.

3. **Put the list to use.** Print out a few copies of your list, trim off the excess paper, and post a copy on your refrigerator. Tell family members to circle any item that you need to buy on the next shopping trip and to write in any items—under the correct department—that aren't already listed. (Use these "write-in votes" to modify the list on your computer now and then.) The next time you go grocery shopping, you will have a list customized to your supermarket and to your family. As you enter each department, you will have a list of everything you need to buy in that area. Gather all of those items before moving on. Your shopping run will go so fast you might just get ticketed for speeding.

If you shop regularly at more than one supermarket, model your list after the store where you do the most business. When you visit a secondary supermarket, your list will still be a perfectly good what-to-buy guide, but remember that the aisle numbers might not match up.

Make a supermarket cheat sheet. Have you ever found chicken on sale at the supermarket—but realized that you don't remember all of the ingredients for your family's favorite chicken dish? There's a simple cure for that, says author and motivational speaker Ally-

SLEIGHT OF HAND

5 Ways a Youngster Can Speed Up Your Grocery Run

Old-time farmers had children so they'd have extra field hands. Surely your kids can pitch in and make your supermarket trip go faster. Children often whine about accompanying Mom to the grocery store, but they won't mind so much if they have important tasks to perform and get to make occasional decisions about which snack foods or cereals to buy. The following little missions also will help familiarize your pint-size assistant with food shopping—good training for the future:

1. Give your child a clearly printed, specific list of orders for the deli counter. Let him run ahead, take a number, and do all of the waiting while you shop elsewhere. If his number comes up before you get there, he can hand the list to the deli worker.

2. If you realize you have passed the aisle that held an item on your shopping list, don't go back—send your youngster.

3. When you're nearly done with your shopping, send your child ahead to scout out the checkout aisles and find the shortest line.

4. Have your child help with bagging groceries, loading them into the car, and hauling them from the car to the house.

5. Once the groceries are in the house, have your child deliver the new goods to the appropriate rooms of the house—toilet paper to the bathroom and soup cans to the pantry, for instance.

son Lewis, based in Jonesboro, Arkansas: On a new computer document, write out the names of the five or six most popular recipes along with their ingredients—enough to fill one vertical column on a sheet of printer paper. Print the list and trim off the excess paper. (Or use the column-setting feature of your word-processing program to put two or three lists on one page, and cut the sheet into strips.) Use the blank side for your weekly grocery-shopping list, and refer to the printed side when you want to make sure you have everything for a favorite recipe.

If you're going for your master's degree in *How to Cheat at Organizing* grocery shopping, combine this trick with the customized shopping list technique mentioned above. Print your recipe ingredients on one side of the paper and your organized-by-department shopping list on the other. It may take a little trial and error with your printer to get the columns to match front and back so you can cut the paper into vertical strips.

Improving on "Scratch" Cooking

On one end of the food-preparation spectrum is the homemaker who insists on making everything from scratch—every casserole, salad, and pie coming from the original, simplest ingredients available. The downside: You're a slave to the kitchen. On the other end of the spectrum is the takeout queen, the frozen-food monger, the doyenne of delivered pizza. There's a downside to subsisting on ready-made food, too: It's usually more expensive and less wholesome.

What's a homemaker to do? You'll find sanity in the middle ground, says Connie Edwards, a cabinet designer for the American Woodmark™ Corp. She's a big fan of "speed scratch" cooking. This has nothing to do with dogs and fleas. It means scouting your supermarket for partially prepared foods that you can take home to complete. Examples:

- In the freezer section, buy bagged ingredients for beef stew all chopped and ready to dump into a slow cooker.

- In the produce section, buy bags of fresh greens—already washed and ready for the salad bowl. You just add the sliced veggies and dressing.

- In the dairy section, buy pre-shredded Mexican cheese, ready to sprinkle onto a taco.

- In the condiment section, pick one of the innumerable exotic sauces to pour over steak or to add to the sauté pan.

"It's a half-and-half kind of cooking," Edwards says. "What's important is getting the family around the table, instead of eating at a fast-food restaurant."

Belly up to the salad bar. Supermarket produce departments often bundle foods in ways that force you to buy more than you want. You may only want a cup of chopped broccoli, for instance, but you have to buy an entire head—and the remainder will go to waste. Edwards has a sneaky way around that: She shops for already-prepared veggies at the supermarket's salad bar instead. She just spoons a cup's worth of broccoli flowerets into a plastic container and takes it to the cash register. Yes, this approach may cost more ounce-for-ounce, but it actually costs less when you consider that she isn't wasting that excess food. "Nobody looks at me funny," she says. "I let whoever shreds carrots for the grocery store do it for me, so I have no waste to throw out. It's funky, but it works for me." Hmm. Sounds like cheating.

Bringing Home the Bacon (and Milk, and Eggs . . .)

Gathering your grocery goods and getting them home—it sounds so simple, but there are myriad ways to waste time, money, and effort. Here are some more sneaky tricks to make your grocery shopping go more smoothly.

Eat first, then shop. Filling your grocery cart with wholesome and practical foods takes discipline, notes John Gabaldon, a home chef and representative for www.cooking.com, based in Los Angeles,

Mashed Peas, Anyone?

When you see John Gabaldon spooning baby food into his mouth from one of those teensie jars, go ahead and stare—he doesn't care. Gabaldon, the representative for www.cooking.com, is a healthy-eating enthusiast. While *you* may turn to cookies or chips for a quick snack, Gabaldon's favorite in-a-hurry food is Gerber®. Mentally, you just have to get past what you see on the label and think about what baby food really is: nutritious, healthful food that's all ready to eat—and there are no additives. No, it's not cheap, but it *is* handy and wholesome. His favorite: banana custard oatmeal. Other faves: mashed peas, spinach, and pureed yams.

California. So he calls this his highest-priority tip: "Never shop hungry. When you do, you buy all sorts of foods you shouldn't— you're not in a good frame of mind for buying food. So eat something before you go."

Also from the Timing Is Everything Department: Don't shop for food in the morning just before work or right after work—the crowds are so mind-numbingly large that you will lose brain cells. During the week, wait until 7:30 or 8 p.m. If you have no choice but to join the crowds in those 30-minute cashier lines, relax and use the time for a mental vacation. Think ahead and take along that enormous *Atlantic* magazine article you have been meaning to read.

Be a brand loyalist. On the surface, it sounds oh-so-simple: When you find a food brand that you like, stick to it. It's actually an important concept, says Judi Gallagher, a chef based in Sarasota, Florida—and it's very easy to be led astray. Here's an example: When Gallagher makes peanut-butter cookies, she likes them best when she uses Skippy® Super Chunk® Extra Crunchy. The taste,

Be the da Vinci of Sauces

A nice sauce will elevate ho-hum food to la-de-da cuisine. You don't have to tell your family that you made the sauce from the simplest ingredients, that it was a breeze to prepare, or that you made it in mass quantity months ago and froze it for occasional use. Here's author-chef Silvia Bianco's approach to easy, "blank canvas" sauce—meaning that it's bland in the beginning but will pick up the flavor of any food that you cook with it. Likewise, you can transform it with a dash of spice or by stirring in a condiment such as mustard.

After preparing the recipe below, pour it into small containers and freeze it so you can use a little at a time, as needed. Or just pour it into ice cube trays, freeze, and then transfer the sauce cubes to a plastic bag and return to the freezer.

Chef Silvia's "Blank Canvas" Sauce

$1/2$ cup olive oil
$1/2$ cup white flour
1 cup dry white wine
4 cups chicken broth
Salt and black pepper (go light on these)

Warm the olive oil in a saucepan on medium heat. Whisk in the flour to make a paste. Turn down the heat and add the wine slowly, stirring until it's all mixed in. Add the chicken broth slowly, stirring. Simmer for 1 hour uncovered. Makes 5 to 6 cups.

texture, and quality of food varies from brand to brand, so sticking to the brand you like best makes you a better, more consistent cook. There's a secondary benefit as well: It's one less thing you have to think about—no need to ponder the differences among competitors. Simply grab your favorite. Ignore the advertising, ignore the promotions, ignore the coupons. Your decision was made long ago, so don't give it another thought. Couldn't be simpler.

Beware of false savings. People get tempted by the "savings" promised when you buy huge quantities. But if you buy a 5-gallon jar of mayo, much of that is going to go to waste, and you don't have room for it anyway. Unless you use tons of relish, buy the teensy jar—it's easier to store and you'll waste less. With food, buying in bulk is not the issue—buying high-quality food is. Save bulk buying for toilet paper and laundry detergent.

Similarly, don't overbuy any item just because it's on sale. If you see a great price on chicken breast, ask yourself first how many packages you have in the freezer. If you already own enough chicken breast to last you for 3 months, buying more doesn't make sense—some of it will be wasted.

Last of all, go fishing. Jennifer Armentrout, test-kitchen manager and recipe editor for *Fine Cooking®* magazine in Newtown, Connecticut, likes to plot out a course in her supermarket that allows her to put the most perishable foods into her cart last. Her store begins with the produce section (as do most). Not a big deal—produce can stand to go unrefrigerated for a while. Then she buys all of her nonperishables. Then she loops back to the dairy shelf, then the meat counter, and last of all the fish section. Because fish is extremely perishable, if she is not going directly home, she will ask the counter workers to pack her fish in ice, which they're happy to do for no charge. "They have tons of ice in the fish department," she says.

Bag by design. Anytime you can, bag your own groceries, says Armentrout. She likes to cluster items in each bag according to where they will eventually be stored in her house. So all of the items bound for the baking section of her pantry go into one bag, and all of the fresh produce going into the refrigerator goes into another. When she hauls her groceries into the house, putting everything away is suddenly extremely simple.

Get your goods delivered. With a few phone calls or a brief session on the Internet, chances are you can make a list of supermarkets and other businesses that will deliver groceries right to your door—for no more than a few extra dollars, and sometimes for free. This is an alluring opportunity for dyed-in-the-wool cheaters at organizing. That's a heck of a lot of driving, cart-pushing, and bag-hauling pared right out of your day. Professional organizer Denise Caron-Quinn raves about the service called FreshDirect®, which, at this writing, will deliver your groceries in the New York City region for about $5—better than the cab fare you would have spent. This solves the age-old "How do I carry all of these bags?" dilemma that's familiar to all urbanites.

So here's my recommendation: For your next grocery run, pick up the phone or log on to your supermarket's web site and have your supplies delivered instead. Even if you don't have your groceries delivered every time in the future, you will understand how it's done and will be able to do it easily when you're really in a bind—say, if you twist your ankle and can't walk or one of your kids is sick and you're reluctant to leave the house.

Coupons: Beyond Redemption

On the "Grand List of Things People Get Really Emotional About," coupons rank right up there with children and pets. So I'm wading into this subject with a little trepidation. But the official, certified *How to Cheat at Organizing* technique for dealing with coupons is this: Round up all of your coupons, along with your foot-thick

Tomato Salad–Tasty and Free

How would you like a healthful–and free–side dish every time you go to one of those quick-service Mexican restaurants? Here's how healthy-eating enthusiast John Gabaldon does it: When he places his order at the counter, he asks for a plastic drinking cup. Then he takes the cup over to the self-service bar and loads it up with salsa, which he eats with a spoon.

Get past the idea that salsa is a condiment, he says. Think of it as a tomato-based salad without the lettuce–fresh, low-fat, nutritious ingredients.

coupon organizing accordion envelope, and drop it all into the recycling bin.

When the steam stops shooting out of your ears, I have a few points to make. Ready? I know, there are homemakers who tear into the Sunday circulars with a blazing pair of kitchen shears. They paw through the neighbors' recycling bins for unused newspaper inserts. They cruise coupon-trading web sites. They sort all of their prized cents-off slips into categorized organizers. And they crow about saving $5 or $10 on a grocery run.

I'm all in favor of saving money. But is couponing really worth the effort? Only a small percentage of coupon fans manage to make the system pay off big time, and doing so requires hours of effort every week. If you put those hours instead into working, or into interacting with your family, the rewards would be much greater. Besides, you're reading this book because you're longing for order in your life without having to work much for it. It's likely that you only save a dollar or two each week on coupons, and it's also likely that three-quarters of the coupons in your organizer (if you use one) have expired. For most of us, couponing is actually the worst-paying part-time job in the world.

And then there are the commerce-and-marketing considerations. Don't fool yourself—product manufacturers do not issue coupons because they're nice folks. They want your money. They issue coupons for products you often don't really want or need, and they hope these products will become a regular part of your shopping list nevertheless. (Did you know that coupon users spend an average of 8 percent *more* in supermarkets than nonusers?) Even if you never use that coupon you clipped (which is likely), the manufacturer has successfully tattooed its product name onto your brain, which sounds a heck of a lot like advertising. Are you really happy when Madison Avenue makes you dance like a marionette while it picks your pocket?

If you are skeptical about the coupon-free lifestyle, give it a test run. For one month, give your kitchen shears a break and leave your organizer behind when you go food shopping. To keep your grocery bills down, follow the example of professional chefs, says healthy-eating enthusiast John Gabaldon: Watch for the supermarket sales on core food products—meat, fruits, and vegetables—and build your menus around those items each week. With the time you save by not couponing, teach your kid to play chess, write a poem, or watch a rerun of *I Love Lucy*. All the while, savor that newly peaceful corner of your life that was once chewed up by frantic but marginally profitable couponing. I bet you'll never go back.

Okay, I'm a forgiving guy. If you insist on making coupons part of your life, I am going to help you anyway. Here are some simple ways to make use of coupons without turning yourself into a paper-snipping obsessive.

Make sure you need it. Only clip coupons for products that you actually use regularly, says Misha Keefe, a professional organizer in Washington, D.C. Conduct a reality check: Are the brand, size, and all other features of the product precisely what you want? Also, make sure the price you're getting on that branded product is better than the price for any equivalent products that are available (store brands, for instance).

Make them easy to grab. Clipped-but-forgotten coupons are a waste of time. So store your coupons in a super-accessible place. One obvious spot is in the kitchen near your shopping list. But an even sneakier place is in the glove box of your car. That way they're available even when you make an impromptu supermarket stop after work. Whenever you clip a new coupon, just leave it with your car keys, cell phone, and other stuff that's headed out the door, and when you settle into the driver's seat, file the coupon away in the glove box.

Play post office. Make your shopping list on the face of an envelope, says Edwards, the cabinet designer. When you clip a coupon, slide it into the envelope. This way, your coupons will be right in your hands when you arrive at the supermarket register. If you fail to use a coupon, toss it out as you leave the store.

Use those familiar categories. If you keep your coupons in an organizer, cluster them in categories that are identical to the categories of food on your shopping list (see the discussion of shopping lists earlier in this chapter). When you enter the cereal aisle, for instance, you will be able to immediately produce all of the coupons that apply to that part of the store.

Storing and Preparing Food

The kitchen is such a hotspot of activity that two of the core *How to Cheat at Organizing* principles you memorized in Chapter 1 are particularly important:

- Cluster like things together.
- The more often you use an item, the handier it should be.

So audit your kitchen with these two ideas in mind.

Are all of your baking ingredients in one spot? Your sauté pans? Your coffee-making paraphernalia? Your crackers and snacks? Your cooking wines, oils, and vinegars?

A Mushy Mystery

A befuddled reader once e-mailed a note to author and chef Silvia Bianco. The reader had made a saffron risotto, put the rice dish—lidded pot and all—into the car, and drove to a dinner party. When he arrived, his once-perfect risotto had turned to mush. Why, for goodness sake?

The reader made a fairly common error, Bianco says. Most people don't realize that some foods—steak and pasta are other examples—will keep cooking from their inner heat. By the time the reader had driven to his host's house, the risotto had cooked itself into goo. The better strategy: Cook the risotto halfway, leave it still firm, and finish the cooking at the dinner party.

Lesson learned: If you're not serving a food right away, always undercook. You can cook it a little more if it's not done well enough. But you can't "uncook" it.

Identify the 2-foot stretch of counter where you do most of your food preparation. Can you grab, without taking a step, all of the following: your favorite chopping knife, a cutting board, your most-used pan, the olive oil, a whisk, a mixing bowl, the kitchen shears, and any other food-preparation tool that you use day-in and day-out? If the answer is "no," then you're wasting way too much time crisscrossing the kitchen. A step or two may seem like a small thing, but they add up to an enormous amount of time and energy wasted over months and years. So reposition these kitchen items now. Cooking will magically become easier and easier.

Make sure the kitchen items that you use only occasionally—particularly bulky items such as your enormous cooking pot, your wok, and your blender—are stored in out-of-the way spots in your kitchen. High shelves are good for this, as is the space on top of your cabinets. An alternative: Stick them in a corner of the pantry. If your kitchen shelves are crowded with decorative, "for display only" items that you never actually cook with (your collection of ceramic teapots, for instance), move them out. Most kitchens don't even have enough space for the *functional* items. Besides, the pots, platters, and other kitchenware that you actually use are probably presentable enough that they add to the décor. So store them on those high open shelves.

Send those silly widgets packing. Do you find yourself buying every clever little kitchen widget that you see advertised on television? Get a grip, says Connie Edwards of American Woodmark. Specialized, one-purpose kitchen gizmos tend to clutter up a kitchen and rarely get used. Try this experiment to pare down the items that you store in your kitchen: The next time a project requires you to box up your kitchen gear (moving, remodeling, or painting, for example), leave all of your kitchen stuff packed away even after the project is complete. When it comes time to cook again, only retrieve the equipment that you absolutely need for that meal. Leave the rest of your gear in boxes. After 2 or 3 weeks of cooking this way, you'll have a clear sense of what items you really need in the kitchen. Get rid of all of those melon ballers and meatball shapers.

Get hooked on pot racks. Arrange the pots and pans in your kitchen so they're convenient and easy to grab without having to unearth the one you want from a pile of clattering metal. If you use pots frequently, a pot rack is the way to go, says Edwards. These typically

hang against a wall or from the ceiling, with hooks for each pot. Warning: Don't just hang pots up there because you want to show off your trendy copper. They will collect a greasy film, creating a periodic cleaning chore. Dangling pots that get used all of the time will be washed often enough that they won't get grimy. Other good pot-storage strategies: Use a roll-out tray inside a cabinet or a lazy-Susan cabinet, the kind that spins around in the corner of your kitchen, allowing you to pluck off the pot that you want.

Get your lids in line. Pot lids are often the sad stepsisters of the kitchen equipment world. They don't store easily with their matching pots, so they end up shifting and sliding around in some odd drawer. Finding precisely the right lid is an annoying puzzle that slows down dinner preparation, too. Don't put up with that, says Gabaldon. Pick up a simple lid-organizing rack to keep them orderly, presentable, and findable in an instant. Such racks are available at cooking stores and on the Internet.

Buy like a chef. Buy your cooking equipment where the professional cooks do, says chef Silvia Bianco—at restaurant supply stores. There are a few good reasons to buy kitchen items this way.

ONCE UPON A TIME . . .

Anchor That Roaming Dishtowel

Does your kitchen towel frequently "take a walk"? Parenting author Pat Saso used to get upset whenever her husband flipped the kitchen towel over his shoulder and sauntered off with it. She would often find it abandoned in some remote part of the house. Rather than brooding or scolding her husband, she opted for a simple and direct cure for the problem: She wrapped a corner of the dishtowel around the oven door handle and secured it with a pin, making it convenient but also immobile.

For the Best Zest

Professional cooks usually turn up their noses at all of the gimmicky gadgets that clutter up the kitchen drawers of us amateurs. But there's a relatively unknown tool that they rave about because it makes a touchy cooking job so easy: the Microplane® grater. These kitchen graters, inspired by the design of woodworking rasps, boast razor-sharp blades, surgical-grade steel, and teeth that won't clog. They're also safe in the dishwasher.

"We use it almost exclusively for removing citrus zest, because it takes the zest off without removing any of the white pith underneath, which tastes bitter," says Jennifer Armentrout, test-kitchen manager and recipe editor for *Fine Cooking* magazine.

Browse the variations of this tool at www.microplane.com. There's a coarser version, for instance, that's perfect for grating chocolate or hard cheese.

"They're used commercially for a reason—it's that they stand up to heavy-duty use," chef Bianco says. Equipment tends to be less expensive in restaurant supply stores than in traditional retail stores. Also, you'll be sure that the equipment you buy won't include fiddly little details and enhancements that chefs would recognize as nonsense.

Conduct an Internet search to see what restaurant supply stores are near you. Many of them have retail areas and are happy to sell to anyone who walks in.

Bag up those extra spices. If you do a lot of flavorful cooking, you probably have a spice rack of some kind in the kitchen that puts all of your most-used spices right at your fingertips. And then you have 56 other little spice bottles filling one of your cabinets—some of them bottles you haven't even seen since the turn of the millennium. So here's an easy way to organize your excess spices, keep them fresher, keep them handier, and free up some cabinet space at the same time. Buy a set of sturdy zip-closing plastic bags, plus a clear, rectangular plastic bin that's just the right width to accommodate the bags inside. Pour each spice into a separate plastic bag, toss out the bottle, and use a permanent marker to label the bag with the spice name and the approximate date of purchase. (If you have no idea when you bought it, it's probably time to throw it out.) Squish the air out of the plastic bag before zipping it closed. Put the spice bags into the plastic bin in alphabetical order. Now these spices are not only easy to locate, they're also much more compact—you can slide them back into their old cabinet space with a lot of room to spare. If you want to add some longevity to your spices, slip the bin into the freezer. Spices in the icebox will last as much as three times longer, says Jackie Keller, a Los Angeles–based author and healthy food expert.

Give spices a spin. A quick visit to the nearest kitchen-and-bath store will give you several ideas for clever hideaway storage of your

HELP!

A Chef's Directory

Here are chef-author Silvia Bianco's favorite Internet sites for purchasing kitchen supplies:

www.johnboos.com: butcher blocks, counters, cutting boards

www.cooking.com: pots, knives, tableware, appliances

www.spicebarn.com: spices

www.americanspice.com: spices, gourmet products

www.instawares.com: professional chef and restaurant supplies

www.chefdepot.net: chef's tools and gourmet products

spices, including narrow racks for the inside of your pantry door or stair-step shelving that shows the label of every bottle. But here's another clever-but-simple way to make sure none of your spices gets lost at the back of a cabinet: Store them all on a lazy Susan and place the lazy Susan on a shelf or counter in your kitchen. Looking for your ground coriander? Just give the lazy Susan a gentle spin and scan the bottle labels. No shy little spice bottle can hide from you anymore.

Mastering Cold Storage

Real estate is at a premium inside a refrigerator. Because an icebox is often crowded and it's hard to see into the back of the compartment, many food items languish way past their expiration dates. This calls for some cold and calculating cheats.

Assign stations in the fridge. Most homeowners will set a half-used jar of spaghetti sauce down in the refrigerator wherever it fits. Bad move. If it gets lost behind that loaf of bread, you might forget about it and open another jar of sauce while the old sauce is still good. Instead, assign official stations for every category of food inside your refrigerator—drinks in one area, deli items in another, fruits and veggies in another, leftovers in another, sauces in yet another spot—and make sure everyone in your family follows the system. A quick check will tell you whether there's already a jar of spaghetti sauce "in play," and you will keep refrigerator crowding and food waste to a minimum.

Make the oldest most accessible. Whenever you have two like items in storage, make sure the oldest item—which should be consumed first—is the easiest to grab, says Jennifer Armentrout, the test-kitchen manager for *Fine Cooking*. In the refrigerator, this means putting the new yogurt container toward the back, behind the older one, for instance. Use the same strategy in the pantry. People in the food service industry call this concept FIFO—for "first in, first out." When you know you've been following the FIFO rule, you never have to stop and scratch your head over which can of beans should be used first.

Squeeze out more space. After a grocery run, few among us have spare room inside our refrigerators. The squeeze is even worse for people who live in cramped quarters with tiny iceboxes. So think strategically about how you use that refrigerator space, says John Gabaldon of www.cooking.com. Instead of storing lemonade in a big round pitcher, use a rectangular container, which is more space-efficient. Also, raise one of your top shelves to within 5 inches of the refrigerator ceiling, and place all of your short-stuff condiments there. This will leave more "air space" for taller items below. To make this shelf easy to navigate, cluster the items that have like uses—group sandwich makings together, burger condiments together, and so forth.

And when you buy fresh produce, purchase a few items that are underripe. When you're putting your groceries away at home, you can arrange your still-hard avocados and pears in a nice bowl on

GREAT GEAR

Condiments on the Go

A condiment caddy will keep your most-used condiments clustered in the refrigerator and will save you lots of walking back and forth, too, says professional organizer Dana Korey. A condiment caddy is typically a basketlike device with compartments that hold mustard, ketchup, relish, and sauces—plus salt, pepper, and maybe a few napkins. A handle sticks up from the center of the caddy, allowing you to pluck everything out of the refrigerator at once and transfer it to the kitchen table or the picnic table in the backyard. (No more, "Hey, where's the mustard?")

Caddies come in various styles, including acrylic, steel mesh, and wire frame. Browse discount stores, home stores, kitchen stores, or the Internet for a style that fits your needs.

the kitchen counter instead of dumping them into the refrigerator. Two days later, when they're riper and some of the food from the fridge has been eaten up, you can transfer these items to the cooler, too. Also, tomatoes often do nicely just sitting on the kitchen windowsill instead of taking up refrigerator space.

Give your produce a raise. It sounds odd, but some food experts have little regard for the fruit and vegetable bins in the refrigerator. *Dang,* you're thinking, *first they declassify Pluto as a planet, and now my fruit and veggie bins are in disrepute?* Yup, there are good reasons for this. Most important: Storing your fresh produce at the bottom of your refrigerator can be a health hazard, particularly if you keep meat on any of the shelves above. Think about it: What happens when the *E. coli*–laden juices from your ground beef drip down onto the tomato that you want to slice up for a sandwich? Not pretty. The solution is to store your meats in one of those lower bins and put your fruits and vegetables on higher shelves. There's another health benefit to this unconventional arrangement: The fresher the produce is, the better it is for you. You'll be more likely to eat these items when you see them every time you open the refrigerator door. Sure, refrigerator veggie bins are designed to supply more humidity to keep your produce from drying out—but if you're giving this fresh food first priority on the menu, spoilage won't be a problem.

Okay, let's say you have an independent streak, and you're not going to rearrange your produce. At the very least, store any raw meat on the lowest shelf possible in your refrigerator and set it on a tray that has a raised rim, which will catch any juices leaking from the package.

Move your milk. That in-the-door storage shelf for milk jugs may be extremely handy, but it doesn't give your milk the most longevity, Armentrout says. Instead, position your milk on a high shelf in your refrigerator, toward the back. In most refrigerators, this is where the cooling vent dumps its frigid air into the compartment. Your moo juice will stay fresh longer.

Double your fridge space. If you entertain a lot or have kids in the house, put a second refrigerator in the garage. Yes, you will have a larger energy bill, but it's a wonderful relief valve for your food storage problems. Use the backup refrigerator for bulky stuff such as extra soft drinks, wine, and ice cream.

Give your fridge an herbal bouquet. When you get fresh herbs home from the supermarket, treat them like a bouquet of flowers, says Armentrout. Pour 2 inches of water into a cup or jar, and place the herbs stem-down into the water. Then take a plastic grocery bag or produce bag and slip it over the herbs, letting the bag tent up loosely over the greenery. Set the arrangement inside your refrigerator. The herbal bouquet does a particularly good job of preserving leafy herbs such as parsley and cilantro. (Woodier herbs such as rosemary and thyme do fine when they're refrigerated in the container you bought them in.)

If the herbal bouquet isn't feasible for you, here's Plan B: Wash your fresh herbs and spin them dry in a salad spinner. Wrap them in dry or very slightly damp paper towels. (You want them semi-moist, but not wet.) Place the herbs and paper towels in a zip-closing plastic bag, press out the air, and seal. This approach is best if you're using the herbs fairly quickly. Use this technique to preserve your lettuce, too, says Armentrout, the test-kitchen manager.

Get an herb garden on ice. Not all of us have herb gardens in the backyard, and the fresh herbs you buy at the supermarket will only last a few days in the refrigerator. But don't fret. You can have fresh herbs at your fingertips year-round now, thanks to innovations in the frozen-food industry. So stop by the freezer section of your supermarket and stock up on your basil, cilantro, parsley, and chives. Your friends will wonder how you became a fresh-herb fanatic overnight.

Leftover liquid? Cube it. How often do you find yourself pouring out broth, buttermilk, cream, and other liquids that grew old in your refrigerator? You can preserve liquids in a way that makes them incredibly easy to use in the future, says Jackie Keller, the author and healthy food expert. Pour your excess liquid into an ice cube tray and slide it into the freezer. Once the liquid has frozen, pop the cubes out into a zip-closing plastic bag, label the bag with the name of the liquid and the date, and return it to the freezer. The next time you need just a little bit of broth, grab a few cubes out of the freezer and drop them into your cooking pot.

Pantry Pointers

In the pantry, the old "place like things together" rule applies in spades. Scores of items can fly into and out of your pantry every day as meals are made, school lunches are packed, groceries are purchased, and snack lusts are satisfied. All of the food-fixing processes in your house will go vastly smoother if pantry items are easy to find. Which means they have to be stored in an orderly way: Soups and broths together, paper goods together, pastas and sauces together, and baking ingredients together.

The venerable S4 technique (Strip, Scrap, Sort, and Store) is a good starting point if you have a disheveled pantry. I won't take up space by repeating it here (flip back to Chapter 1 if you need a refresher course). Once you have your food storage shelves in good basic order, here are some fine points for making your commissary run even more smoothly. (Pay attention: Each of these items appears on the exam for the *How to Cheat at Organizing* Pantry Operator's License.)

Design by frequency. Let your cooking preferences guide the way you stock your pantry, says chef Judi Gallagher. If you make pasta three times a week, the dried pasta, canned tomatoes, sauces, and related ingredients should be the most accessible on the shelves and closest to the kitchen. If you bake a lot, put the flour, sugar, and brown sugar within easy reach.

Your list of pantry "must-haves." If you make sure you always have a handful of core items on hand in the pantry and refrigerator, you will never be at a loss in the kitchen. Even when you don't have any "real food," you can still whip up an impromptu meal, says chef

SLEIGHT OF HAND

The Dot System: A Time for Every Wine

What do you do if you're a wine snob and your spouse . . . well, just wants something to drink while watching basketball? Use chef Judi Gallagher's color-dot system. Go to an office supply store and buy a set of those sticker dots, the kind people use to price-tag items in a yard sale. Establish a message that each color of dot will represent, and affix a sticker to the bottom of the appropriate wine bottles—an inconspicuous spot where guests won't see it. Here's how Gallagher's dots are translated:

Pink dot: "Don't you dare drink this—it's way too expensive."

Yellow dot: "Caution—this is a mid-priced wine for dinners and other nice occasions."

No dot: "Sure, drink this cheap stuff while you watch sports on TV."

and author Bianco. In the pantry, keep a permanent store of flour, pasta, rice, and olive oil—all versatile ingredients that will carry you far. Likewise, in the fridge, keep butter, milk, wine, and eggs. And always in the freezer: boneless chicken breast. With the aid of your spice rack, there are hundreds of ways to combine these ingredients to make satisfying meals.

Pick narrow shelving. Whenever you have a choice, use narrow shelves in your pantry instead of deep ones, says John Gabaldon, the rep for www.cooking.com. Let's say you have a walk-in pantry and you have enough room for either one deep shelf along one wall or two narrow shelves both to your left and your right. On the deep shelf, the items at the back will grow dusty and forgotten. On the two narrow shelves, every food item will get star billing.

For tiny food items, such as spices or baby food, buy a small stair-step shelf. Gabaldon had special shallow shelves built in his pantry that were just the right height to accommodate canned food. With this arrangement, there's no wasted "air space" above the cans.

Whatever shelving you install, make sure you have a flexible system that allows for repositioning. As needs, tastes, and trends change, your shelving will have to adapt.

Use containers. If you're stuck with deep shelves in your pantry, all is not lost, says Dana Korey, a professional organizer in Del Mar, California. Rather than stacking cans, jars, and boxes individually on those shelves, place them in containers or drawers that sit on the shelves. This way, you can pull out the container and easily see everything inside—even the food that would have been hiding at the back of your shelf. Put like things in each container—for instance, baking goods in one, napkins and paper plates in another, and soups and broths in another.

Brighten up that pantry. Make sure you have good lighting in the pantry, so you can see everything and no items will get forgotten in a dark corner. If possible, install an automatic switch on your pantry door so the light will go on and off as you come and go. This way, you won't have to mess with light switches when your hands are full of food items.

Get see-through storage. Clear plastic containers are a great idea because you can tell in a split second what's inside. This is particularly important in the pantry, says Gabaldon, especially for such foods as grains and pastas. "Easy access and stackability in a tight pantry make a less stressful kitchen," he says.

Work the angles. It's a natural instinct to want to line up your pantry items in rows, but that makes it hard to see objects that are in the back. The result, says Gabaldon: You won't be able to find the foods you need readily, and some of those items will be forgotten and go out of date. The solution is to arrange your pantry items in zigzagging or V-shaped lines. They'll still be orderly, but you will be able to see every container at a glance.

Keep like items in line. If you have a broad range of one kind of ingredient—chef Gallagher has several grades of olive oils, for instance—arrange them on the pantry shelf in an order that you will instantly recognize. Gallagher positions her olive oils from lightest to heaviest, left to right. This way, she can quickly grab precisely the grade of olive oil she wants without having to ponder the labels.

Chopping, Cutting ... and Short-Cutting

Everybody who's been to cooking school knows the core strategy for making the preparation of a meal go incredibly smoothly. And now you know, too: Before you apply heat to any food, have all ingredients assembled and prepared (measured, chopped, sliced, peeled, and grated). Also, gather all pans, bowls, tools, and utensils you will need and arrange them within easy reach on the counter by the stove.

The French call this strategy *mise en place,* which translates as—no, not "mice on the plate," but more like "setting in place." What makes this simple concept so effective?

- If an ingredient or crucial tool is missing, you can fix the problem before the cooking actually starts.

- You can take care of small-but-time-consuming tasks well in advance—letting meat warm up to room temperature, for instance, or toasting sesame seeds.

- With the ingredients and tools arranged in an orderly way, according to the steps in the recipe, you will be able to grab up everything you need in a split second.

- You'll be shocked at how quickly you're done with cooking and how simple the food preparation process suddenly seems.

Home cooks who don't follow this approach make their food preparation 10 times more harried and complicated than it needs to be. They run frantically between the stove, the pantry, and the refrigerator. They panic when they discover they're out of chicken stock. And their eyes tear up when they realize that the shrimp should have started marinating an hour ago.

Watch out for common ground. If you're making a big dinner involving a number of different recipes, review each of those recipes in one sitting, says *Fine Cooking's* Armentrout. Identify the ingredients that the recipes have in common—say, crushed garlic or chopped parsley—and prepare those ingredients all at one time. This will save you several rounds of rinsing produce, chopping, and cleaning utensils.

Chop those veggies early. Don't just leave your fresh vegetables in the refrigerator whole, says psychologist Susan Fletcher. Whenever possible, slice and chop them up in the way they're going to be used later in the week and store them in the icebox in zip-closing plastic bags. If you do this during the leisure of a Sunday evening—as a family activity, so you don't have to do all of the work—you will save tons of time during the workweek. For instance, Fletcher is a working mom, but she still manages to make the occasional omelet for breakfast in the middle of the week, because the onions and green peppers are already prepped.

Planning a Movable Feast

A picnic may be an informal shorts-and-sandals event, but in some ways it's more complex than a formal dinner party. Not only do you want to delight your guests with creative food, but the entire production needs to be easily transportable. Here's how food and kitchen experts map out their picnics in advance. A tip of the baseball cap goes out to Silvia Bianco, Connie Edwards, and Scott James for their input.

3 weeks ahead: Plan your menu. With this much lead time, you'll be able to wait for the best prices at the supermarket. Reserve the date of the picnic on the family calendar and invite friends. If any friends are bringing food, coordinate who's making what now.

1 week ahead: Buy all nonperishables. Bake any special items you had in mind—those crab cakes everybody raves about, for instance—and freeze them.

1 day ahead: Do any cooking necessary for chicken salad or pasta salad and refrigerate—but don't mix the ingredients yet. Toss your pasta in a little olive oil so it doesn't stick together. If you have room, pick up bags of ice and sock them away in the freezer. If you're going to grill at the picnic, marinate your meat and vegetables. Refrigerate your beverages.

3 hours ahead: Blend the ingredients for the chicken salad or pasta salad (you'll see—waiting makes a big difference in taste and texture). Pick up ice if you haven't already. Establish a staging area in your home and gather all of your picnic stuff that doesn't require refrigeration—if you have a walk-in pantry, that's a good place.

30 minutes ahead: Make sandwiches. (An alternative: Just pack up a couple of loaves of interesting bread with a bread knife, plus sandwich fillings in containers. Slice the bread at the picnic and take orders.) Slice tomatoes and put them into a plastic container.

10 minutes ahead: Transfer ice, food, and drinks to the coolers.

Picnic time: Load up the car and go.

Don't try to make it all. You ought to look forward to a picnic. Naturally, you want to wow everyone with the food you provide, but who wants to be an anxious wreck in the weeks leading up to the event? The certified *How to Cheat at Organizing* approach takes the pressure off: Select two picnic foods you're famous for—say, your homemade lemonade and those yumptious chocolate-chip

cookies—and make those for the picnic. For the entire rest of your menu, go store-bought: potato salad, spicy wings, chips and salsa— the works. You will have put your personal touch on the event for a tiny fraction of the effort. "Remember," says Edwards, "nobody ever complains if you bring a bucket of KFC®."

Go ahead—get sauced. Oh, what the last couple of decades have done for home cooks! If you have been turning a blind eye toward the supermarket aisle that's crammed with bottles, jars, and envelopes of prepared sauces, you're missing out on a major *How to Cheat at Organizing* culinary trick. All you have to do is cook a core food in the simplest possible way—say, sauté a pork chop— then you add an exotic sauce that you pulled off the shelf, all prepared and ready to consume. Sprinkle a little water on your shirtfront, and your family will think you've been sweating up a storm in the kitchen.

"Our grocery stores today have great condiments from all over the world," says chef Bianco. She's a particular fan of the Hoboken Eddie's® sauces that are available in her stores. She also adores Marie's® bleu cheese dressing. Just a couple of possible uses for prepared sauces: Pour blue cheese dressing as is over steak, or spoon store-bought sautéed peaches or apricots over salmon—or onto ice cream, for that matter.

So jump into prepared sauces with both feet. Play a sauce-of-the-week game with yourself: Pluck an unfamiliar, exotic preparation off the shelf at the supermarket and make use of it within the next week. Also, stockpile various sauces in one area of your pantry so you can perk up a tired old recipe in seconds.

Entertain your guests—with cooking duty. If you have guests coming to dinner, do all of the time-consuming chopping, slicing, and sifting ahead of time—and then stop. From that point on, you will be able to throw the meal together in no time, says Bianco. Complete the cooking right in front of your guests. Don't worry—they'll find it entertaining. You can even ask a few of them to participate.

Raising Your Barbeque IQ

Here's one of the most vexing things about grilling outdoors: You have to recreate the kitchen environment yards—and sometimes miles—away from the comfort of your kitchen. Here are clever ways to cut corners on your trek to the "outdoor stove."

Station tools at the grill. Keeping a few tools permanently stationed at the grill solves a number of organizational issues. You don't have to go searching for those super-tongs, for instance, when you're in the midst of grilling ribs. You don't have to carry your gear back and forth. And you alleviate the clutter issue in your kitchen drawers. At a minimum, says Armentrout, keep tongs, a grill brush, paper towels (if you can get them under cover), and a container of oil for cleaning the grate. If your grill isn't quipped with a rack for hanging tools, look for such a device where grilling products are sold.

Protect the platter. One of the big hassles of grilling is carrying all of those serving platters and containers from the kitchen to the grill and back again. Here's how to cut your carrying duties in half, says Armentrout: When you're taking raw meat out to the grill, cover your dish or container with plastic wrap before setting the

Charcoal: The Surefire Method

Many a small child has learned interesting new words from parents who were trying to get the charcoal lit in the backyard. With a few simple tricks, however, you'll have those coals glowing in no time. Here's how chef Scott James does it.

First, pick up a little device called a charcoal chimney, available where grilling supplies are sold. This is an aluminum cylinder that you pour your charcoal into. At the bottom of the chimney is a little compartment where you stuff some fire-starting material (really dry paper works well). Set the chimney in your grill, loaded with charcoal, and light the fire-starter at the bottom. The fire-starter ignites the charcoal inside the cylinder, aided by the concentrated heat and the chimney-style updraft. When the coals are covered in gray ash, dump them into the grill and go find the steaks.

Now, that alone is enough of a shortcut to qualify as a cheat, but James even cheats at cheating. His sneaky secret: When he's filling his charcoal chimney, he places in the bottom three—and only three—of those charcoal briquettes that come pretreated with starter fluid. Then he fills the chimney the rest of the way with conventional charcoal and adds paper at the bottom. Why only three supercharged briquettes? If you use too many, there's a chance of getting the fuel taste on the food you're grilling, James says. But never fear: Three pretreated briquettes are more than enough to get the charcoal blazing.

meat on it. This way, you don't contaminate the actual plate. Put the meat on the grill, remove the plastic and throw it away, then put the cooked meat back onto the bare plate. You don't dirty two plates this way.

Grill your side dishes, too. Grilling always presents a quandary: When the cook is outside working over the grill, who's minding the vegetables that are cooking in the kitchen? Sure, you could make food preparation a two-person job on nights that you grill. But chef Scott James of Raleigh, North Carolina, has an easier approach.

Wrap your vegetables in aluminum foil; add some butter, salt, pepper, and other seasonings; close up the foil packet; and place it on the grill to cook while you're charring the steaks. Allow 20 minutes for red potatoes (cut into quarters) and 10 minutes for other veggies.

Great grate-cleaning. The number one thing to remember about cleaning your grill grate is that you aren't really trying to clean it. At least, not in the sense of returning it to its original, shiny-steel condition. Here's an easy, nonfinicky way to clean the grate: When you're done grilling, leave the grate in place and cover the grill for a minimum of 15 minutes. This will cook off much of the food that's stuck to the metal. Then, the next time you grill, all you have to do is remove any remaining chunks that could get stuck to your food and change the flavor. So heat up the grill and give the grate a once-over with the wire brush—right there over the fire. Then moisten a paper towel with oil. Using your tongs, wipe the grate down with the paper towel. The grate doesn't have to be 100 percent clean—no germs can live on the grate of a fired-up grill.

GREAT GEAR

Get a Beeper for Your Meat

John Gabaldon's all-time favorite cooking gizmo is his digital thermometer probe, designed for grilling meat. Made by Weber®, his meat thermometer includes a remote beeper alert that you can drop into your apron pocket or clip onto a belt. You stick the probe into your barbeque ribs, put them onto the grill, and the beeper goes off when the internal temperature hits the correct level. That takes all of the guesswork out of grilling, letting you know exactly when the food is done.

But Gabaldon "cheats" even further, which is why we love him. The home chef and PR dude for www.cooking.com figured out that the beeper system works equally well indoors, in his conventional oven. So he now knows precisely when his Thanksgiving turkey is done. It "pages" him!

Chapter Five

Storage Spaces

The World's Easiest Attack Plan

IT HAPPENS TO ALL OF US. At some time in your life, you wander into the attic, or the basement, or the crawl space, and you notice that what was once an innocent collection of six cardboard boxes (old record albums and low-priority kitchen gear) has now been joined by a scuffed-up golf bag, boogie boards from your last beach trip, a tent, sleeping bags, two defunct lamps, ancient tax files, and all of the junk that didn't sell in your last yard sale. The pile grows every week. It's a random, rolling heap. The room is gridlocked and unusable. Finding any specific thing in that mess would be a project all in itself.

A magic wand would be handy just now. But until you find Tinkerbell, the *How to Cheat at Organizing* storage-area attack plan is a reasonable substitute.

8 Rules for Buying Containers

It sounds so simple on the surface: Buy a box and throw stuff in it. Well, it's *almost* that easy, but keep these eight rules in mind when you buy the bins, baskets, and boxes that keep your storage spaces organized. Thanks go out to Mona Williams, vice president of buying at The Container Store, and Laura Ray, professional organizer, for their input.

1. **Take your time.** Merely loading a shopping cart with storage containers will not solve your organizing problems. You might be buying the wrong size or shape of container, and your unusable containers will become clutter themselves. Only buy containers when it's clear exactly what you need, information that will only come late in the S4 process (let's all say it together: Strip, Scrap, Sort, Store). Buy only containers that are a good fit for the stuff you need to store.

2. **Consider the storage space.** Containers can help you convert odd spaces around your home into storage—underneath your bed or under a stairway, for instance. Consider shape (wide and flat for under the bed). Measure the space, jot down the specs, and take a tape measure with you when you shop for containers.

3. **Think vertically.** An easy way to multiply the storage capacity in your home is to make good use of the vertical space. Putting your containers on shelves is one way to go about it. Another is the use of stacking containers. When stacking, buy containers all in the same style and brand so they'll create a stable vertical structure. In some situations, it helps to buy the kind of bin with side access, so you don't have to unstack your containers every time you want to grab something.

4. **Look high and low.** Choose containers based on where they will be stored. For high shelves, get small containers that you can lift easily. On low shelves, you can use bigger, heavier containers.

5. **Remember color.** The color of your storage bins may be important in a couple of scenarios. If the bins are highly visible in the home, you may want the containers to blend well with your décor. If you are organizing by

color—say, each family member has a different storage bin on a particular shelf—you may want to buy the same-size bin in different colors.

6. **Make it apparent.** You want it to be immediately obvious what you have stored inside any container. Transparent containers make this easy. Use opaque containers for stuff that can be damaged by light. In that case, have a good way to label your containers on the top and the sides.

7. **Consider the future.** Kids grow up, you move, your interests change—all of these inevitable things mean that your storage needs will shift as the months and years pass. When you buy a storage container, ask yourself whether it can be put to other uses once your current need has passed.

8. **Think about heft.** How sturdy do your containers need to be? If you need to store bulky or sharp objects (leftover bathroom tile, for instance), heavy-duty tubs are the way to go.

Storage Magic in 3 Easy Steps

With the minimum possible effort, we're going to convert that heaping wasteland of a storage room into an orderly depot where you can locate any of your possessions at a moment's notice—and we'll leave open floor space to boot. You'll be happy to know that the following strategy borrows heavily from Chapter 1's S4 technique, which, by now, you have tattooed to your forearm (Strip, Scrap, Sort, and Store). This plan is broken down into three stages. I highly recommend that you be nice to yourself and not attempt more than one stage per day. Complete a step, and then go out for an ice cream cone, the *How to Cheat at Organizing* all-purpose salve. A feather-duster salute goes out to Connie Edwards, a cabinet design expert for the American Woodmark Corp., for her contributions to this plan.

DAY 1: The Strip-Scrap-Sort-Store steps are probably all the easier, because many of the items in storage areas are often already boxed up and clustered by type. Check the contents of each box. Move the boxes and the loose items around the room, forming three clusters:

- **I'm keeping this stuff.** Be hard on yourself. Do these items really hold a place in your future? If they do, they get to remain in the storage room, albeit in a more orderly fashion.

- **This is usable, but let's get it out of my life.** Good for you— donate it to charity or leave it on the curb where passers-by will snatch it up. If there are no takers, then that's the surest indication that it really belongs in the category called . . .

- **This is junk.** Throw it away—immediately.

Now categorize all of the possessions that you have decided to keep—for instance, all of the golf gear goes together, the kitchen equipment goes together, and the entertainment stuff goes together. When that's done, leave the room and get some ice cream.

DAY 2: Our second round of organizing work will be even easier: just a little analysis. Consider the size and the shape of the room— better yet, take 10 seconds to sketch the room out on a piece of paper, with approximate measurements of the walls marked. Also make note of the size and shape of the stuff you have decided to keep in storage here. This information will heavily influence the kind of storage devices you install in this room. It would take an

entire book just to list every one of the nifty little options, but you're a smart person—and you've been in a home improvement store before—so I won't bore you with such detail. In very broad terms, here are some of the choices to think about:

- **Freestanding open shelves.** Very flexible, since you can move the shelves around if you want to reconfigure the room. You get easy access to the stored stuff, since the shelves are open, and you can see all of the stored items easily.

- **Freestanding lockers and cabinets.** Storing your stuff behind closed doors will lend a more orderly look to the room if that's important to you. It also will keep dust off your possessions, meaning there's less cleaning in your future. This approach costs more.

- **Wall-mounted open shelves.** They don't eat up any floor space, and you get easy access to the stored items. Mounting shelves on the wall is more hassle, though, and they're a trial to move if you decide to reconfigure the room.

- **Wall-mounted cabinets.** Again, you get a more orderly look when you close the cabinets, plus better protection for your stuff. But they're a more permanent, less flexible fixture.

- **Wall-mounted storage systems.** You cover a wall with special paneling (most famously, pegboard) or wire mesh. Hooks, brackets, and bins attach to it, providing storage for all manner of tools and gear, from screwdrivers to electrical cords to skateboards. An excellent way to make scores of smallish objects super-handy and organized.

- **Independent hooks and brackets.** These include everything from a delicate little hook you hang a key on, to monster brackets you suspend from the ceiling to hold your surfboard.

So it's decision-making time. After analyzing the room, the nature of items you want to store, and the storage gear options, come up with a combination that best meets your goals. Factor into your plan any bins or other storage containers you will need to use in combination with your shelving and cabinets. Complete the sketch of your room, indicating the position of all storage units. As you plan the room, try to cluster all of your storage in one section so that floor space is left over for other purposes—such as an exercise area, a workbench, or a sewing table.

Now, what's that sound? Oh, it's an ice cream cone calling your name!

DAY 3: Time to gather and install your storage hardware. Take precise measurements for all of the storage features you need (more on measuring on p. 101) and make a thorough shopping list—from the big stuff (shelves and cabinets) right down to the number of hooks you need and mounting screws. You can buy everything at a home improvement store, a discount store, a hardware store, or a container store. Install it and slide your possessions into place.

Tired of ice cream? Treat yourself to a big steak dinner. You deserve it.

Stashing Your Stuff Smartly

Here are some more general tips and tricks for getting the best use out of your home's storage spaces.

Can they take the heat? Consider the environment of each storage room in your home and whether those conditions will be hard on the items you want to store there. Crawl spaces, for instance, are notoriously humid, so unprotected books and papers will not last long there. Garages are often exposed to the elements, which could spell trouble for electronic gear, clothing, and books. Attics will get unbearably hot, even if you have an attic fan, so photos, albums, kid artwork (especially glued projects), candles, and many holiday decorations are out of the question.

Avoid stacks. It may sound obvious, but whenever possible, arrange your storage containers so that they don't have to be stacked on top of one another or one in front of the other. Containers you can see and reach easily are convenient storage. Containers that you cannot see or easily reach are merely time capsules—when they're out of sight, you might not even think about them for decades. An exception to the don't-stack rule: your eight or 10 containers of holiday decorations. These are all stored in the same place, they're pulled out at the same time, and they're put back into storage all at the same time. So stacking them is fine, says New York City professional organizer Gillian Wells.

Contain consistently. Use the same style and brand of container consistently. Rectangular containers fit together better and therefore conserve space.

SLEIGHT OF HAND

Vacuum Storage: A Smash Hit

How much of your storage space is eaten up by soft goods such as sweaters, mittens, scarves, pillows, and comforters? When these items are out of season, there's an easy way to protect them and at the same time smoosh them down so they take up minimal space.

The makers of those vacuum-sealing food-storage appliances (such as Seal-a-Meal® and FoodSaver®) tell me that, lo and behold, some of you folks out there are cheating! You're using vacuum-sealing appliances—machines intended for food storage—to compress clothing for storage instead. (For the uninitiated, these machines will roll out a stretch of plastic bag, you insert the food—or your sweater, as it turns out—the machine sucks the air out of the bag, and then it seals the plastic.)

If you want to compress items that are too big for these plastic food bags, such as comforters and pillows, grab a trash bag out of the pantry. Insert the items into the bag and stick the end of your vacuum cleaner's hose inside. Hold the plastic tightly around the hose and turn the vacuum cleaner on. When the bag is compressed, fold the mouth of the bag over to create a tight seal and wire it shut with a twisty-tie.

Let 'em roll. If you have limited space in your storage room, outfit the room with heavy-duty rolling shelves. When they're not in use, roll all of your shelves against each other at one side of the room. When you need to find something, roll the shelves out to create an access corridor between them. Wells has a client who successfully uses this tactic in a tight basement storage locker in New York City. The commercial-grade Metro® shelves she likes are pricey, but they're super-sturdy and have lockable 5-inch wheels.

Store between supports. A lot of storage rooms have open rafters and open studs on the walls instead of drywall. While these features are not much of a decorating statement, they are a great storage opportunity. Nail a few wooden strips from one rafter to the next to create convenient, out-of-the-way storage for long and slender objects. Pipes, garden stakes, and unused lumber will rest neatly between the rafters. Between those vertical wall studs, the horizontal cross-supports make handy shelves for tools or storage jars. Cut up a board to make more between-stud shelves if you like. Two feet above the floor, nail a strip of wood across two studs to create a storage slot for long-handled tools such as hedge clippers and rakes.

Mapping Out Your Garage

Now, I didn't mention garages in the storage-space attack plan described above. That's because your garage is a little different. It's the fourth-most-used room of your house (after the bathroom, kitchen, and bedroom). Unlike other storage rooms, it's actually a multiuse activity center. You might have a sports equipment depot in there, a potting bench, a workbench, a yard-tool center, and food storage all at the same time. Heck, some oddballs—just a quarter of the population—report that they can actually fit a car in there, too.

With all of these varied activities, and the attendant equipment and materials, the family garage *ought* to be a highly organized room. Unfortunately, according to one survey, half of all homeowners say the garage is the most disorganized room of the house.

Rock-Solid Storage Shelves

The ultimate *How to Cheat at Organizing* storage-room shelving would have to be extremely durable and rigid, easy to set up, easy to clean, and presentable (although it needn't be fine furniture). Connie Edwards, a cabinet design expert for the American Woodmark Corp., votes for "chef-style" wire shelves. You can throw these sturdy shelves together in minutes—all you need to do is count the grooves on the poles to make sure the shelves are set up evenly. Because the shelves are thick open wire, they don't hold dust and grime, simplifying cleaning. They're handsome in a high-tech way, so they work as well in the kitchen as they do in the garage.

This is "Rock of Gibraltar" shelving, Edwards says, and she has a unit of her own in a sewing closet. I have one, too, holding books and office supplies right beside my desk.

You can buy a freestanding chef-style wire shelf unit from home improvement stores for about $75.

Even more unfortunately, it's the only room in the house where the wall rolls up two or three times a day, exposing the interior to the entire neighborhood.

Ouch. This sounds like a big organizing project. And big projects call for big-time cheating.

Let's get one core question out of the way first, because it will affect all other organizational issues in your garage: Do you want to be able to park your car in there or not? Michael Dagen, founder and CEO of the HouseWall® garage storage systems company in Miami, is very hot on the idea of getting your car under cover. After all, your car is probably worth several times the combined value of everything else you have stashed in your garage. If you agree, then all of your other plans for the garage need to anticipate leaving that central space free for your car or cars. Leave plenty of free room on the periphery of your cars, too. You don't want to bonk the lawn mower or a hanging surfboard every time you open a car door.

Now for a second planning question: What will the other core uses of your garage be? You can't successfully rearrange all of the junk in your garage unless you have a clear idea of what belongs there and what doesn't. Depending on the size of your garage, you probably will have space for three to five core activities permanently stationed there—jot them down in a list.

Then make a quick sketch of your garage's floor plan and identify the best place for each of these activities. For instance, if you have your washer and dryer in the garage, they should be as close as possible to the entrance to the house. That goes for food storage and your backup freezer, too. A potting bench and garden tools go

Toss That Gift, Guilt-Free

How many cubic yards of your precious storage space are eaten up by "gifts" you don't have the nerve to get rid of? The Unwanted Gift Headache (UGH) has done untold damage to garages, closets, and basement shelves. While your intentions are honorable, this pain is largely self-inflicted, says Laura Ray, a professional organizer in Atlanta.

So stop it now. Apply this rule to all of those old wedding gifts moldering in the crawl space and every new gift that enters the house: If it's useful to you or you just love it, find a home for the gift right away. If it's not useful to you or you just don't like it, get it out of your life right away. Return it to the store and exchange it for something you do like. Or donate it to the Salvation Army[SM]. Or drop it into the box of stuff you're saving for the next yard sale. Life is too short to turn your house into an UGH museum.

Don't worry, says Ray: Gift-givers almost never ask months later whether you're still using the salad spinner they sent. There's one exception to this rule, however: A mother or a mother-in-law with a strong personality just might ask about a gift she gave. In that situation, stash such items under the bed and bring them out when she comes to visit.

How to Cheat at Organizing

hand in hand, so those areas should be side by side or just blended together. Similarly, a craft table should be near the place where you store hand tools, it should have electrical outlets nearby, and it should have good light. Bicycles, sports equipment, and yard tools should be near the exit to the outside.

Pick a Station, Any Station

Now, I can see the half-moons of sweat darkening your armpits. So far, I have asked you to do nothing more than scribble on a piece of paper for 25 seconds. But you can tell that it's now time to roll up your sleeves and create some order out of that messy heap on your garage floor. Never fear, my friend, this is where we are going to cheat like nobody's business. Pick one and *only one* of those several activities you listed for your garage. Choose the activity that's dearest to your heart, the pursuit that is most frustrating because you can't easily get to the gear that you need.

Let's say you chose gardening. Go to the newly assigned gardening storage area in your garage and use the S4 technique on this one little area alone:

STRIP every single thing out of the vicinity except the garden tools and materials. Round up any stray garden tools from elsewhere around the house and deposit them here.

SCRAP any broken tools, worn-out tools, and materials you never use.

SORT all of the remaining items by type—fertilizers, trowels, stakes, work gloves, and rakes and hoes, for instance.

STORE the items. Review all of your storage options mentioned in the section above about attics and basements— shelves, baskets, cabinets, and hanging systems. In your mind, assign a home to each and every gardening item, then make out a shopping list of storage equipment you need. Buy and install the equipment, and slide your gardening tools into their new homes.

I know, I know: You're dusting off your hands, pleased with a job well done. Then you turn around and ask yourself: What about all of that junk in the rest of my garage? And what about all of the other activities I want to station here? Well, we're cheating, remember? Walk away from that mess, and take a week off from organizing the garage. Every time you walk through the room, your picture-perfect gardening section will glow with orderly precision. You'll feel warm inside every time it takes you just a split second to find your weed-digging hand tool on the pegboard. Friends and family will *ooh* and *aah*. Bluebirds will land on your finger and chirp happy songs. After a week of this, wild horses will not be able to hold you back from organizing the sports equipment. A week later, it's the shop tools—and so on until all of the activity stations in your garage are organized.

Or not. Stop with the gardening station if you want. It's your business, and I'm not your mother, after all. At least you got your beloved gardening center up and running, and now you know how to get the rest of it done when you're ready for the job.

Speaking of Garages . . .

Here are a few more garage-specific organizing issues to consider:

Stick to the activity focus. Because of their proximity to the rest of the house, garages are best used as the center for multiple activities, as discussed above. This is a splendid strategy because all of the bulky paraphernalia is kept orderly and easily accessible. But this strategy also means that there are a number of things commonly stored in garages that really don't belong there, including:

- Your grill. Get it into the backyard or onto a patio.

- Holiday decorations. You don't need day-in and day-out access to your holiday decorations, so put them into long-term storage in your basement.

- Long-term storage boxes. The same reasoning applies—find some other place for those boxes of memorabilia, old files, and books that have nothing to do with the activities stationed in the garage.

Get 'em coming and going. If you have a garage entrance or a mudroom where family members typically come and go, outfit that spot with some handy storage devices that will keep everyone's personal possessions organized, says Connie Edwards, the cabinet expert. These features can include:

- pegs for coats and jackets
- lockers, cubbies (open), or cabinets (closed) for stashing lunches, mail, and homework
- a bench for putting on shoes, with storage underneath
- hooks for keys, handbags, book bags, scarves, and umbrellas

Make sports easy. Imagine a bored teenager. If she knows she has to root around in the basement to find a basketball, is she going to get any court practice done? No way. But if the basketball is in a handy bin in the garage, she just might shoot some hoops. The lesson, says New York organizer Gillian Wells: In-season sporting equipment needs to be at the family's fingertips. The garage or the mudroom is a good spot. Hooks, cubbies, and lockers are helpful in storing this often-bulky stuff. Overhead racks suspended from the

ceiling are superb for storing skis and other long, bulky objects and keeping them from being underfoot.

Guard your health. Do some poison control in your garage. Get all personal possessions off the floor and onto shelves, racks, or hooks. This way, if you have to spray for pests, you won't get insecticide squirted all over your golf bag. While you're at it, make sure all potentially harmful chemicals are locked in a cabinet or on a high shelf, out of reach of youngsters and pets. Store any potentially dangerous tools out of the reach of kids, too. Keep all flammable materials away from heat sources, such as pilot lights.

Intelligent Installation

I'm not questioning your competence. You are human, however, which means that you have limitations. You might be a genius at teaching third grade, picking stocks, or driving a bus, but that doesn't mean that you're a genius at hanging a storage cabinet on the wall. And that's exactly the mistake that many homeowners make, says Edwards, the cabinet design guru. It's more complex than locating a stud inside the wall and driving a few screws. Unless you're really adept with your hands, hire out a job like this and get it done right the first time—you'll save yourself a wheelbarrow load of grief.

I know it's been, heck, several minutes since you read Chapter 1, so the *How to Cheat at Organizing* HIRE principle is worth repeating: If you have a job around the house that's Hard, Important, Rarely done, and Elaborate, pay a pro to do it for you. So we're not going to talk about how to hang a cabinet. We're cheating here—we're going to talk about how to get someone *else* to do it. Someone who knows what he's doing. Who are you looking for, then—a professional "cabinet technician"? Such an animal exists and would do a bang-up job. More than likely, however, a good all-around handyman (or handywoman—they exist, too) could easily handle mounting a storage cabinet on your wall.

Finding a Dandy Handyman

You'll find plenty of handypeople advertised in the yellow pages and the classifieds of your local newspaper. However, one of the most reliable ways to find one is to ask your friends and neighbors. How do you know whether you have found a good handyperson? Look for a professional who:

- has a broad range of abilities—light plumbing, electrical work, carpentry, and carpet-laying, for instance

- has good references (don't be shy; ask for a few names of recent customers and phone them)

- does high-quality work for a reasonable price

- shows up when he says he will

- has his own tools

- arrives with a truck that's stocked with the most common materials that a household repairperson is likely to need, such as caulk, spackle, screws, and nails

When you find a good handyperson, treat him well. Make him feel welcome, offer him coffee and a croissant, ask him about his kids, pay up promptly, and give him lots of business. You want this person to like you and to leap into action immediately when you have an emergency. Also, take a tip from Edwards and just schedule your handyperson to visit twice a year. Edwards spends the interim time jotting out a to-do list for him.

Make Sure You Measure Up

When you buy shelves or cabinets for your storage rooms, the success of your installation depends heavily on how well you measured the space they will occupy. Way too often, people plop down hundreds of dollars for cabinets that don't fit in the assigned space. "I can't tell you how many times that's an issue," says Edwards.

Perception vs. Tape Measure

I had to buy another computer for the house (the old kids-and-homework story), which meant I also had to buy another computer workstation for one of our living areas. At my local mega office store, I settled on a couple of choices—until I whipped out my tape measure as a final check. I was shocked. The computer desks I had *thought* I was interested in were way too big for the assigned space. Instead, I bought what appeared to be a dinky little corner unit. When I got it home and installed the desk, it suddenly took on perfectly appropriate dimensions.

The big lesson: Inside a showroom the size of an airplane hangar, no furniture looks too large. Measure your space at home, every time, before shopping.

So let's get it right. Here's a primer on proper measuring for storage devices:

- Make sure you know how to read fractions on a tape measure. You may have a tape measure that has inches and feet marked off on one side and centimeters and meters marked off on the other side—know the difference. The inches typically will be subdivided down to 16ths of an inch, and the centimeters will typically be subdivided into 10ths. If fractions baffle you, consult a 9-year-old for a refresher course.

- A good-quality steel measuring tape that's at least 25 feet long is a must-have for any household.

- Answer quickly: What's 108 inches, translated into feet and inches? If you didn't come up immediately with the answer "9 feet even," then you need a tape measure with the feet *and* inches printed on it rather than just inches. (If you came up with the answer "7 feet, 4 inches," then you need to consult that 9-year-old again for a refresher course in basic math.)

- Have a partner help you measure any space that's longer than a few feet. It takes two people to hold a measuring tape tight and snug enough to get an accurate reading.

- Don't forget about baseboards, which can take up three-quarters of an inch of floor space. If you measure all the way to a wall, but you have bought a shelving unit that stands freely on the floor and will bump against the baseboard, your figures will be off.

- Always measure to the nearest one-eighth of an inch. When you're buying shelves and cabinets, $95\frac{3}{4}$ inches is not the same as $95\frac{7}{8}$ inches, which is not the same as 96 inches.

- It sounds like a no-brainer, but many people forget: Always measure your space before you go to the store to buy shelving. As well as you think you know your living spaces, you cannot eyeball a shelf on a store's showroom floor and be sure it will fit in your home.

- While you're measuring, take note of any other features of the room that may cause a problem. Will your shelf cover an outlet? Will that light fixture be too close to the top shelf?

- If you're taking a long measurement inside a room, remember that floors and ceilings are not always perfectly level. This means that the floor-to-ceiling height of a room in one spot may not be the same as in another spot.

"This is the upfront work that makes the back end of the project much easier," Edwards says.

Rental Space: The Final Frontier

What happens when your home's storage, every last nook and cranny, is totally maxed out? When stuff you wish you could cram into storage is eating up your living areas? One solution is to transfer a significant amount of your possessions to storage outside of your home. Unless you have a shockingly friendly neighbor with an empty basement (an extinct species, actually), you need to rent some storage.

But first, let's conduct a reality check. There are good reasons and not-so-good reasons for renting storage space.

- You've just moved from a large house into a small retirement apartment, and you have downsized your possessions as much as humanly possible, but a mountain of beloved possessions still remains. In this scenario, pledge to pare down those possessions over the next 6 months. Rather than willing your worldly goods to friends and relatives, give them away now. Simplify your life and make that rental temporary.

- You're in the midst of a complex household move, and for logistical reasons you need a place to stash some bulky furniture for a couple of months. Fine. Just don't let "a couple of months" turn into "a couple of years."

- You're selling your house and, being a sneaky person, you know that a sparsely furnished house looks roomier and therefore more inviting to buyers.

- You're going to spend a year hiking the Appalachian Trail and you don't want to pay rent on an apartment all of that time. Have fun. Donate your pants to charity in advance— none of them will fit when you get back.

- You live in New York City, where homes are notoriously cramped, and the expense and hassle of a storage unit are worth it to you.

NOT-SO-GOOD REASONS:

- Your possessions have been just growing and growing, and you need to rent a space to handle the spillover. Don't get offended, but you don't really need rental storage space— you need discipline in your buying habits and a better program for getting rid of stuff.

- You're thinking of a storage locker as an auxiliary basement. Now and then you'll hop in the car, motor out to your rental unit, and get the items you need—a spare set of dishes or that box of backup tools. Sorry, but you're dreaming. People who *think* they will visit their storage lockers frequently actually do it . . . well, just about never.

Rental Options Are Multiplying

If you have weathered all of the abuse I dealt out above, and you're still convinced that you need a storage locker, then you have a choice to make—what *kind* of storage locker.

You are probably most familiar with the traditional self-storage unit. You just rent a large box with a locking door, one that sits on a lot in some commercial neighborhood. This is the least expensive option, but you do everything yourself—all the packing, renting a truck if necessary, loading, unloading, and driving goods to and from your home.

However, there have been a lot of developments in the moving and storage business in the last several years. It's worth studying the yellow pages and calling around to get a sense of the extra services that such companies are offering. If you're starved for time, if you aren't able to move heavy boxes around, or if you need other

Locker Talk: Choosing a Unit

Okay, you have decided to rent a self-storage locker. Here are crucial factors to consider.

Leave walking room. If you need to visit your do-it-yourself storage unit frequently, get a locker with extra space in it. You will be opening up storage containers to retrieve items that you need, which is a royal pain if your containers are stacked solid floor to ceiling, front to back. So if you are storing enough stuff to totally fill a 5-foot by 5-foot storage unit, get a 10-foot by 10-foot unit instead.

Ask for the specs. When you're shopping around for a storage unit, make sure you ask what price you would have to pay for a specific size of locker. This allows you to make valid comparisons from one company to the next.

Check accessibility. Before you rent a storage unit, find out the specific location of the locker you would be assigned. Make sure you have a clear idea of how accessible it is. With some storage companies, you have to trudge down long hallways, take elevators, and sometimes even schlep your possessions up stairs. These obstacles can be time-consuming—and expensive, too, if you're hiring movers to put your stuff away or retrieve it.

Check the clock. Remember to ask what hours your locker will be available. If you need to pick up that portable generator from your locker at 10 p.m. on a Saturday, will you be able to get in?

Play inspector. Before you rent a storage locker, visit the company site and take a look around. Drop by on a rainy day and make sure your locker is dry inside. Are the grounds clean and secure? Any sign of vermin? In case of fire, are there smoke alarms and a sprinkler system?

Assess your risk. Call your insurance company and ask whether possessions stored out of the home are covered in the event of damage.

Check their reputation. Ask the Better Business Bureau whether there have been any complaints against the company you are thinking of renting from. Also, find out how long the company has been in business—more than 5 years is a good sign.

specialized help with storing your stuff, chances are there's an innovative company in your town that has the solution. A couple of examples:

The pod people emerge. Pod-style moving and storage was a smash hit when it entered the market several years ago. With this arrangement, the moving company delivers to your house an enormous storage container. You get to take all the time you wish packing your goods into the container yourself. When you're done, you call the company and tell them to pick up the container. They take it wherever you tell them to—a warehouse for storage, your new house across town, or the other side of the country. To find out more, conduct an Internet search on the term "pod storage."

Full-service container storage. Ram Katalan, president of North-Star Moving Company[SM] in Chatsworth, California, is pioneering a unique menu of moving services. His company will send professional movers to pick up belongings from your home, inventory them, and take them back to a warehouse, where they will store your stuff in a container for you. Any time you wish, you may call the company and say, "Please bring me items 5 and 8 off my inventory." Or you can call ahead, drive to the warehouse, and movers will have your container on the loading dock so you can pull out whatever you need. Such services will cost you a little extra each time, but you'll be darned certain that you're a cheat-at-organizing champion.

Ironic, isn't it? Our humble storage rooms—the garage, the attic, the basement, and other drab spaces that we hide away—are actually the soul of the home from an organizational standpoint. When they function well, the rest of the home can function well. But when they're cluttered and clogged, you can be sure the same will be true for the conventional living spaces. So if it's been a while since you dared to crack open the basement door, you can do so now fearlessly, armed as you are with a laser focus on what's important and the planet's sneakiest shortcuts for organizing storage rooms.

Chapter Six

Rescuing Your Home Office from the Data Deluge

THE RULES CHANGE when you walk into a home office. This is a place where business happens, there's expensive equipment all around, and the paperwork on the desk and in the files is often crucial to the family livelihood. So it's not a place for tomfoolery or child's play. It needs to be distant from the hustle and bustle of daily family life. And the décor and layout must be far more utilitarian than in the family room.

If you're among the wise and adoring throng that snapped up this book's predecessor, *How to Cheat at Cleaning,* you're probably wondering what more can be said about home offices. The subjects of home cleaning and home organization overlap frequently, and *How to Cheat at Cleaning* already addressed not only physical cleaning in the office, but decluttering, office layout, filing, computer maintenance, and virus protection as well.

What's left? Easy: One of the biggest home office organizational issues of our day is not how to obtain information, but how to winnow the information we truly need out of the glut we are bombarded with daily. This calls for some shortcuts—some unabashed, bald-faced cheating at organization. First we'll examine how to focus in the midst of information overload—that is, ignore a lot of the junk input people throw our way. Then we will discuss how technology itself, ironically, can help us simplify our overdigitized lives.

First, a couple of notes: While this chapter is aimed toward home offices, much of the advice applies equally well to the conventional working environment. Also, writing about computer technology is tricky because it changes quickly. So in many cases I have avoided mention of specific brand names and web sites. In the cases where I do make such mentions, understand that this information is current as of this writing but may change by the time you put this advice into play. The spirit of the advice will likely hold up for a long time, however.

Information Overload: Cures and Shortcuts

The good news is that information these days is cheap and plentiful. The bad news is that information these days is cheap and plentiful. We're up to our hyperventilating noses in e-mail, phone calls, and paperwork. Buried somewhere in that overload of data are the crucial bits and pieces that we need to do our jobs well and keep our personal affairs in order. With our livelihoods and personal well-being at stake, cheating our way out of this fix is out of the question, right? Oh, ye of little faith . . .

E-Mail: Taming the Modern Monster

Isn't it odd how e-mail has taken over our lives? A couple of decades ago, e-mail was unheard of, and you wrote pronouncements on paper—"memos" and "letters," we called them—and dropped them into a physical container called an "outbox" or "mailbox."

HELP!

Are You Chronically Disorganized?

Sometimes the roots of disorganization run deep, and fixing the problem requires some specialized help. Does this sound like you?

- In the past, self-help efforts at getting organized haven't worked.

- Disorganization affects your quality of life.

- It appears your disorganization will continue.

If so, you could be what's called chronically disorganized. There is a broad range of possible causes, including problems involving neurology, your environment, emotions, attitudes, addiction, aging, physical problems, learning, and grief. A nonprofit group called the National Study Group on Chronic Disorganization can provide you with helpful literature and point you toward professional organizers who specialize in cases like yours. On the Internet, go to www.nsgcd.org.

E-mail as an institution is in its infancy. This means there are major improvements ahead in e-mail hardware and software. It also means that we humans aren't very good yet at managing the messages that come our way. Our systems aren't very highly evolved. In its current form, e-mail can often be an unproductive distraction from your work. Here's how to coexist with e-mail and still be able to focus on the things that are important.

Turn off e-mail notification. Imagine having a playful child standing in your office, poking you in the ribs every 30 seconds. Distracting, yes? For the same reason, you should never have notices pop up on your screen when e-mail arrives. Each notice interrupts your train of thought, and you have to fight the temptation to see who has sent you a message. It's worse when your curiosity gets the best of you. Ninety-nine percent of your e-mail is marketing junk or newsletters you have lost interest in, but you get sucked into dealing with them anyway.

Schedule your e-mail time. Establish just a couple of specific times of the day when you will weed through your e-mail and respond to the worthy ones. Say, "I will read my e-mail at 2 p.m. and 6 p.m. before I quit work for the day." Erika Salloux, a personal and business organizer in Cambridge, Massachusetts, calls this "containerizing your time." Throughout the day, you will be able to assure yourself that any important e-mail will be dealt with soon. Your anxiety level will drop a notch, and your ability to focus will rise.

Sort e-mail before reading. Make sure you have a folder in your e-mail system that corresponds to every current project, plus folders for the individuals you correspond with frequently. When you first confront a screen full of fresh e-mail, don't start reading the messages one at a time. Glance at the topic and quickly sort them first into your folders. (Don't worry—you won't lose track of them. In most systems, the folder label will turn bold when it contains unread e-mail.) Now you can move from folder to folder, focusing on all of the related messages as a group. Your brain will work at full capacity when it doesn't have to repeatedly leap from topic to topic.

Trim down your e-mail volume. Create a folder in your e-mail system called "Unsubscribe," and drop into it distracting and unwanted e-mail you receive—the marketing pitches and newsletters you no longer read. When you have a few free minutes, go through the folder and look for ways to unsubscribe to this e-mail. Better yet, have your teenager or an assistant do it for you. Think of this as an investment: Each little message may seem insignificant, but spread over a year, repeated e-mail from the same source represents hours lost to distraction.

Send the clowns packing. We all have goofy friends who can't help but circulate jokes or bizarre Internet links to several hundred of their closest friends. Remove this distraction from your workday. When you receive such e-mail, send back a genial note asking your friend to take you off of the mass list. Say, "Don't take this personally, but I'm trying to focus and cut down my e-mail volume."

CHECK THIS OUT

5 Wise Ways to Size Up Software

You wouldn't waltz into a car dealership and buy a car off the lot without doing some advance research, would you? Blindly buying your organizing software from that mega computer store is just as foolhardy—unless you make these five moves before you take it to the register, says Adam Fingerman, an expert in organizing software.

1. **Decide what you want.** Jot down what you want your new organizing software to achieve, and match these notes up against the attributes of the software you're considering buying.

2. **Test-drive it first.** Go to the software company's web site and see if it offers a trial version, which will be limited either in the number of days you can use it or the number of files it can handle. Also check computer magazines for "cover mount" CDs that often offer dozens of pieces of trial software.

3. **Check the reviews.** Stop in at web sites that post reviews from real-life consumers, such as www.amazon.com and www.cnet.com.

4. **Check the prices.** A comparison shopping web site such as www.pricegrabber.com will show you what your target software is selling for at various locations. You may not get the rock-bottom price at your local store, but at the very least you want to pay somewhere in the middle.

5. **Talk to the clerk.** In the computer store, see what the sales clerk has to say about the software you intend to buy. However, consider this input just one more opinion. There are too many titles on the market for a store clerk to know them all intimately.

If you'd rather shift the blame elsewhere, say, "My boss monitors my e-mail, and I get in trouble when stuff like this arrives."

Write up stock replies. We all find ourselves answering a certain set of questions over and over again in our e-mail correspondence—for instance, driving directions to your home, or the specifications of a product you sell. Rather than typing your reply every time, write a set of stock replies and store them in a folder in your word-processing program, says Salloux. When a common question arises, just open up the folder of stock replies and copy-and-paste the appropriate answer into your e-mail. If necessary, spend three seconds tailoring it to the individual. If you handle a lot of e-mail, this technique will put hours back into your workweek. Sure, it's an impersonal approach, but we're cheating here, right?

Looking Gift E-Mail in the Mouth

I know it goes against your genteel nature to get picky about something that you get for free. But with free e-mail services, you might as well. You have a number of options, after all (including Yahoo[SM], Gmail[SM], and Hotmail[SM]), and their features and ease of use vary. These services are tweaked all of the time, so I won't attempt to say who's offering which feature. It's more important that I give you a rundown of technical issues to think about before you open a new e-mail account and tell all of your contacts to start shipping your electronic messages there. Thanks go out to Philadelphia techno-whiz Rafi Spero, cofounder of NeatReceipts, for these observations.

Is it user-friendly? If, like most computer users, you use Outlook® e-mail organizing software, an e-mail service that mimics Outlook is going to be easiest to use—you don't have to mentally switch from one system to another.

Is your e-mail searchable? You want to be able to conduct easy searches to retrieve old e-mail.

Can you download e-mail? Not all e-mail services offer a feature called POP (Post Office Protocol), which allows you to download an e-mail to your computer or PDA.

Is your information private? At least one major service allows software to browse the content of your e-mail and then target you for marketing offers. Spooky.

Can you import and export contacts? Often you want to pass contact information from one electronic device to another—say, from your e-mail service to your PDA. Make sure your e-mail service allows this.

Is adding a contact automated? Look for features that allow you to automatically add a person's e-mail address to your contact list when you send or receive messages.

When you sign up with an Internet service provider, at least one e-mail address generally comes as part of the deal. So why would you want to set up another e-mail account at one of the free services? There are several strategic reasons, says Spero:

- Use it to deflect spam. When you register with an Internet site in order to conduct business, you typically have to supply an e-mail address. You can count on them sending you junk marketing e-mail later. So why not have it all go to an account that's separate from the one you use daily?

- Some free e-mail accounts come with generous amounts of digital storage, which you can use to keep all kinds of data.

- Separate your business e-mail from your personal e-mail. For instance, you could give your friends your e-mail address on Yahoo and clients your e-mail address at work. Never forget that your e-mail at work is not private.

- Use it to get through firewalls. Ever notice that certain people don't seem to receive your e-mail? That could be because they have spam-blocking software that mistakenly thinks you're trying to send inappropriate e-mail. Spam blockers typically allow any e-mail coming from services such as Yahoo and Gmail.

- If you travel, a free e-mail account can be a godsend. From a rickety coffeehouse Internet connection, it might be hard to reach your conventional service provider—but you can reach Yahoo from anywhere.

Telephones: You're Calling the Shots

E-mail isn't the only persistent distraction in the working environment. There's the time-honored device called the telephone, too. Thank goodness, some modern technology and some old-fashioned management skills will whip those hunks of noisy plastic into submission.

Line up a second phone line. If you're going to conduct any kind of business out of your home, call the phone company and ask them to install a second telephone line, says Scott Simmonds, an insurance consultant in Saco, Maine. (Call it a residential line—otherwise they'll gouge you with a "business" rate.) Many homes are already wired to accommodate a second phone line. In any case, installing a second line is a simple matter for a phone technician. Train all family members to stay away from line two at all times. They are not to use it for personal calls, and if it rings they are to let it switch over to voice mail. Simmonds has two-button telephones accessible around the house—in the bedroom, the den, the office, and on a portable wireless phone.

Ignore that ringing. When you are in a productive phase of work, let the telephone keep ringing and switch over to voice mail, says professional organizer Salloux. If you can't resist picking up the receiver, turn the ringer off. Later, you can respond to all of your collected phone messages at once. Separating work time from phone time makes you more efficient.

Toss out your answering machine. Sign up for your telephone company's voice-mail service, says Simmonds. It's easy to use, and it allows clients to leave messages even when you are using the line. Your clients will never again hear a busy signal. This approach also will save you a shopping trip to the electronics store every two years when your answering machine goes kaput.

Cluster your calls. Organize the phone calls you make by topic—for instance, make all of your sales calls at the same time and make all of your summer-camp-registration calls at the same time. This way, you will stay centered on the individual topic and will not have to fight your way through a learning curve for every phone call.

Manage your clients' expectations. *Whoa,* you're saying by now. *Ignoring my e-mail and telephone may make me more productive— but I have clients who need to communicate with me!* Right you are, smarty-pants. That's why you should map out your average work-week and analyze the times when you get the most work done and the times when you need to be most available to your clients. Make it clear to your clients when you will be easiest to catch, and give them a way to reach you in a genuine emergency—a cell phone number, a special phone line, or a beeper number, for instance. When you have set up the right expectations with your colleagues and customers, you will be able to ignore e-mail and ringing telephones guilt-free.

More Ways to Sharpen Your Focus

Now that your e-mail and telephone are behaving themselves, let's look at other ways to remove distractions from your work environment and sharpen your focus.

Find a quiet corner. If you have any choice about where you set up a home office, select an area that's away from routine foot traffic, says New York City professional organizer Denise Caron-Quinn. When your teenager decides to bounce a basketball through the kitchen, you won't be distracted or—worse—have to explain that odd noise to a client. Having an office door you can close is a bigger issue than you might think. It blocks out sounds and distractions, of course, but it also sends a message to passersby that you don't want to be interrupted. There's a more subtle benefit, too: When you are done with work, you can close up your office and free your mind to focus on your private life.

Work when you're at your best. Every worker's energy and productivity rise and fall throughout the day. These "circadian rhythms" are different for each of us, says Caron-Quinn, so you need to map out the times of day when you are hitting on all cylinders. Schedule your work accordingly. You want to do your most important work when you are at your best. Save rote work for the times when your creativity will not be so sharp. Schedule break times throughout the day, too, to give you longer stretches of high energy.

Do one thing at a time. "Multitasking is a myth," says Salloux. If you're talking on your cell phone, cooking, and paying bills all at the same time, you aren't doing a good job of any of those things. Psychologists have proven it—every time you switch between tasks, your brain slows down to reorient itself. So focus on one task at a time. Say, "I am now doing this," and get it done efficiently. The exception to this rule: You can get away with multitasking if one of the things you're doing is truly mindless—say, watching *Gilligan's Island* reruns.

List tomorrow's priorities. Before you stop working for the day, list the top three things that you want to accomplish the next day. When you arrive at your desk the next morning, ignore your e-mail—attack the items on your list. If you go directly to your e-mail or other distractions, you will spend your day reacting to other people's priorities, not your own.

Preserve those ingenious thoughts. Plant a pad of paper and a pen permanently in your car, says Tiffany Mock, an organizing consultant in San Francisco, California. It sounds so simple, but people lose track of important ideas, dates, and to-do items when they try to store such data in their heads. Jotting down this information when you're out and about ensures that your brilliant concept for a product innovation, or the phone number to call for Springsteen tickets, will be preserved. Just be sure to park your car before you do any writing.

Layout by Convenience

Missy Cohen-Fyffe, an inventor and distributor of baby products, says she's lazy—when she's working, she doesn't want to get out of her chair unnecessarily. Well, there's a highly honorable term for that: a cheater at organizing. Here are tips from the Pelham, New Hampshire, proprietor of www.cleanshopper.com for arranging your office for maximum convenience.

Keep the "popular" equipment close. Put the items you use a zillion times a day within easy grasp while you're sitting in your desk chair—either on your desktop or in a handy drawer. For Cohen-Fyffe, this includes a supplies organizer (for pens, paper clips, and such), a calculator, a telephone, a planner, a Rolodex™ (slowly being converted to digital), and a set of hanging files containing immediate projects. Also place a trash can and a recycling bin at your fingertips.

Create a supply depot. Make sure it's easy to resupply your immediate work area with the materials you use frequently. Cohen-Fyffe converted a closet in her office area to a supply station, but a bookcase would work nicely, too. Here you would keep your extra printer paper, pens, markers, computer disks, paper clips, tape, and sticky notes.

Get plenty of counter. An L-shaped desk is a handy configuration, because it places worksurface on two sides of you. Cohen-Fyffe fashioned a desktop from a piece of scrap wood left over from her husband's factory. It's supported by file drawers on the end.

File in three stages. The less frequently you need a file, the farther away from you it should be. Put the files you need every day—current projects—in some kind of open, vertical holder within easy grasp. Files that are still active but you only need once a week or so should be in a file cabinet—which can be a few paces away. Inactive files that you still have to hold on to go into deep storage in the basement.

Chew up those personal papers. Sure, if you're that hungry, go ahead and use your teeth. But for most of us, a mechanical shredder, available at office stores, is what we need for destroying unwanted papers that have personal data on them—credit card solicitations and old bank statements, for instance. At a minimum, keep a shredder by your desk. You might want another one positioned wherever you open your mail.

The Cheater's Guide to Paper Clutter

The filing cabinet is the perfect symbol for the dreariest aspects of work—tedium, bureaucracy, and perfectionism. The good news is that there are perfectly reasonable ways to cure the paper clutter in your home without resorting to color-coded folders and computer-generated labels.

The perfect system for stackers. You might have the idea that professional organizers all abhor stacks of paper. Then you will be

Missing the Boat

Janet Luhrs, author of *The Simple Living Guide,* loves to travel. When she wasn't visiting exotic locations, she used to avidly clip and save articles about potential destinations.

She and a friend once decided to go on a houseboat vacation together, and they made their arrangements over the Internet. Upon her return from the trip, Luhrs discovered to her dismay that she had a complete hard-copy file devoted to houseboat vacations—which she had forgotten about and never consulted. After years of careful filing, she never thought to go to her own cabinet for the information.

Lesson learned: To heck with paper files. That massive electronic filing cabinet called the Internet often provides all the research you need.

shocked by this admission from Dorothy Breininger, a professional organizer based in Canoga Park, California: Her personal paper-management system is based on stacking. Her brain just isn't happy with going to files to retrieve the papers she wants. So she sorts her paperwork into stacks that are arranged along shelves. On the edge of the shelves she has affixed labels for each stack, such as "Events," "Bills," "School," "To Read," and "Church." Other stacks pertain to her upcoming media appearances ("Dr. Phil" and "QVC").

Breininger finds that her shelf system takes a level of procrastination away—she immediately has a proper place to put any paper she thinks is important, the papers are easy to retrieve, and they don't clutter up her desk or other surfaces.

If her shelves are full of paper, where does she park her books? In those unused filing cabinet drawers, of course. Lay them in the drawers spine up so you can find each book at a glance.

Presort your "to file" pile. Karol McGuire, a public relations professional in Colorado Springs, Colorado, has her home office on a different floor from her filing cabinet. So it would be easy for her stack of "to be filed" papers to quickly grow out of control. Her solution: She keeps a box under her desk where she drops all incidental papers that she needs to keep—such as receipts, tax papers, and warranties. In the bottom of that box are folders with broad labels on them ("Auto," "Insurance," and "Repairs," for instance) that correspond to the files in her official filing cabinet. Every few months, McGuire pulls out her "to be filed" box and slides each of those papers into one of the folders in the bottom of the box. Then she carries the folders to the filing cabinet, where they are easy to empty into the correct files.

Subdivide judiciously. No self-respecting cheater-at-organizing would make a filing system any more complex than it has to be. Look at it this way: If you have separate file folders for your SUV, your subcompact, your boat, and your bicycle, you have to hunt down each of those folders to file the corresponding papers. However, if you have one folder labeled "Vehicles," all such papers go into the same place—much simpler, says professional organizer Caron-Quinn.

First of all, divide all of your home paperwork into two broad categories, she says: personal and business. Keep these categories totally separate, with different filing areas for each. Then subdivide these categories judiciously. For instance, if your "Insurance" folder grows too bulky, split it up into "Insurance—Home," "Insurance—Life," and "Insurance—Automobile." But only create such subcategories when it's necessary.

Put event papers on the rack. The papers that you *really* don't want to lose track of are those pertaining to important events that are coming up—train reservations, directions to a wedding, and notes about your pumpkin-carving party. Breininger has an easy way of keeping such papers at your fingertips. Go to your office supply store and buy a tiered wire rack, the kind that holds file folders upright in a stair-step arrangement. In the rack, place one manila folder for each upcoming event. Place a small rectangular label on the tab of the folder and jot on it the following information:

TOP LEFT CORNER: the date of the event

TOP RIGHT CORNER: the event's time of day

BOTTOM LEFT CORNER: the name of the event

BOTTOM RIGHT CORNER: the location

Place inside each folder the relevant notes, receipts, tickets, directions, and other papers. Arrange the folders in chronological order, with the soonest event up front, staring you in the face. When you're dashing out the door to that wedding, all you have to do is grab the folder, and you'll know that the invitation and directions are inside.

Bind up those projects. Papers pertaining to projects are a breeze to keep track of if you dispense with file folders altogether and use three-ring binders instead, says Michelle Anton, author of the book *Weekend Entrepreneur.* She assigns one binder to each project. She keeps a three-hole punch handy, of course, but she also does all of her computer printing on prepunched paper from the office supply store. She also keeps a supply of dividers for her binders so she can categorize all of the information within each project. For example, when she was writing her book about personal entrepreneurial stories, she had three categories in her binder: an ongoing list of to-do's, personal stories, and entries for the resources section of the book. She can print out the name of each project and slide this label into the exterior plastic sleeve and spine of the binder. When she is on her way to a meeting, all she has to do is grab the right binder off the shelf and go.

Turn off the tap. Janet Luhrs, author of *The Simple Living Guide*, keeps paper clutter from ever entering her life in the first place. For instance, when clothing or furniture catalogs arrive at her home, she calls the 800 number listed and asks the customer service representative to take her name off the mailing list. Stopping an unwanted catalog, newsletter, or magazine before it crosses your threshold is far better than figuring out what to do with it inside your home. "I don't want to spend my life organizing and reorganizing—it just drives me crazy," she says.

Give papers a way station. What happens when sports schedules, take-out menus, and programs from your kid's play enter the house and you don't decide where they belong? They get added to those random stacks on the kitchen counter, the dining-room table, and the coffee table. Instead, intercept those papers with a clever little way station for unsorted items, says organizing consultant Tiffany Mock. Park a basket or bowl by the door or on the kitchen counter. When a flier enters your home and you don't have time to file it properly, drop it into the "unsorted" basket. Once a week, pull these papers out and sort them as a group. Throw away everything you possibly can, and find the proper homes for the rest.

Small Skills, Big Career Boost

Can organizational skills make a difference in your career? Listen to this story from personal and business organizer Erika Salloux, of Cambridge, Massachusetts, and decide for yourself.

A government attorney asked Salloux for help because she was reprimanded for not preparing reports on time. Also, her office was such a paper jungle that coworkers could not find the files they needed. So Salloux helped the attorney institute some simple systems. They created a "tickler" system to remind the attorney of important dates. They organized her computer files and established an "action bin" where crucial to-do items reside. Then they created another system for minor tasks: a handwritten to-do list on a pad. A tiered vertical file held a folder for each current client. Suddenly, the beleaguered lawyer could tell a coworker how to find any file in the office within seconds.

The foundering career took an about-face. Soon the attorney was being rewarded with extra vacation time. Eventually she landed a great new job as an executive director managing 55 people spread over three offices. And perhaps the sweetest touch, the attorney has a new assignment for Salloux: Come back to the office, she says—some of her underlings aren't organized enough.

Calling a Powwow

Whether you toil in the corporate world or behind a desk in the basement of your home, now and then you will need to gather in the same room with other people to share information. Good meetings are focused, productive, and no longer than absolutely necessary. Unfortunately, good meetings are astoundingly rare, too. To make sure your next meeting gets off to a professional start, we consulted organizers Erika Salloux and Denise Caron-Quinn.

There are a zillion kinds of meetings, of course, so let's say we are speaking of a gathering of eight colleagues to discuss the next steps of an ongoing project. If that doesn't sound like your next meeting, we trust you to adapt.

1 week in advance: Reserve the meeting space, make sure the key players can attend, and circulate an agenda. Include on the agenda a specific run time for the meeting, which will keep you and your coworkers on task. In your personal notes, write down points you want to cover under each agenda item.

4 days in advance: Gather input from meeting participants and revise the agenda if necessary.

3 days in advance: Order a deli platter.

2 days in advance: Send out a reminder about the meeting, with the revised agenda. This will catch the attention of the less organized participants and improve attendance at the meeting.

2 hours in advance: Check your presentation materials. Call and confirm that lunch will arrive.

15 minutes in advance: Check the room and get it ready. Distribute information materials. Make sure all needed equipment is working. Fill a cup with water and put it at your seat.

Zero hour: Start the meeting on time, instead of waiting for lagging participants. Starting late teaches people that arriving on time doesn't matter.

High-Tech Help

These are wild times for home computers. Every time you turn around, computers have gotten more powerful and less expensive. Software makers are falling all over themselves to make home software easy to use—because the market consisting of us everyday klutzes is far bigger than the techno-nerd market. And new ideas and new technologies for managing your personal affairs are springing up left and right without pause. Here's a collection of ways to cut corners in the computerized areas of your home office.

Scanners Emerge as a Hot Organizing Tool

Imagine this futuristic scenario: A businesswoman is avidly making contacts at a trade show, but instead of stuffing her pockets with business cards, dinner checks, and cab receipts, she slides all of these bits of paper through a pocket-size wand. This device reads the paper, identifies what kind of document it is, plucks off all of the information, and sorts the information into a searchable database. Well, that's not really far-fetched at all. This paper-reducing technology is in use right now. As organizationally challenged consumers cry, "Get this paper out of my life!" scanners are emerging as an intriguing solution.

As scanning technology becomes faster, higher quality, and more intelligent—and as digital storage space becomes cheaper—letting paper inundate your office space is making less and less sense. Some homeowners are experimenting with the paper-free lifestyle, dumping insurance forms, articles to be read, children's finger-paintings, recipes, warranties, report cards, and certificates into their computers, where the scans can be easily dealt into digital folders. Of course, unlike the folders in your filing cabinets, computer folders take up zero extra space in your home.

Will homes ever be truly paper-free? Such predictions are tricky, but Philadelphian Rafi Spero thinks we're going quickly in that direction. He and his father founded the company NeatReceipts, offering a portable scanning tool that allows businesspeople to keep track of their receipts while on the road. But they discovered that their customers were cheating—that is, using the product for other purposes. Customers were asking for special features that the Speros had never considered. One caller even used a scanner to track which spouse was spending what during divorce proceedings. Another used it to track contractor expenses during home building. Now the Speros are planning to offer a broad pick-and-choose menu of features for their portable scanners.

Am I telling you to run out and buy an advanced scanner for your home right now? Not necessarily. But do recognize that there are very few bits of paper in your life that aren't being converted to digital form. (Aside from thank-you notes or invitations, when was the last time you actually wrote a letter instead of e-mailing? Do you use a paper desktop calendar anymore? How about a Rolodex?) If you don't own a scanner now and want to stick a cautious toe into the water, buy an all-in-one machine that will scan, copy, fax, and print for you—all out of one box. Such machines don't tend to do a superb job of any of those functions, but they do an adequate job of all of them—the perfect choice if you don't require cutting-edge technology. Buy an all-in-one machine, see how it feels to scan all of your magazine recipes rather than filing them, and decide a couple of years later whether you're ready for a faster, smarter scanner. Your technical needs will be clearer by then.

"That makes a ton of sense," Spero says.

Quick Quiz: What's Your Techno Profile?

Have you ever gotten an inkling that you were lagging behind the rest of the world technologically? That you might be more connected, more in synch, and more organized if you took the leap into cutting-edge equipment for communications, business, and entertainment? Here are a few questions that will help you clarify where you fall in the spectrum that ranges from technophobe to technophile.

1. Do you own a home computer that's less than 3 years old?
2. Do you *always* own a home computer that's less than 18 months old?
3. Do you have a cell phone?
4. When you're told that you qualify for a free cell phone upgrade, do you accept it immediately?
5. Do you have a personal e-mail account (not provided by an employer)?
6. Have you ever bought anything over the Internet?
7. Do you do more than 50 percent of your holiday shopping over the Internet?
8. When you need to research a medical issue, do you start by going to the Internet?
9. When you are standing in line, do you occupy yourself with a PDA or smart phone?
10. Do you own a portable device that you download recordings onto?

Answered yes to three questions or fewer: If you're a working professional, you probably are being held back by a lack of technology in your life. Invest a little in getting connected to the digital world. The best place to start: Review your situation with a tech-savvy friend. If you're retired, know that you can stay connected with loved ones if you adopt some basic, easy-to-use technology such as e-mail and Internet access.

Answered yes to four to eight questions: You're in a good position. You have at least one foot solidly in the digital world, but you don't splurge unnecessarily on every new piece of technology that presents itself. High-tech companies are dying for your business.

Answered yes to nine or 10 questions: Well, aren't you the techno-geek? Careful: When you acquire all of the cutting-edge technology, there's a chance you like playing with electronic toys more than you like being productive.

Let Software Organize Your Digital Life

Whether you're busily scanning expense receipts into your computer or loading your hard drive up with vacation photos, something will quickly become apparent: If you're not careful, the inside of your computer can be as messy as the real-life office it resides in. It makes little sense to acquire and store any kind of digital files if you can't find them again easily, share them with friends, incorporate them into projects, or put them to other uses. Software manufacturers know this. Your local computer store offers any number of programs that will make your digital life easier. But knowing what to buy isn't quite as simple as buying a carton of eggs. Here are some tips from Adam Fingerman, the resident organizing software expert for Sonic Solutions® in Santa Clara, California.

Buy no more than you need. Some software companies develop a broad range of digital tools that are interrelated. You will find them on the store shelf packaged in different configurations. The limited, more narrowly focused package of software (say, for sorting and manipulating digital photos only) will typically cost less. The all-inclusive packages of software (perhaps photo and video editing, music library, web site construction, and presentation building all in one product) will cost more. Buy only the software that you need at the time. Not only will you save money, but you will not be burdening your computer with software that won't be used. If you decide that you want the broader capabilities in a year or two, it will be easy to buy an upgrade—and you will be getting the latest version of the software.

Break down and read the manual. You may pride yourself in being able to fire up any software and, using nothing but stark naked intuition, make the programming work for you. However, if you take this approach, you're missing out. Yes, manufacturers make their software as intuitive and user-friendly as possible. And yes, there are often built-in tutorials to guide you along. But if that's as far as you go in learning about your software, you aren't using its full potential—you've only had beginner's training. Many of the subtler tools and techniques will only be found in the manual. So crack the book, too.

Get bargain alerts. If you want to save money on software, sign up for e-mail notification from a bargain-hunters' information clearinghouse, such as www.dealnews.com. The members of this outfit send each other alerts when they run across great deals. They report on a broad range of consumer goods, but specialize in computers and electronics.

Fear no software. A lot of consumers are reluctant to adopt organizing software because they're afraid they're going to do something wrong and break their computers. Get over it, says Fingerman. "They're hard to break."

Here are more easy ways to get more organizing power out of your home hardware and software.

Get two screens. It sounds bizarre, but insurance consultant Scott Simmonds finds that hooking up two monitors to his home office computer gives him a huge boost in efficiency. With two screens running, he can have his calendar up on one screen while he writes a report on the other, for instance. Setting it up was easy: Most computers have only one monitor input, so he bought a $100 adapter that converted the second monitor's cable to a USB connection (computers often have extra USB ports). An alternative: Have a technician install a second monitor port. Once the second monitor was hooked up, the operating system walked Simmonds through an easy, 45-second setup routine. (It asked, for instance, which monitor was supposed to be on the left and which on the right.) A feature that makes the dual monitors work all the more smoothly: His mouse-guided cursor slides easily left and right from one monitor to the other as if they were one screen.

"It is incredibly efficient," says Simmonds. "I've thought about adding a third monitor."

Put your contact list to work. Learn how to make your computerized contact list work harder for you, says Simmonds:

- As soon as you have a conversation with a client, use the notes section of each contact's record to jot yourself a memo about what was discussed. Use these notes to refresh your memory the next time you talk.

- Common contact list software can be set up to dial phone numbers for you, he says, "like a big speed-dial list." Just a couple of clicks will reward you with that familiar beep-beep-bop computerized dialing, and it will kick your phone into speaker mode (if you're so equipped).

- Shop around for a program that uses the caller ID system to figure out a caller's phone number, search the contact list for a matching number, and pop that entire record up on your computer screen. Your notes about the last caller will automatically be thrust in front of your nose as soon as a call comes through—"which is very cool," Simmonds says. "My object is to work as little as possible. Any time I can save 15 seconds, I will do it."

Instant Advisor

High-tech entrepreneur Rafi Spero of Philadelphia, a cofounder of the company NeatReceipts, is never at a loss. He was in New York City one day when he and friends had a hankering for Middle Eastern food. Not knowing the SoHo eateries that well, he typed "hummus restaurant" plus the zip code into his cell phone and sent the text message off. Within seconds a cyber-world database had conducted a search and sent back a message listing all of the suitable restaurants within an easy walk.

Yes, you can find information companies that will gladly take your money for this kind of service. But the Short Message Service[SM] (SMS), Spero notes smugly, is free (at this writing, anyway). It's just one of many tools that the search engine company Google™ posts on the World Wide Web with not a peep of advertising to point you there.

SMS offers a long menu of information offerings, including stock quotes, local weather, phone listings, an area code translator, sports scores, language translations, movie locations, driving directions, and currency conversions—all available to you over any text-messaging cell phone. To send in your query, you simply type 466453 ("google") in the "to" field and enter your search terms in the message field. For more information on how to use SMS, go to www.google .com/sms.

"To me, this is one of the great unknowns," says Spero. Well, not anymore.

Get remote backup. Back up your important computer files on an off-site server, says Eva Rosenberg, a tax expert based in Northridge, California. This will ensure that if your office is ever wiped out by fire, flood, or teen toga party, you will merely have to replace your damaged computer—not re-create all of that data. For several dollars a month, you can rent space on a storage server that will keep a copy of your important electronic data. She notes that www.xdrive.com and www.backup.com are two popular sites. You also can check *PC Magazine* for reviews of data storage sites. Internet connection to data storage is a hot topic among software innovators, so a lot of big companies are entering the market. Most companies will offer you a 30-day tryout period and offer good support if you're having trouble. Find out where your data storage company keeps its servers, however. If they're in a famously hurricane- or earthquake-prone region, keep looking.

Bookmark the best sites. If you're not in the habit of bookmarking your favorite Internet sites, start doing it, says Erika Salloux, the personal and business organizer. There are way too many useful web sites—you can only keep a handful of them in your head. Categorize your bookmarks using a folder system that mirrors the categories you use for e-mails and for hard-copy files. You'll be able to find the site you need more intuitively that way. Some Internet browsers allow you to keep notes about why you bookmarked a particular site—an extremely handy feature.

Chapter Seven

The Budget-Free Path to Orderly Finances

YOU CAN'T AFFORD to "cheat" at personal finances by neglecting them. You cheat by taking a laser focus on what's necessary, using the most efficient tools and techniques, and ignoring all of the myths, misconceptions, and unnecessary processes. Being secure financially is a matter of survival, so you have to get the basics right. But frankly, as a group, we consumers are just plain lousy with money. We find credit card debt more addictive than salted nuts, and our savings rate is a pitiful zero. To "cheat" at finances, we're going to ignore the overcomplicated systems that repel consumers in droves. In this chapter, you will find a core collection of easy steps you can take to make sure you are handling your money in the wisest way possible. You'll find surprising ways to let technology take the tedium out of financial tasks. You'll find simple ways to assess your financial condition (without budgeting!), to eliminate fees that nibble away at your cash flow, to pay bills effortlessly, to

Addicted to Debt

Some fun, and frightening, facts from Freedom Financial Network:

- The average household has more than 16 credit and debit cards.
- Seventy percent of households live from paycheck to paycheck.
- Twenty percent of all credit cards are maxed out—meaning their owners have spent the limit.
- Seventy-five percent of all couples say money is a major sore point in their relationship.

put savings on autopilot, and to scoop up scholarship money for your college-bound child.

None of these tips is difficult or time-consuming. If you follow all of this advice, you will be far ahead of 95 percent of the population. So wake up and put these minimal basics into place right now. You can't afford to snooze through this. Ignore your money, and it will go away.

Daily Cash Flow

Sometime in your youth, you gave up your piggy bank and opened a checking account. Things have gotten more and more complicated ever since. While the daily ebb and flow of your money may seem wildly circuslike, there are some simple ways to intercede and make sure your cash is behaving itself.

I am psychic, you know. Right now I am peering deep into your soul, and I'll prove it: When you read the phrase "household budget," beads of sweat break out across your brow. Your eyes start to cross at the prospect of the terrific tedium of shuffling financial papers, penciling numbers into neat columns, and click-click-clicking at the calculator. So relax—I'm not going to tell you to budget. I'm going to give you the pain-free, budget-free way of managing your spending, recommended by consumer debt expert Brad Stroh, the co-CEO of the Freedom Financial Network[SM]. (Okay, he does believe budgeting is a good idea, but he acknowledges that not many people do it.)

So use the "rearview mirror" approach to managing your spending. Once a month or once a quarter, just pull out your checkbook, your credit and debit card statements, and your bank statement. Look at how much money came in. Then look at how much money went out. If the second number is greater, then you need to look for ways to change that trend. Decide how you're going to adjust your spending for the next month to at least break even—and preferably create some savings. There are probably some big payments you can't do much about—the mortgage and the car loan, for instance.

Cool Down Your Card Spending

If you have trouble controlling your credit card spending, here's the cure: Go to the box where you store your extra books of checks. Swipe a spare checkbook register and one of those plastic covers. Slide the register and your credit card into the plastic cover. If you don't have an extra register or cover, drop by your bank and ask for spares.

When you use your credit card, act as if you've written a check—enter the amount in the register, says tax expert Eva Rosenberg. Enter payments to your credit card company as deposits, and also register any fees involved if you let part of your balance roll over to the next month.

Tape to the outside of the cover a note reminding you how expensive it is if you overspend or pay interest on your balance. For instance: "Each time I use this card, I give up two hours of my life to pay the interest."

These two visual reminders—the register of all of your purchases, plus the note on the cover—will cool down your overheated spending pattern.

3 Ways to Stop Deficit Spending

You've added up all of your income for the month and all of your expenses for the month. Yikes! You're spending more than you make! It doesn't take a Ph.D. in economics to realize that this trend has to stop. There are three ways to fix the problem, says Brad Stroh, co-CEO of Freedom Financial Network. A blend of all of them will work most powerfully. Stop making excuses, and get to work on this.

1. **Cut expenses.** Attack leisure spending first, and tighten up the routine daily expenses as well.

2. **Make more money.** This is not easy to pull off, but your options are to put in overtime hours, get a promotion, get a higher-paying job, take on another job part time, or turn a hobby into a paying sideline business.

3. **Eliminate credit card debt as quickly as you can.** The fees involved in credit card debt are an enormous drag on your cash flow.

So take a line-by-line look at the discretionary spending (that is, the spending that wasn't absolutely necessary). "Sometimes when you add up all of your lattes at Starbucks® and your DVDs, that number can be shocking," Stroh says. Such "leisure spending" should be your first target for cutbacks, but you can trim your spending on core living expenses as well—relying more on sales at the supermarket, taking a bag lunch to work rather than eating out, and adjusting the home thermostat so you put less demand on the heating and cooling systems, for instance.

The rearview mirror is a quick, informal assessment. But it will alert you to financial trouble and point out the solutions. Consider this the rock-bottom minimum you should be doing to guide your financial empire. There's no one else on the planet who will monitor this for you, so start doing it. After all, you may be able to skip the budgeting process, but you can't just let your finances wander willy-nilly like a free-range chicken.

Take the Leap to Online Payments

Not too many years ago, the only people who paid their bills online were financial whiz kids with MBAs from Wharton. No more—anybody can do it now, and should. The system for having money drawn out of your account electronically and sent to other people is as easy to use as a crossing signal. If you have been resisting adopting this method of bill payment, you will be shocked at how much time and effort you save once you get started.

Drop by your bank or consult your bank's web site to find out how to sign up. Almost all banks offer this service free to their customers,

CHECK THIS OUT

Find the Right Bank

When you're shopping for a bank, here are crucial issues to think about, says Brad Stroh, co-CEO of Freedom Financial Network:

- Do you have a lot of assets? If you have a lot of cash that you will want your bank to hold on to for you, make sure you're getting a good money market rate. Also see that there are low fees on your bank's investment products.

- Are you low on cash? If you don't have a lot of assets, make sure your accounts have low minimum balances.

- Is the bank tech-savvy? Make sure you can pay bills and manage your accounts online.

- How broad is the ATM network? Identify all of the places where you're likely to want an automatic teller, and make sure your bank has one there. You don't want to pay fees for using ATMs out of your network.

- Can you get financial advice? Ask whether you can walk into the bank monthly or quarterly and talk to a real human being about your budget, accounts, investments, and any fees charged. Is someone available to help assess your financial situation?

says Stroh. When you log on to the bill-paying system for the first time, you will spend a few minutes entering the names and addresses of the people and institutions you regularly send money to, and this data will be stored permanently (unless you change it). The local utilities will probably be entered for you already. From that point on, all you have to do is enter a dollar amount in the appropriate blank and click on the "pay" button.

No longer will you have to spread all of your bills out on the kitchen table, gather your checkbook, pen, scratch pad, calculator, and stamps, and then spend two hours writing checks and licking envelopes. No more paying for stamps. No more trekking to the post office. Your payment records are all kept for you online under your secure log-on.

And speaking of security, if you have been resisting paying bills online because you're concerned about safety, Stroh has three words for you: "Get over it."

Never pay late fees again. The benefits of online bill-paying go on and on. You can use this system to ensure that you will never have to pay late fees to your credit card company again, for instance. Glance at your credit card bills for the last 12 months. What's the largest "minimum payment" you can find on these statements?

Let's say it's $17.95. Go to your bank's web site and set up a regular monthly payment to your credit card company that's just a tad more than that minimum—in this example, $20. Schedule that payment to be made to your credit card company every month well before the due date. Minimum payment made, no late fee.

Whoa, you say, *I'm a savvy consumer and I know that it's wisest to fully pay off my credit card balance every month—not just the minimum.* Well, right you are. There's nothing to say you can't make a second payment to your credit card company each month to get you fully caught up while you're paying the rest of your bills. With this setup, you won't be paying late fees even if you pay the remainder of your balance a few days after the due date.

Travel worry-free. Bill payments are the traveler's classic quandary. While you're lapping up the sun on a Mexican beach or ogling the ruins of ancient Rome, how are you going to get the household bills paid? Sending out hundreds of dollars in advance would work, but few of us like to let go of so much cash prematurely. The better option: Go online and schedule future, onetime payments for all of your bills that come in regular amounts. Schedule the payment to happen just before the due date rather than weeks in advance.

Get a web site's help. If your bank doesn't offer free online bill payment for some reason, you can have its advantages by going to a web site such as www.bills.com, says Stroh. For a small monthly fee—still cheaper than buying stamps—you will be able to pay your bills by having the cash drawn straight out of your checking account.

Locate the complaint line. Banks are not perfect, online or off. If a bank's online bill-payment system slips up and pays a bill late—costing you late fees—the bank is duty-bound to correct the situation for you. (This assumes you provided the correct bill-payment data in the first place.) The bank may contact the company charging you the late fee, or it may just reimburse you. Most banks make it easy to start the complaint process online, but a direct call to the bank will work, too.

Pay Your Bills Like Clockwork

Out of all of the paper that the mail deliverer drops onto your doorstep, a few items require special, immediate handling on your part—bills, for instance. If you adopt just a few simple habits, your checkbook and your creditors will be happy.

Pick one spot for bills. Assign a single spot in your home for keeping unpaid bills, a spot that's near the place where the bill-paying happens—perhaps a vertical file marked "To Pay" near your computer or a specific desk drawer where you also store your checkbook. When bills arrive in the mail, immediately place them there. You don't want bills to get buried in the pile of junk mail that accumulates on your kitchen counter, says Fred Cyprys, managing partner of Cypress Financial Consultants in Rochester, New York. At bill-paying time, you won't have to hunt and scrounge for bills, and you won't be left with the haunting feeling that you've missed one.

Automate your reminders. In the crush of everything else you have to do, it's easy to forget to pay your bills on time. The solution is simple, Cyprys says. Go to your computer calendar function right now and enter recurring reminders to pay your bills. Cyprys has a reminder scheduled in his electronic calendar for every week, plus a monthly reminder to pay the mortgage. "You can set that up forever," he says.

Shred what you don't need. As soon as you have paid a bill, shred it, says Cyprys. You don't need the extra papers lying around your office, and they're a pain to file away. For tax purposes, usually all you need is proof of payment, which is still recorded online (assuming you're following our recommendations). The exception would be bills that contain a mixture of tax-deductible and non-tax-deductible line items—business phone calls made on your home phone, for instance. Shredding, rather than recycling whole paper, makes it less likely that your personal information will wind up in the wrong hands.

Your Number One Target: Credit Card Debt

How would you react to a financial advisor who promised that you could make nearly triple the average return of the stock market? You would tar-and-feather the guy, of course, and send him on his way with a boot in the pants for extra momentum. Except that such a return is actually easy to accomplish for a staggering number of consumers, says Stroh, the consumer debt expert.

Here's how it works. The average yearly return on stocks is around 8 percent. Triple that would be 24 percent—an eye-popping return, indeed. Now think about your credit card. How much of that balance do you allow to go unpaid each month? A thousand dollars? Five or ten thousand? Stroh says a quarter to a third of all people who have credit cards pay nothing but the minimum payment each month. You're paying an outrageously high interest rate on that money, often in the low 20s. So the very first place where you should "invest" your money is in paying that balance off. And keep it paid off. *Not* paying 24 percent interest on a credit card balance is three times as good as *earning* 8 percent on stocks or mutual funds.

Despite all of the pitfalls inherent in having a credit card, there are actually good reasons to have one in your wallet, says Eva Rosenberg, a.k.a. Tax Mama, a personal finances expert based in Northridge, California. You can't rent a car without a credit card, for instance, and without a good credit history you won't be able to get a mortgage for a house or a loan to finance a business. Credit cards also create a good spending record for tax purposes.

Do careful card-hopping. Until you do manage to pay off your entire credit card balance every month, you want to use cards with the lowest interest rates possible. "Even if you don't qualify for 0 percent, you probably qualify for something lower than you have right now," says Rosenberg. Watch those credit card offers that arrive in the mail five or 10 times a week. Some will offer a 0 percent interest rate for a few months, and the rate jumps up after that.

If you play your cards right, so to speak, you can cancel your old card just before the rate rises and transfer your balance to a new 0 percent card for a few more months.

This takes a little work and organization, but it's better than paying loan-shark-type fees—so add this technique to your cheatin' repertoire if saving money is a top priority. If you're going to attempt this trick, enter a warning in your electronic calendar when it's time to start scouting for a new credit card, Rosenberg says. Also, beware: If you fail to make at least the minimum payment on these very-low-rate cards, you will lose the privilege and your interest rate will bounce up.

Pay your taxes—without fees. If your credit card has a rewards program—giving you merchandise, cash back, or airline miles, for instance—you want to run every possible necessary purchase through that card in order to maximize your rewards. It's even possible to pay your taxes by credit card, says Rosenberg, although there's a trick to doing it inexpensively. If you're paying your taxes online, you don't want to charge it straight to your credit card. Why? Because your card company charges most merchants a fee when you buy from them, but the government doesn't pay such fees. So your card company instead will charge you a "convenience fee," often 2.5 percent of the transaction, when you pay your taxes. There are a couple of ways to get around this fee:

1. See if your credit card company offers no- or low-fee checks that draw on your account. Sometimes you're mailed such checks, or you can call the company and have them sent. Use these checks to pay your taxes.

2. Accept a credit card offer that comes in the mail if it offers no-fee checks, then use one of these checks to pay your taxes. Get a cash advance from your old credit card and transfer that money to the new card to cover the amount of your taxes.

Get late fees removed. Anytime you have a late payment fee show up on your credit card bill, call the card company and ask them to remove it—no matter how small the fee is. If late payments are unusual for you, your card company will comply—they'll typically give you a break once a year. Why bother with this? The point is not saving the small amount of money, the point is that you don't want the late payment showing up on your credit report. Late payments on your record could jeopardize approval for a loan in the future.

Monitor your card account—any time. A credit card user can have some anxious moments between monthly statements. Are you near your spending limit? Did your husband make a purchase he didn't mention? Is someone making unauthorized use of your card? Is your child at college keeping her spending under control?

There's an easy way to track your credit card account between statements. Many credit card companies allow you to monitor your account over the Internet. An up-to-the-moment summary of the activity on your account is just a couple of mouse clicks away. Check your latest hard-copy statement, or your card company's web site, for the easy instructions for signing up for this password-protected service. Never again will you have to wring your hands for that month between statements.

Discipline yourself with a debit card. Brad Stroh is a big fan of debit cards, particularly for people who need to bring a little discipline to their finances. Credit cards and debit cards may look the same, but their function is significantly different. Each credit card purchase you make is like a mini-loan. If you're managing your money carefully, you pay this loan off at the end of each month to avoid finance charges. The card company is betting you *won't* pay off your balance every month—and they're dead right with way too many consumers. On the other hand, debit cards immediately draw money straight out of your checking account. "It's your own money, just like cash," Stroh says. This forces you to keep your spending within the constraints of the cash you have available in the bank.

Debit cards do not involve interest charges, and the statements you receive provide a good record of your purchases—making it easy to monitor your spending.

Take Your Banker Some Cookies

Dropping in to say hi to your local banker sounds so old-fashioned, so *It's a Wonderful Life,* particularly in this age of impersonal corporations. But you really can do it, and this simple act can save you bucketloads of cash, says financial consultant Fred Cyprys. "They're much more friendly than they used to be." Why? Because they know they need to please customers in order to keep them. Here are ways to make a personal visit play to your advantage:

- If you don't already have free checking, insist on it. Too many competitors offer free checking for your banker to hold out.

- Get your banker's direct phone number. If you ever have a banking problem, you'll have a person to call who will remember your face. No more pecking your way through an automated phone system.

- Ask your banker to set up a home equity line of credit for you—and then don't use it. Use this loan-at-your-fingertips for emergencies only. For instance, if you get inundated with credit card debt, use your line of credit to pay it off rather than carrying the balance forward and paying those outrageous fees. A home equity line of credit, secured by the money you have invested in your house, may provide a better interest rate than a personal loan or borrowing from your 401(k).

- If you're starting up a new business, have your banker set up a new checking account for it. (Get a separate business credit card, too.) Keeping business accounts separate from personal accounts will make your record keeping much simpler, says tax expert Rosenberg.

Securing Your Future

Sure, it's tough enough keeping track of what's going on in your wallet. But taking a look at the big financial picture now and then is important, too, to make sure you reach your long-term goals. Retirement, for instance. Or buying that beach house. Or sending your kid to college.

Here, in plain and simple terms, we're going to outline some basic long-term strategies you should be taking. The importance of getting this right can't be overemphasized, so don't hesitate to hire financial experts to help you with such details as picking investments, determining insurance needs, and preparing your taxes.

Save More, Borrow Less

Debt weakens your financial condition just as forcefully as saving strengthens it. Here's a good rule of thumb for what is worth taking out a loan for and what is not, says finance pro Brad Stroh. Only borrow to pay for things that grow in value over time. A home is a good example. Even though the market turns soft now and then, real estate is often worth more and more over time, so taking out a mortgage to buy your home is a sound strategy. A less obvious example, he says: college education. Having a college degree

generally results in a higher salary for the long haul, meaning that taking out a loan to pay tuition is a sound investment.

There's a flip side to that rule: It's unwise to take out a loan to buy things that don't hold their value long term. So if at all possible, pay cash for your automobile rather than financing it. Unless you think that you can make more by investing the cash you'd spend up front for the car plus the cost of your loan, this is a huge

Make Your Cards Work Harder

It's amazing all of the invisible transactions that go flying around cyberspace every time you swipe a credit card, debit card, or discount card. The example that most people are familiar with is the credit card rewards program—a setup where you get cash back, points toward merchandise, or travel miles with an airline. Your cards can work even harder, however, particularly if you shop frequently online. The details of such programs change more often than your underwear, so you're going to have to do a bit of research yourself. But to get you started, here are a couple of interesting arrangements that channel cyber dollars back into your pocket.

Upromise.com[SM]**:** This is a rewards program that accumulates cash to be used toward your children's college tuition. You register your cards with the web site and select a 529 plan, one of the special accounts that allow U.S. taxpayers to grow their invested college money tax-free. When you use those cards to spend with certain companies and brands, a trickle of cash goes into your account. First, make sure that a 529 plan is the right tuition savings vehicle for you.

Ebates.com[SM]**:** When one Internet site refers you to another Internet site and you make a purchase there, the first site often gets a kickback—a small percentage of the transaction you just made. Ebates.com has established this kickback arrangement with a zillion online businesses, only Ebates.com doesn't keep the money. When you link to a store through this site, they dump the kickback into an account for you, let the cash build up, and then send you a check.

Cars: Lease or Buy?

The question of whether to lease or buy an automobile depends on the individual and the car involved, but these general guidelines will steer you in the right direction, says Fred Cyprys, managing partner of Cypress Financial Consultants:

- If you like to drive cars that have high resale value and you're good about maintaining your car, then buying works out best financially.

- If all you need is an inexpensive set of wheels to get you from Point A to Point Z, you're not finicky about maintenance, and you don't care whether the car lasts forever, then leasing probably will work out for you okay.

- If you're getting a car to use for business, lease it. You can deduct most of your lease payments. If you were to buy your business car, you would be able to deduct the loan interest—not nearly as big an advantage.

money saver. You will get the best deal on your car this way (commonly thousands of dollars "cash back" is available to people who don't buy with a loan).

If you absolutely must take out a loan to buy your car, shop for a rate that's 5 percent or less—preferably 0 percent, of course. Don't fall for those "0 percent interest for 6 months" come-ons. Make sure you're getting a permanent rate for the life of the loan, not a "teaser" rate that jumps up after some period of time. Also, to limit the amount of money you're financing, save up for your new car and pay at least 30 percent of the car's value as a down payment.

Credit card debt fits under this rule, too. If you pay for your laundry, pizza, books, CDs, and movies with a credit card and then fail to fully pay off your balance each month, you are taking out a very-high-interest loan to pay for these things—and none of them hold value over time. Stop that.

Max out your 401(k). The 401(k) is hands-down the best form of investment available. For the uninitiated, this program allows you to have money automatically taken out of your paycheck and put into an investment account. Often, employers add some matching funds to the accounts as well. These accounts grow like weeds because the money is never taxed until you withdraw it, presumably in retirement when you're being taxed at a lower rate. Investment advisors routinely tell consumers to put every dollar allowed into such accounts. Nevertheless, among the people whose employers offer this savings option, a pitifully small percentage participate, says Stroh. Why? One study suggests that people are just too lazy to fill out a couple of pages of routine information to get the accounts set up.

HELP!

Find a Certified, Unbiased Investment Advisor

When it comes to mapping out your economic future, not just any ol' financial advisor will do. Make sure you know how much training your financial advisor has had and how your advisor is being compensated, says Fred Cyprys, managing partner of Cypress Financial Consultants.

If at all possible, select a professional who's a Certified Financial Planner—a credential bestowed by the Certified Financial Planner Board of Standards, indicating the advisor has met rigorous educational, experiential, and ethical requirements.

If possible, choose one who earns a living through "advisor-based" fees, meaning he or she is paid by a direct fee and not by a commission on the investments you make. This helps to ensure that you're getting unbiased guidance. At the very least, find an advisor who can earn his fee either way—through fees, commission, or a combination of both. You don't want an advisor who only gets paid when he steers you toward a particular fund.

"There's no such thing as free advice," says Cyprys. "Understand how that person is being compensated."

If you're among these laggards, spend the 7 minutes to sign up, for goodness sake. It's the optimal way to put your savings on autopilot.

Pull your investments together. People who have changed jobs several times often end up with several different retirement and investment accounts. There are two very good reasons for having an investment advisor consolidate those accounts into a central place, says Fred Cyprys, managing partner of Cypress Financial Consultants:

- You have fewer fees nibbling away at your profits.

- You can have a coordinated investment strategy, rather than money spread all over the place without a plan.

Conduct an Insurance Review

Most people don't need to be sold on the wisdom of having an accountant handle complex taxes. But how many people do you know who have a professional analyze their insurance coverage? Take your paperwork for all of your insurance coverage—home, auto, life, disability, long-term care, and anything else—to a financial planner, says Stroh. You may discover that you're paying for much more insurance than your situation requires, or you may discover that you are underinsured in certain areas and exposing yourself to financial ruin. You need to play the odds wisely, protecting yourself from the most common disasters. Insurance needs vary vastly from one individual to another, but here are some points to discuss with your financial planner:

- Save with high deductibles. When you smash your car fender against a tree and report it to your insurance company, the deductible is the amount of money you pay to fix the damage, and the insurance company pays the rest. If you have a small deductible, say $100 or so, you're paying high insurance premiums for coverage you might not need (assuming you're not accident prone). If you habitually keep a little extra money in the bank for contingencies, you can pay for small, incidental accidents out of pocket. Use your insurance to protect you against huge, costly mishaps. Ask your financial planner about raising your deductibles as high as you can comfortably manage, and pay the lower premiums.

- Don't just buy insurance based on a big fat round number that a salesperson throws out: "You need a million dollars in coverage." Decide the amount of insurance coverage you want by analyzing your needs. Insurance helps you manage risk, so establish what money your family would need under various scenarios. If you were to die, for instance, would your spouse be making enough money to meet living expenses? How long will dependents be in your home, and will they need college tuition? How long until your home mortgage is paid off?

- Having disability insurance is even more important than having life insurance, particularly if you're self-employed, says tax expert Eva Rosenberg. Becoming disabled—at least temporarily—within the next several years is a lot more likely than dying. Resist the temptation to deduct your disability insurance premiums as a business expense, she says. Sure, taking that deduction may save you a little pocket money. However, if you don't deduct the premiums, then when you actually draw disability income, it's not taxable. That's huge. Still not convinced? By taking the deductions, you're gaining a little money each year at a time of your life when you might not need it so much. But if you're disabled and you're getting your income tax-free, that benefit is enormous at a time when you need all the financial help you can get.

- Don't be frightened into buying narrowly focused insurance—flight insurance, for instance, or mortgage payment insurance. Such policies are usually highly priced for the coverage you're getting, and usually a broad life insurance policy will cover you sufficiently in these areas anyway.

Taxes: Buy Some Advice

You remember the HIRE criteria from Chapter 1, right? If a task is Hard, Important, Rarely done, and Elaborate, it's worth paying an expert to take care of it for you. Let a professional who does the task regularly keep up with the training that's required. If you try to blunder through the task yourself, your mistakes could be more costly than the professional's fee.

The HIRE criteria easily apply to cleaning out your chimney, fixing your car's brakes . . . and doing your taxes. Yes, the certified, hard-core, *How to Cheat at Organizing* approach to taxes is simply to hire a certified public accountant (CPA) or to visit a tax preparation service such as H&R Block℠. Your accountant will relieve you of all of the paperwork and will represent you if any problems crop up with your return. Money well spent.

There's one thing an accountant can't do for you, however: track your expenses throughout the year. Somehow, you need to devise a method for drawing together all of your tax-related materials and handing them over to your tax preparer in a comprehensible form. Financial consultant Fred Cyprys has a trick for that: Every month, he makes up a little computerized spreadsheet that lists his expenses. He prints out the spreadsheet, attaches any receipts, slides it into a manila envelope, labels the envelope, and files it. When tax time approaches, "It takes you 20 minutes to get ready for the accountant at the end of the year," he says. Enter a recurring reminder on your calendar for the end of each month.

If you want to save money on tax preparation, using tax software such as TurboTax® or a web site such as www.taxbrain.com is a reasonable approach, says Stroh. Just remember that there's a trade-off: You will spend more time doing research. If your finances are simple, tax software might take half an hour. If they're complex, the chore could take 8 hours or more.

Finding Scholarships the "Cheating" Way

If you have a child in her junior year of high school, the word *scholarship* enters your mind more and more frequently. A thorough scholarship hunt is virtually a full-time job in itself. It may require sending out as many as 75 applications during the last 2 years of high school. And now you're wringing your hands, thinking, *Oh, no—teenagers are notorious procrastinators and drift off-task easily.* Fret no more. Here's corner-cutting advice for organizing a successful scholarship campaign.

Divide the labor. As a parent, you get the easy job: When you and your child identify a scholarship that she qualifies for, your role in the project is entering the application deadline on a calendar. Your child's job: writing the essays and filling out the application forms. Prod your child as each deadline approaches, keeping in mind how long it typically takes her to get one into the mail. Just to be safe, plan to send off all applications a month early.

Prepare essay templates. Every scholarship application must be individually crafted for the granting organization. But you can still cut corners on writing all of those essays. After your child has written several scholarship essays, note the themes and styles that emerge most frequently. Your child will be able to store on her computer five different basic essays, which can be quickly adapted to meet the requirements of any application.

Gather recommendations. Encourage your child to nurture relationships with her favorite teachers and advisors throughout high school, says Shayla Price of Thibodaux, Louisiana, who as a teenager raised a six-figure nest egg to pay for college. She's the author of *The Scholarship Search: A Guide to Winning Free Money for College and More.* At the beginning of your scholarship campaign, have each teacher write a template recommendation—a stock letter to be used again and again—and store it on his or her computer. When your child is preparing a new scholarship application, she can give each teacher the relevant name and address so those recommendation letters can be tailored for the granting organization—an impressive touch.

Hit the books. Scholarships that are touted on the Internet have high exposure, so there's a lot of competition for those dollars. Do apply for such scholarships, but also go to your library and ask for the fat volumes that list scholarships. Many organizations listed in such books have no need for Internet publicity and are therefore less known—meaning your odds of success will be higher.

Go local—again and again. Many students mistakenly think they have to land a scholarship worth of tens of thousands of dollars in order to pay for college. Actually, many students pay for college by accumulating scores of smaller scholarships—$500 here and $1,000 there will add up to an impressive nest egg. So track down scholarships offered by local businesses, churches, and civic organizations.

A Cautionary Tale: When Divorce Looms

If you and your spouse are headed for divorce, keep in mind that monumental financial changes are about to happen that can affect you for decades to come. Here are some steps to take in advance of a divorce to ensure that you get your fair share, says Jessie Danninger, a financial analyst for the Rosen Law Firm, based in Raleigh, North Carolina.

- **Copy statements.** There's usually one spouse who handles the finances. If that's not you, make copies of all of the financial statements that come in so you will have documentation of where all of the money is.

- **Track monthly expenses.** You and your spouse are about to start operating separate households—an expensive proposition. To get a handle on what this is going to cost, review the expenses for operating your current home, including bills, credit card statements, and insurance premiums. Don't forget that someone's going to have to acquire a new home and new furnishings, too.

- **Establish your priorities.** The divorce process will be easier and go more quickly if you know what your priorities are and communicate them to your attorney. Be realistic. "You're not going to be able to keep everything," Danninger says. For instance, you may feel most strongly about keeping your current residence, the art collection, the family dog, or your retirement account.

- **Settle tax issues with your spouse.** Come to an agreement with your spouse about what tax filing status you will use, who will claim exemptions for the children, and who will use which itemized deductions, for instance. Remember that if you're separating but you sign a joint tax return with your spouse anyway, the IRS can hold you responsible for the entire tax bill. If your spouse should suddenly be hard to find, the IRS could make you pay.

- **Order your credit report.** This will show whether you and your spouse have any joint credit cards. If your spouse were to run up charges on a joint card, you could be held responsible for those bills. You may want to freeze or cancel such accounts. When you call the card company, don't take an employee's word that the change has been made—get it confirmed in writing.

- **Document your valuables.** The laws vary from state to state, but usually anything you owned when you entered the marriage will be yours afterward. Gather any documentation you can find that demonstrates when you acquired such valuables. Usually, gifts and inheritance given to you will remain yours as well.

If your brain is now swamped with financial information, don't fret—no one expects you to implement all of this overnight. But do return to this chapter every week, or every month, and pick out a new item to implement. This is just like the decluttering process for your home: Take one narrowly focused section at a time. You'll be astounded and proud at how your finances fall into line and secure you a brighter future.

Chapter Eight

Your Schedule

Boost Your Productivity—
and Leisure Time—with
a No-Frills, No-B.S.
Calendar System

YOU CAN'T KEEP IT ALL in your head. No human being is capable of remembering all of the data that are necessary for conducting a productive life. So we write down the stuff that we need to remember and refer to these records in order to accomplish what we need to do.

A funny thing happens to this schedule management process, though. Because we jot down dates, check our appointments, and fulfill our commitments many times during the week, we fall into routines. The long-term habits we develop for organizing our lives may not be the most efficient. And habits that waste 5 minutes here and 20 minutes there may not seem significant, but over a week they translate into hours lost—over a year, weeks squandered. All invisibly. This is time you could have spent enjoying your family, reading a book, exercising, or eating chocolate.

Numerous forces are constantly pressuring you to manage your schedule inefficiently. This is a complex blend of fads, economics, conflicting priorities, your desire to please others, and plain ol' inattentiveness. As you delve into this chapter, cheating at managing your schedule may sound like a selfish thing to do sometimes. But what's at stake is nothing less than your survival, your success, and your sanity. So let's pick apart those counterproductive forces and put them in their place.

We're going to ignore the fads and embrace function. We're going to spend money to cut corners—when we'll get a good return on the investment. We're going to be alert for shortcuts and time-saving tricks. We're going to reject the demands on our time that don't jive with our priorities. We're actually going to say "no" to people we love and admire. And we're going to get people to do stuff for us—one of the most delightful ways to free up time on the calendar.

Scheduling Basics

Before we start cutting corners, it helps to understand the stripped-to-the-bone basics of managing a personal schedule—the core functions we can't do without.

A busy person's schedule is an enormous amount of information that is constantly being revised. We organize this data in ways that make specific details easy to retrieve when we need them. Even the very simplest system for managing a personal schedule will include these categories of information:

Times and dates: A schedule of what you're supposed to be doing at any particular time.

Tasks: A running list of the things that you have to get done.

Contacts: The information you need in order to interact with other people.

These categories of information work in tandem. For example, if your boss tells you to make a sales call on the XYZ Corp., you add that to your task list. When you make the appointment, it's recorded among your times and dates, and the person you're going to visit is added to your contact list. When the big day comes, you see the appointment and check your contact list for the address so you can get there. After the meeting, you cross that item off your task list.

If these fundamental components are not part of your schedule management system, it's time to redesign your system from the ground up, using this model. It can be as simple as you want it to be, and the payoff will be immediate and enormous. The *cheating* part of schedule management does not mean dispensing with one of these tools—it means cutting corners in how you use these tools, which we will get to shortly.

Deciding on Your System

You *could* get by managing all three categories of information—dates, tasks, and contacts—with just a pad of paper and a pencil. However, even the most inveterate simplify-your-life enthusiast would agree that commercially printed calendars and address books are a helpful step up from mere blank paper. And from there, it's not much of a stretch to embrace planning notebooks, which combine calendar, address book, tasks list, and other functions all in one binder. They're available at any office supply store. So if you're new to the concept of managing your personal schedule, that's where I recommend you start. Planning notebooks are convenient, portable, modestly priced, and easy to work with. You might never need any other system, or you might start adopting enhancements once you get the hang of it.

Now, you're aware that personal computers automate schedule management functions nicely. And in recent years, there's been an explosion of highly portable mini-computers that can handle schedules, e-mail, phone calls, photography, video, music, the Internet, and more—all in one unit that can slide into your pocket. Personal digital assistants (PDAs) and the fancier "smart" cell phones

Quiz: Am I Ready for a PDA?

Would a personal digital assistant (PDA) be a sensible, hardworking tool for you—or just a showy and expensive toy? It's not easy to be sure. Take this quick quiz to find out:

1. Do you frequently use a personal computer?
2. Are you at ease with software and electronic gadgets?
3. Are you frequently away from your desk—attending meetings, conducting business, and running errands?
4. Would you describe your schedule as jam-packed or hectic?
5. Does spending a few hundred dollars for a long-term, time-saving solution sound like a reasonable trade-off?
6. Do you frequently wish you were more on top of things and better connected?

Count up the number of times you answered "yes." Here's where you stand on the issue of whether to buy a PDA:

Said "yes" six times: You're ready for a PDA.

Said "yes" three to five times: You're borderline. Read up on these devices, browse electronics stores, and ask friends to let you test-drive their PDAs. Reevaluate where you stand once a year.

Said "yes" one to two times: Pens, paper, hard-copy organizers, and desktop software are fine for you.

unquestionably put a number of high-tech cheats at your fingertips. For instance:

- Categorizing your tasks (maybe all personal errands are highlighted in green, while business appointments are blue) and the ability to "hide" tasks that aren't relevant to your current location (you won't be able to pick up the dry cleaning if you're in a meeting, for instance, so you can hide that errand for the moment).

- Ordering your tasks by priority and creating links between tasks and people in your contact list.

- The ability to tap on a contact's name—anywhere it's listed—so your gizmo will automatically dial that person's phone number.

- Voice commands for operating your PDA or phone. Just say, for instance, "Dial Suzanne at work," and you'll be yakking with her in seconds.

- Accessing the World Wide Web.

- Using your little electronic friend as an MP3 player for listening to music, books on tape, or the day's news.

- Software for making shopping lists and managing your passwords.

These pocket gadgets are by no means perfect. Making new entries into your calendar, task list, or contact list is usually awkward. You might have to peck at a screen with a stylus, type with your thumbs on a teensy keyboard, or use a telephone numeric pad to convert numbers into letters. The screens on portable devices also are notoriously small, so it's hard to display your calendar for the week or month ahead—which you often want to do when you're planning. And don't start thinking that a PDA will magically turn you into an organized person. As with any helpful tool, you still have to employ it wisely.

The scheduling tools you're already using fall somewhere in the spectrum ranging from pencil and paper to the latest, cutting-edge, computerized widgets. Have you ever attended a meeting where all other people in the room were typing with their thumbs on PDAs? You may have felt like grabbing your pen and legal pad and crawling under the table. But stick to your guns. Every person's circumstances are different, and therefore their schedule management tools are going to be different. In fact, adopting more technology than you need is counterproductive—you'll spend more time

PDA Data Entry Made Easy

Becoming dependent on a PDA or high-tech cell phone has a couple of considerable downsides:

1. These little handheld devices are easy to misplace, and if you lose one, an enormous amount of personal data vaporizes with it.

2. Entering information directly into these gadgets is inevitably a clunky, time-consuming process.

Michael Fritsch, a.k.a. the Gizmo Ph.D., says one solution will fix both dilemmas. Back up your gadget's data frequently on some other digital storage device—preferably your home computer. This way, if you lose your PDA or "smart" phone, all you have to worry about is replacing the hardware—not reentering all of that information or reconstructing your calendar from scratch.

Also, if your system "synchs" with a desktop computer, you can use your conventional computer keyboard for entering your new data (much easier), and then transfer the information to your portable device. PDAs and phones often interact with desktop computers through a desktop cradle that doubles as a recharger. But even if you have a less fancy phone, you probably can find a kit (software and cable) that will allow you to do your data entry on your PC and load it into your phone. Such add-on software typically sells for about $40. Check the Internet or airline magazines.

learning how to use your tools and playing with their features than you will actually working.

The most organized people I know cherry-pick their tools from the full range of options—some can't live without PDAs and some despise them. Some love e-mail and cell phones for communication, but prefer printed calendars for keeping track of appointments. Some print out their home-computer calendars and take them on the road as "paper PDAs." I spend my working life at a home-office computer, so desktop software is perfect for organizing

my professional appointments. But my task list is handwritten on a legal pad. And when I go out, I carry only a simple cell phone (no photo, music, or Internet capabilities), plus a pen and a folded sheet of paper in my pocket for listing errands and other reminders. Just enough to meet my needs.

The crucial thing is that you remain aware of your options for managing your schedule and that you adopt new technology and techniques when the benefits outweigh the cost or hassle of doing so. Think of your schedule management system as a perpetual work in progress. What you can't do is drift through life with *no* system—or a system that you only use sporadically. That's the path to failure and frustration. Pick a system that fits your situation and use it religiously.

Committing to Tasks

Whatever scheduling system you arrive at, you need to be able to perform these two simple functions, says Guido Groeschel, a workflow expert based in San Diego, California:

- Display both calendar and task list at the same time. This combo serves as a "dashboard" helping you control your life.

How to Cheat at Organizing

- Copy an item from your task list to your calendar. This is a pivotal moment in being productive—committing to getting a task done.

On the surface, it all sounds so simple: Make a list of the things you gotta do, put them on the calendar, and do them at the assigned time. For busy people, however, there's much more to think about (and we're all so swamped that we're barely clinging to sanity, right?). The main problem is that there are more things crying out for your attention than there are spaces on the calendar, so there's this perpetual heap of unfinished business on your task list. It depresses you, following you around like a dark cloud.

Groeschel has made a science out of eliminating such distractions. A task list needs to be carefully groomed, he says. If it grows too big, that mountain of unattended items will distract you from the things that really matter. So cheat: Identify some perfectly valid tasks and decide not to do them—not in the near future, anyway—and banish them from your mind.

How do you go about this? Allow onto your task list only the items that you can reasonably accomplish within the next 7 to 10 days. Put all other items onto a separate list—a list of deferred tasks, your "back burner," so to speak. This way, you will know that the deferred items have not been forgotten, but they also are not competing for your attention here and now.

Apply the two-question test. Don't agonize over prioritizing your tasks. Use Groeschel's quick-and-easy shortcut—asking yourself two questions:

- Do I *have* to get this done?
- Do I *want* to get this done?

If both answers are no, then move the matter to your deferred-task list.

Divide and conquer. If that doesn't whittle your to-do list down to a manageable size, assign every remaining item a rank of high, medium, or low priority. Be brutal—give yourself at least twice as many "lows" as you have "highs." Move the high-priority tasks onto your calendar. Move the low-priority tasks to the deferred list—particularly if they have been riding on your task list for more than 2 months.

Now, your high-priority items are scheduled, your medium-priority items are still under your nose (but not sapping your mental energy), and the "lows" are off your radar altogether. No longer overwhelmed, you are in a better position to make good decisions about the things that are most important.

Pad your calendar. Be realistic about adding commitments to your calendar, says Michael Fritsch, an expert in time-saving gadgets based in Austin, Texas. Sure, you can fill up all of the open spaces on your calendar—but that doesn't mean it's humanly possible to accomplish all of the tasks you scheduled. If you overbook yourself, you will always be in a rush, you will make more mistakes, you will perpetually disappoint colleagues, and you won't complete everything you had committed to. Schedule ample time for each task, plus a little extra time to accommodate the unexpected—getting

SLEIGHT OF HAND

Double-Duty Businesses

A well-run business will help you take care of more than one errand at the same location. Publicist Vanessa Wakeman of New York City prefers a salon that will do both her hair and her nails at the same time, for instance.

"That's the only way I can get it done," she says.

Here are other ways that businesses can do double duty, helping you cut corners on your errands: Have your car worked on at a garage that will also wash it for you, and do your grocery shopping at a store that has a bank and pharmacy under the same roof. Also, frequent businesses that offer free wireless Internet access (typically coffee shops and copy stores) so you can work on your laptop while you're there.

lost, equipment failures, or long-winded discussions, for example. "Padding" the calendar with extra time might feel like lying, but that's okay—we're cheating, remember? If you discover downtime during the day, just consult your task list for a way to fill those surplus moments.

Set an alarm. If you tend to drift through the day oblivious to time, you're probably famous for showing up late at meetings and missing deadlines. Technology will help you out. Some watches have alarms that can be set to go off at certain times of the day. If you have a 3 p.m. staff meeting every day, set your alarm to go off at 2:50 p.m. Computer software and PDAs also can be set to give you a warning minutes or hours in advance of an event. Or keep a digital kitchen timer at your desk (the ticking mechanical kind is too noisy) and set it to go off shortly before your next meeting.

Avoid the Trivia Trap

All of the "in-boxes" in your life are a distracting drain on your productivity, Groeschel says. These include the literal in-boxes—where memos arrive at work, mail arrives at home, voice mail arrives on the answering machine, and e-mail arrives on your computer. But they also include various abstract in-boxes—oral requests from friends, family, and colleagues, for instance. These newly arrived items are pleading for your attention—begging to jump onto your to-do list, although very few of them deserve to be there. The trick is to prevent this barrage of input from building into an annoying mountain. Clear out those in-boxes systematically by selecting one of these four quick decisions for each item:

Delete it: Dispose of the item and don't give it another thought. Use this as often as you possibly can.

Put it on your task list: This means you could reasonably deal with the matter within the next several days, although you're not committing to a specific time.

Enter it onto your calendar: This means you're committed to working on the matter at a specific time.

File it for reference: There's no action to take, but you want to keep the material for future use.

Notice that none of these decisions requires you to do anything immediately. That's important psychologically. This approach allows you to clear out all of your distracting "in-boxes" quickly, eliminating trivia and preserving the important stuff. You don't get suckered into working on matters that are not your top priority.

Why should you care about this? Studies show that when an office worker gets distracted from the task at hand, it takes an average of 25 minutes for that worker to get back to the task—and another several minutes to fully reengage. "So you lose twice," says Groeschel—time lost to the distraction and time lost getting back up to speed.

There's a flip side to the concept of keeping trivial matters off your schedule: Make sure that your most important long-term goals get *onto* your calendar, says Fritsch. In your heart of hearts, what do you most want to accomplish over the next 3 to 5 years? Write a novel? Run a marathon? Learn to play the piano? Plot out all of the incremental steps that lead up to those goals. Before your schedule gets overwhelmed with PTA committee meetings, enter the work sessions and the milestones that carry you toward your highest-priority accomplishments. If low-priority items get shouldered off the calendar, so be it. The cheating way of life means focusing on your priorities and letting the rest go.

Making Your Life Work

Now let's talk about setting up your life so that the routine hassles no longer drive you crazy. First, we're going to go deep—with a look at two monumental decisions that lay the groundwork for how easy, or difficult, your schedule is to manage:

- how you work

- where you live

Now, you're not going to change jobs or sell your house based on a couple of sentences that you read in *How to Cheat at Organizing*. (Surely you will wait until the end of the chapter.) But the thinking here will prepare you for the next time you *do* make such a decision—and it will also arm you with some strategies that will help you cope in the meantime.

You'll also find in this passage a host of other "cheats" for managing your schedule—corner-cutting techniques for conducting routine family business, strategies that provide an enormous payoff for very little effort.

Talk to Your Boss about Flexibility

The old-fashioned work schedule went like this: You walked in the door at 9 a.m., took a break for lunch, and clocked out at 5 p.m. The explosion of two-career couples and single-parent households destroyed that notion. If you're still working rigid, conventional hours, you'll be shocked by how much easier your daily life is when you switch to a flexible arrangement.

Cell phones, portable computers, and Internet technology make it easy to do many kinds of work at any time and from any location—including home, of course. After all, savvy managers judge their employees by how productive they are, not by how many hours they spend warming an office chair. So redesign your workday in a way that relieves pressure on your personal life. If your company resists—well, how long to you intend to work for such a shortsighted outfit?

Stephanie Worrell, a public relations executive in Boise, Idaho, says her productivity earned her the trust of her boss—and the right to split her workday into two shifts: roughly 9:30 a.m. to 3 p.m., and then a few more hours at home, starting at 10:30 p.m. That's right, late night into early morning—a schedule she gleefully accepts, since it buys her more time for her family. Between those two daily shifts, she picks up her children, takes them to sports, feeds them, and puts them to bed. Her clients understand her unusual schedule and are happy to work around it.

Another reason to work at unconventional times: You get to avoid rush hours. Worrell analyzed her commute and found that her drive took as much as 45 minutes at certain times of the day but only 15 minutes at other times. Thus, her flexible schedule saves her hours a week in driving time alone.

Double Your Productivity

Even for extremely busy people, the typical day is rife with opportunities to get two tasks taken care of at once. Here are ways to make constructive use of the minutes and hours that typically get squandered, offered by publicists Stephanie Worrell and Vanessa Wakeman:

While on the telephone: Sort through e-mail on your computer or clean around the house.

While watching TV: Write thank-you notes, holiday cards, and client correspondence. Review the family calendar and organize the week ahead. Read or clean.

While waiting for a child to get out of school: Fire up your cell phone and call clients, schedule a home repair, or order a birthday cake. Or use your PDA to answer e-mail.

While commuting in the car: Find books on tape that are related to your profession and listen to them while you're driving. You'll find that you actually look forward to your time in the car. You can buy such recordings at any bookstore, online, or through mail-order clubs. Your local library also has a great selection for free. Wakeman likes to listen to recordings of old radio broadcasts she made, gathering pointers for future appearances.

While driving the kids around: Nothing! Use the time to interact with your children.

So talk to your boss about creating flexible hours for your job. You might be surprised at how receptive he or she is. Clever managers know that a stable, workable home life makes for happy and productive employees. "It's a matter of asking—a lot of people just don't ask," Worrell says.

Reecanne Joeckel agrees. A partner in an advertising and public relations company in Fort Worth, Texas, Joeckel feels strongly about spending time with her four teenagers while they're still living at home. Often, she will leave work at 3 p.m. if one of the kids needs to be picked up. On other days, she will compensate by working late at the office or by putting in extra work hours at home. Working odd hours around their schedule is worth it. "Flexibility is just a huge part of my whole system," she says.

How Close Is Your Supermarket?

Romantic notions can turn your personal schedule into a nightmare—particularly when you're deciding where you're going to live. Think you'd like to live on a mountaintop? Or beside a river in some remote valley?

First, ask yourself some questions:

- How long will my commute be?

- How far will I have to drive to buy groceries, deposit a check, see a movie, or dine out?

- Where will my kids go to school, and how will they get there?

- Where does the local soccer team play?

- How easy will it be to get a plumber out to the house?

- How long does it take to clear the snow off that driveway?

With those answers in mind, ask yourself which is more sensible: Living out in the wilds, but driving long distances for every modern amenity? Or living close to the modern amenities, and taking a trip when you need your nature fix?

Publicist Stephanie Worrell didn't hesitate the last time she moved. The convenient location of her home "was the whole consideration," she says. Her digs are central to supermarkets (she can get groceries delivered), a drugstore, restaurants, and a movie theater.

Managing the Family Calendar

When multiple people live under the same roof, their lives intertwine. They work together to make all of the details of daily life happen smoothly—food, transportation, shopping, laundry, school, sports, socializing, and entertainment.

The number one rule for managing a family's schedule: Make sure there's one and only one family calendar—and one and only one Master Planner designated to manage it. Everyone must participate: Train all family members to get important dates onto the calendar the moment they're known. This includes medical

5 Signs Your Family Is Overbooked

Everybody needs some "downtime." Adults should be able to take a break from the daily hubbub—say, to take a walk or to listen to some music. Children need time for just flopping on the couch or unstructured play with the neighborhood kids. Here are some signs that your family is overbooked:

1. There's no white space on the family calendar.

2. The past week is nothing but a blur of appointments, errands, and driving kids around.

3. The children are so tired that they go to bed on time without protesting.

4. You see a personality change in your kids. Perhaps they get uncharacteristically withdrawn, sullen, or cranky.

5. It's been weeks since you heard a child say, "I'm bored." Occasional boredom is a good thing—that's when kids get creative with their play.

How to Cheat at Organizing

appointments, cheerleader practices, concerts, sports games, club meetings, teacher conferences, parties, and more.

"The minute they have a date, they have to communicate that date to me," says Joeckel. "One of the best ways to get me wound up is to let me know something at the last minute."

All schedules and fliers need to be dropped into a designated "in-box," which may be a bin by the door, a folder that accompanies the calendar, or just the kitchen table. The Master Planner is in charge of watching for conflicts, briefing other family members about logistics, prodding forgetful children, and raising a red flag when the schedule is so jam-packed that there's no leisure time.

The family calendar is typically a hard-copy desktop or wall calendar with plenty of space for handwritten entries. Post the family calendar in a central spot in the home—probably the kitchen or the most frequently used entrance. This way, any family member can tell at a glance where parents or kids are. Having a telephone near the calendar is a good idea.

Use personal calendars, too. The central family calendar isn't enough for a busy household. Every family member also needs a personal calendar for matters that don't affect other parents or siblings. For adults, this would be a calendar with professional appointments that don't require coordination with the family, as well as errands, birthday reminders, workout schedules, and such. Kids—even elementary school children—can manage their own calendars to track homework, test dates, book-report due dates, and project milestones.

If your school system doesn't provide planning calendars, look for kid-friendly versions where school supplies are sold. Train your child how to use it, let your child customize it with drawings and stickers, and check it occasionally to make sure the planner is being used consistently.

Brief the troops. Once a week, hold a quick family meeting to review the family calendar for the upcoming days, says Sharon Mann, an organization expert for Pendaflex®, the filing supplies company. Find a leisurely time when everyone's present—perhaps right after dinner on Sunday.

ONCE UPON A TIME . . .

Slumber Party Plan

Not every little girl has an event management expert plan her slumber party. But that's your privilege if Vanessa Wakeman of New York City happens to be your aunt. Here's how Wakeman pulled off the ultimate slumber party for her niece and several guests. The young lady wanted to include swimming in the festivities, so they reserved a suite in a hotel that had a pool.

6 weeks in advance: Define the budget. Decide what the maximum spending will be, including breakdowns for the various components.

4–5 weeks in advance: Send out invitations.

3–4 weeks in advance: Plan activities, reserve hotel suite, and touch base with the parents of the guests.

2 weeks in advance: Involve the kids. Get niece's ideas for "dream themes," gift bags, and pajamas for the guests.

1 week in advance: Confirm pick-up and drop-off arrangements with the parents.

3 hours in advance: Set up the space in the hotel.

Motivate the youngsters. If you have trouble training children to check the family calendar regularly, pencil in the occasional treat—"Ice Cream Sundae Night," for instance. These could be events you hold routinely anyway, but when they're formally scheduled, the kids will start consulting the calendar religiously.

Pass around the cell phones. If you think giving your children cell phones is an extravagance, think again, says Joeckel. She has four teenagers. If there's a change of plans or she needs to remind her kids of something, the text messaging function on their cell phones will save the day. Also, if the kids find out at school that they need materials for a project, they can send a message to Mom, who can pick up the goods on the way home from work—thus saving her an evening errand. Shop around for a cell phone plan that gives you a discount for having multiple phones on the same account, plus unlimited text messaging.

Add a binder. Use a thin binder, stored near your family calendar, to hold handy reference information. Include emergency phone numbers, names and contact info for doctors and dentists, names of commonly used service people, fliers for upcoming events, and sports team schedules.

Squeezing Time Out of Your Schedule

We're all creatures of habit. We fall into patterns for all of the things we do routinely—running errands, feeding our families, celebrating birthdays, and cleaning the house. Inevitably, there are wasted minutes and hours lurking in those routines. So apply the Thinking Wins Out (TWO) philosophy to your daily routines—you know, thinking strategically about cutting corners rather than daydreaming. Award yourself TWO points every time you use a new time-saving trick, and give yourself a reward (earrings? a professional massage?) when you reach 10 points. The cheatin' life will be your new routine. To get you started, here are ways to shake up

A Musical Wipeout

When Ivan Mann was a youngster, he wrote to the Beach Boys letting them know he could fill in on vocals if any band members ever got sick. To this day, he still knows all of their sun-drenched lyrics and harmony parts. So it was quite a thrill when his wife, Sharon, bought tickets for a Beach Boys concert at the Jones Beach Amphitheater on Long Island.

Sharon, a professional organizer, kept the big date in her head. But when they arrived for the concert they noticed something strange: The Beach Boys seemed to be drawing a much younger crowd that evening—rather than the baby boomers you'd expect. Finally, the ticket-taker burst their bubble with the comment, "That performance was *last* night." On the current evening's stage: Sinead O'Connor.

The big lesson: Don't try to keep important dates in your head. Write them down on your schedule so you can't miss. "I was so embarrassed—that's what happens when you don't plan or schedule correctly. My husband will never let me forget," Sharon says.

your standard methods for doing things and whittle some time out of your schedule.

Keep a time diary. Worrell keeps running notes of how she spends her time. This helps her analyze where she can pick up extra minutes in her daily schedule. Every day, jot down in a notebook the amount of time you spent at each activity. (If it's easier for you, reconstruct this at the end of each day.) Include everything you did—chauffeuring, talking on the phone, writing e-mails, cooking, eating, sitting in meetings, working at your desk, commuting, exercising, chatting with the neighbor, and reading to the kids. Once a week, tally up the times and calculate what percentage of your average day is devoted to each activity. Are you spending enough time focused on your highest priorities—your family, for instance? The results will inspire you to cut even more corners at the time-consuming tasks that mean little to you.

Get others to help. When you see that your calendar is filled with wall-to-wall events and no downtime, it's time to share your duties with other people, says Misha Keefe, president of an organizing company in the Washington, D.C., area. Here are ways to spread the joy and loosen up your family calendar:

- If your spouse works near a shoe repair service, hand him that bag of shoes that need new soles.

- Assign your kids to household chores that they can handle at their respective ages. These duties can include feeding the pets, walking the dog, scooping out the cat litter boxes, folding laundry, emptying the dishwasher, watering plants, vacuuming, and shaking the doormats outside.

- Set up carpooling arrangements for each recurring event that's attended by multiple kids—sports practices, scout meetings, and play rehearsals, for instance. Making a phone call or two to set up the arrangement is certainly easier than doing all of that driving yourself.

Outsource the small stuff. Vanessa Wakeman, owner of a public relations and event management company in New York City, likes to take the lessons of business and apply them to home life. "Only take on the things that give you the biggest return on investment in your personal or family life," she says. If paying a modest fee for a service will give you more time with the spouse and kids, that's an attractive investment. Some examples:

- buying a cake instead of making one

- hiring a housekeeper to do at least part of the cleaning

- dropping off laundry to be washed and folded

- buying food at the supermarket that's already partially prepared, such as mixed salad greens and taco kits

Learn to say "yes." You've done it a thousand times. A neighbor offers to babysit, or your mother-in-law offers to cook dinner one evening a week. Something prideful prompts you to say "no thanks." You're a competent adult—you can take care of your family needs. Well, loosen up. Accepting help is not an admission of failure. Think of it as found time—an extra bit of relief in a high-pressure week. So memorize this response and get comfortable with it: "Yes!"

Errands Made Easy

Don't think of your errands as self-contained little missions. A few moments of strategic planning will save you hours of driving time and tons of hassle. Here's how.

Don't wait for emergencies. Wakeman is a big believer in preemptive strikes. During the less hectic hours of the weekend, she likes to take care of errands that aren't even necessary yet. For instance, on her trip to the supermarket, she will also fill up her gas tank (even if it's half full) and visit the ATM for cash (even if she

ONCE UPON A TIME . . .

When Labor Starts, Work Should Stop

When PR executive Stephanie Worrell was about to give birth to her son, she made 15 frantic calls to professional contacts during the 20-minute ride to the hospital, despite her labor pains. Each contact had essentially the same response: "This can wait—get off the phone, and go have your baby!" Embarrassed, she learned two big lessons:

There's a time to worry about work, and there's a time to worry about yourself and your family. Draw a firm line between the two.

Worrell's coworkers could have made any necessary phone calls for her, and they felt bad because she didn't ask them to. Let people help you—they'll be happy to deliver, so to speak.

has plenty for the next day or so). This ensures that she won't have a gasoline or cash emergency in the middle of a busy workweek.

Bunch up those errands. Plot out your personal errands for the week—both the recurring errands (grocery shopping) and the incidental errands (buying stamps at the post office). Cluster together the errands that are in the same vicinity and schedule them on your calendar as a single run.

Shop while you chauffeur. Reecanne Joeckel, the advertising and PR exec, likes to structure her errand-running around her kids' schedules. When she drives one of her teenagers to a sports practice, she identifies what businesses she needs to visit in the same vicinity. "If the kids are going to work out for 2 hours, then I'm going to run errands for 2 hours," she says. What if she has no errands to run at the moment? She hauls her laptop to the closest coffee shop that has an Internet connection, and she does advertising work there until the sports practice is over.

Go in the off hours. Many people save up their errands for the weekend. If you do the same, you're going to encounter jammed parking lots and long lines at the registers. Pick a weeknight to run errands. There will be little traffic—on the streets and in the store.

Work on Relaxing

Do you spend a major portion of your life behind the steering wheel of a car, picking up kids and dropping them off at lessons, sports practice, play dates, and parties? Stop that. It's a sign of Super Parent Syndrome, says Patrick Snow, a professional speaker and author of *Creating Your Own Destiny*. If you stop driving your children around so much, you're actually doing them a favor, he says. They'll learn to become independent. Be more of a mentor to your kids and less of a chauffeur.

Let them take the bus. If at all possible, quit driving your kids to and from school. Most children either live close enough to walk to school or have bus service available. They'll discover that riding the bus is actually fun—they'll be sharing the ride with friends, and they'll gain a measure of confidence that comes with handling their own transportation logistics.

Limit outside activities. Here's another way to keep your kid-driving duties under control: Put a limit on the number of out-of-school activities. Each season, each child in Snow's family may participate in only one such activity—they can't take drum lessons *and* play on the basketball team *and* play on the lacrosse team all in one season. "There's just no way you can do it all," he says.

Put rest on the schedule. Here's the surest way to give your family a restful break from a hectic schedule: Put R&R on the calendar and stick to it just as religiously as you would any other important event. When "Joeckel Family Night" is blocked out on Reecanne Joeckel's household schedule, no one's allowed to make other appointments. Family members spend the evening grilling steaks, watching rented movies, and hanging out at home.

Head for the hills. Another Joeckel relaxation tactic: Scheduling the occasional weekend at a lake house, where there's little to do but play and interact with each other. In that remote setting, "There's nowhere to go except for the Wal-Mart," Joeckel says.

Donate Your Time—Judiciously

You're a good person, and you want to make the world a better place. It's admirable that you want to volunteer your time for coaching Little League, maintaining the church grounds, or managing the finances of the Band Parents Association. Volunteering is good for your soul and a good example for your children.

But don't forget: A volunteer organization has many helpers. You, however, are the only person on the planet in charge of managing your schedule. Cheating at organization means that you stick to your priorities—and your work, your family's needs, and your personal sanity are big ones.

Here's how to keep your volunteer hours under control:

Budget your volunteer time. Rather than accepting volunteer duties willy-nilly, study your schedule and decide how many volunteer hours you can handle in any given month. That's your budget—stick to it.

Learn to say "no." It's such a harsh little word—hard to force out of your mouth sometimes. If you prefer to keep your genteel nature intact, practice a few responses that say "no" in polite terms, such as: "Too bad that event's not *next* weekend—my schedule is looser then," or "Sorry, that would cut into family time that is dear to me," or "I barely got my bills paid last month—gotta get more work time in."

3 Cures for Procrastination

Do you have trouble finding the energy or the emotional oomph to get started on a project? Do those calendar pages keep flipping by with that task left forlorn and undone? Organizing expert Sharon Mann offers these tricks for breaking the mind-lock that's so familiar to procrastinators.

1. **Think small.** Tell yourself you're going to do just 10 minutes of work on the task. Sit down and put in the time right away. Once you've started the job, you'll probably find that you don't mind sticking with it and finishing. Even if you stop after those 10 minutes, you'll now view the task as something that will be easy to resume.

2. **Put it on a list.** At the start of each day, jot down the things you hope to accomplish—including that task you've been avoiding. Make a note estimating how long each item will take and when you can reasonably tackle each. With this game plan guiding your day, you'll be more likely to complete the work.

3. **Start early.** Research shows that people tend to be more productive in the morning, so that's when you'll have the energy to jump into that task you've been ignoring.

Count on a sympathetic ear. If the organization you're helping is well run, its managers are highly aware of the issue of volunteer burnout—that is, making such heavy use of the same good-natured people that they get resentful and angry. You'll be surprised how understanding people will be when you explain that you have no more free time.

Declare a moratorium. If just glancing at your personal schedule makes you hyperventilate, put your foot down and take a break from *all* of your volunteer activities. Tell your contacts at each volunteer group that you need the next three months to be distraction-free, and they'll have to get along without you. At the end of the three months, resume volunteering on a limited basis—only the one or two activities that are most gratifying to you.

So here's the bottom line on the scheduling process: You can't afford to ignore it. Sure, you check the calendar every day, but are you also checking that all of the elements that go into your schedule are being managed in the best corner-cutting spirit—setting priorities, weeding out trivial matters, coordinating with family members, and squeezing extra minutes out of your routine duties? Your sanity is at stake: Pick a system, and manage it relentlessly. As Reecanne Joeckel says, "I don't ever take a day off from that."

Make Family Members Pitch In— for Their Own Good

IF YOU WERE TO RUN your family the way you'd run a business, what would your family's mission statement be? For purposes of discussion, I'll propose two that are vastly different:

1. "This family's mission is to provide for its children until they are adults."

2. "This family's mission is to raise responsible and competent adults."

What makes these two statements so different? In the first, the children play a passive role. You are fulfilling their needs, which is fine as far as it goes—but kids need to learn to provide for themselves. The second mission statement indicates a learning process—the children are engaged in their own growth, finding out how to do things for themselves. They will enter their 20s knowing how to run a washing machine, balance a checkbook, and cook an omelet.

Any family counselor would wholeheartedly prefer mission statement 2 to mission statement 1. So I'm sold already. But the *How to Cheat at Organizing* side of me can't help but recognize that number 2 is also a heck of a lot easier on the parent than number 1. Every time a kid can pack his own suitcase or fix his own lunch, the pressure is taken off you. Spread that relief over several years, and you might just get through parenthood with your sanity intact. In the midst of that chaotic life you have running a family—that errand-running, clothes-washing, egg-scrambling, PTA-going treadmill—put some thought to your overall approach to family life. Are you merely fulfilling immediate needs, or are you educating your kids about the fundamentals of life, too?

So let's take a look at organizing and the family. Newborns, toddlers, teens, college kids, spouses, and other relatives all present different organizational challenges. There are plenty of corner-cutting tricks here—simple and easy ways to save you a ton of time, effort, and worry.

Managing Kids–Ages and Stages

As tempting as it may be to try, you're not going to teach your 2-year-old how to wash her own clothes. Organizational issues change as your kids grow. Younger children may need more basic things done for them, but there are labor-saving organizational shortcuts at every stage.

Little Munchkins

A newborn baby draws into the house a tidal wave of new clothing and care products that you may be unaccustomed to. You may not have established permanent "homes" for them in the way that you have a spot for wineglasses and a spot for DVDs. Two months

before the arrival of your new family member, arm yourself with at least a half-dozen clear plastic bins. Sort into them all of the baby-care products that you stock up on in advance. Cluster diapers, diaper rash treatments, wipes, onesies, jingly toys, and pacifiers all in separate containers, says Ginny Snook Scott, a vice president and organization expert for California Closets. Open tops on the containers will help, since you often have one hand occupied with the baby while you're using the other hand to grab the item you need.

Park your containers on shelves built into your changing table or on wall-mounted shelves above it. A plastic changing table organizer that hangs off the side will provide handy pockets for holding many of these items, too.

Keep a mobile diaper reserve. Taking your baby out in public without a fully stocked diaper bag is like swinging on a circus trapeze without a net. You have to be ready for accidents because, as they say, "it" happens. The trickiest part is remembering to restock your diaper bag after you've used the last diaper. Michelle Neujahr, author of *The Family Plan: Keys to Building an Awesome Family,* has a simple solution: When you buy diapers at the supermarket, buy two packages. When you're unloading the groceries, leave one diaper package in the trunk of your car so you always have a supply nearby when you run errands, even if the diaper bag runs out.

Set a Potty Alarm

You can accelerate your child's potty training by asking him once every hour whether he needs to go to the bathroom, says professional organizer Maria Gracia, author of *Finally Organized, Finally Free*. To remind yourself of this duty, get a watch that has an alarm and set it to chime once per hour. Or set the kitchen timer. On the other hand, just think of how much money you'll save not buying diapers—that alone may inspire you to remember to the hourly potty check.

Keep those sizes straight. When you have a newborn in the house, you have to become a master at juggling clothing. Just a couple of weeks makes an enormous difference in what fits and what doesn't. Several storage bins will streamline this little corner of chaos in your life, says closet pro Scott. Buy several plastic bins, all in the same size, with sealing tops to keep dust out. New parents often receive gifts of clothing that's meant for babies who are 3 months, 6 months, or even a year old. Fold such clothing into bins that are labeled by age and keep them in near-at-hand storage (you'll need them in the blink of an eye). The closet of your baby's room is a good place. Or station them in the laundry room, so you can easily wash the new clothes as soon as you need them. Remember that the sizing of baby clothing isn't an exact science. For instance, your 6-month-old might easily need clothing that's labeled for babies a few months older.

When your baby outgrows clothing, move it out of your life immediately so it doesn't become clutter. If you intend to have more children, place old baby clothes into bins, again labeled by age—only this time the bins go into deep storage (the basement or crawl space, for instance). If you don't intend to have more children, place the too-small clothing into shopping bags that are headed out the door—either into the hands of a friend or a charity.

Consolidate the baby gear. When baby toys and equipment sprout up all over the house—baby swing, bouncer, play gym, and such—it's easy to feel as if you've been overrun by a plastic, primary-colored jungle. This will wear thin quickly. To give yourself some sense of order and visual relief, consolidate these items to one room or one area of the house, says Maria Gracia, a professional organizer and author of *Finally Organized, Finally Free.* By the time the baby

Disorderly Teen?
5 Words Preserve a Parent's Sanity

You have a teenager who flings clothing and other personal possessions about wantonly. If she speaks to you at all, it's in an ear-splitting scream. In her opinion, nothing you do is right. And she'd rather be "out"—wherever that may be—than spending time with the family. Does this mean you're a terrible parent and your family is plunging into chaos?

No. Smile, if you can manage it—your youngster is right on course. These are all typical behaviors for a teenager, and they will pass, says Pat Saso, a family therapist and coauthor of *Parenting Your Teens with TLC: The "Time-Limits-Caring" Way to Survive Adolescence.* "If parents are prepared for it, they're not going to be thrown off by these changes," she says.

Until these phases do pass, here's a powerful tool that Saso recommends for preserving your sanity. Every time you have a frustrating encounter with your teenager, repeat this phrase to yourself: "This is not about me." It's about your teenager—ill at ease with the changes in herself, being critical of herself, or on edge because of relationships or pressure in school.

Your new mantra is free, is easy, and will help you cope with what appears to be an explosion of disorder in your home. Use it often: "This is not about me."

is in bed for the night, you'll be ready for some peace and quiet. Set aside your main relaxation area—the living room, for instance—as your toy-free retreat.

Stem the toy tide. When you're a new parent, well-intending friends and relatives dump truckloads of infant toys into your living room. If you anticipate this phenomenon, you will come out way ahead. It doesn't take much to entertain a newborn, notes Gracia, so just a few wiggly, nursery-rhyme-playing toys will take you a long way. Ask your friends to give you toy store gift certificates that you can use several months in the future or, better yet, to make a small contribution to a college fund for the new member of the family.

Rethink the kid's closet. The typical bedroom closet is designed for adult use—lots of tall hanging space for dresses, trousers, and shirts, plus a shelf or two for shoes, hats, and sweaters. If a young child uses the bedroom, however, that closet arrangement is impractical, says Scott, the California Closets VP. Itty-bitty clothes rarely fit well on hangers, and even those that do hang well don't require all of that "air space." Small clothing is easy to store folded and takes up little space inside drawers, bins, or sliding baskets. So turn some of that hanging space over to labeled, compartmentalized storage. And reserve the remaining hanging space for "Sunday best" and other special clothing. Clever use of this space will take some of the pressure off the furniture and shelving elsewhere in the room. You'll get a lot of mileage out of your bins or drawers, too—Scott says this approach will serve you well until your child reaches age 8 or 10.

As Kids Grow, So Do Challenges

Wouldn't you know it? Just as kids get better at caring for themselves, their lives also get more and more complex. Once upon a time, all they cared about was eating and sleeping. Now we have math tests, backpacks, and allowance to worry about.

Keep your eye on this phenomenon: At age 10, your child enters what's called her Master Year, says family therapist Pat Saso, coauthor of *Parenting Your Teens with TLC: The "Time-Limits-Caring" Way to Survive Adolescence.* In her Master Year, your child is finally physically and mentally equipped to handle basic tasks around the house, such as vacuuming and laundry. She'll still need supervision, but she can complete such jobs satisfactorily from start to finish. So dance a little celebratory jig on her 10th birthday.

Make before-school assignments. If you have a big family, getting everyone ready for school in the morning feels like an unmanageable stampede. Motivational speaker Allyson Lewis, author of *The Seven Minute Difference: Small Steps to Big Changes,* knows how to get every kid's needs met: Assign each large child a smaller child to supervise. It's the older child's responsibility to make sure the little tyke gets dressed, eats breakfast, gathers school materials, and remembers to take lunch. The parents might even have time to enjoy a cup of coffee.

Get the hang of wardrobe planning. How many times have you heard a squeaky little voice cry this during the morning rush: "Mommy, where's my underwear? Where are my socks?" To avoid

SLEIGHT OF HAND

Learning on the Installment Plan

Any teenager who works to pay off a substantial loan is going to be better prepared to cope with the same process as an adult. Michelle Neujahr, author of *The Family Plan: Keys to Building an Awesome Family,* had a son who took out a loan to buy a car when he was only 16. Okay, he bought the car from his parents, he got a great deal on it, and the money he borrowed was from his parents, too. Nevertheless, he made regular payments to meet the expense and learned a valuable money management lesson at a young age.

such last-minute panics, work with your youngster to line up her wardrobe in advance, says Lewis. For instance, on Sunday evening, put together a week's worth of outfits—or let your child choose the clothes. Put all clothes for one day on a single hanger—shirt, pants, underwear, and socks. Line up the hangers on the closet rod, in order by day. In the heat of the morning scramble, your child will have no clothing decisions to make and no items to hunt down on an emergency basis.

Get hooked on backpack control. Do you have a kid who can't seem to keep track of his school supplies and homework papers? Institute some simple controls that prevent school materials from getting dispersed throughout the house—and therefore forgotten or lost. Here's how it works in the home of parenting author Neujahr. In the entryway to the home, there's a wall hook for each child's backpack. When a child comes home from school, he does his homework in the kitchen, returns all books to the backpack, and places the backpack on the hook. Backpacks are not allowed in the bedrooms, where school paraphernalia might get mixed in with other possessions.

Start a clothesline gallery. Young artists love to see their best work on display in the home. Here's an easy, mess-free way to accomplish this, says organizing author Gracia: Run a clothesline or twine across the length of one wall of a room, fastened to hooks at each end. Use clothespins to hang your little Picasso's work on the line. When your child has new artwork to post, he can choose which picture will come down and go into storage. The advantages to this approach: You don't have to tape pictures to the wall (damaging both the wall and the artwork) and the number of pictures your child can display is automatically limited by the space on the clothesline.

Chart financial progress. When children are learning to save money toward a financial goal, a visual depiction of their progress will help keep them on track. It makes the abstract practice of saving feel more real. Therapist Pat Saso's family used a simple thermometer-style chart—a drawing that showed the financial goal at the top and a narrow channel leading up to it, colored in as the money stacked up. For instance, when Saso's daughter wanted to buy a cockatiel, she babysat for neighbors' pets and performed other chores to earn money. Seeing the "mercury" rise every time she brought home a fee kept her on task.

Let kids find their own solutions. You can't force children to be organized in their personal affairs. Threats, punishment, and shouting only teach a child how to keep Mom or Dad from getting angry temporarily—and how to push their buttons when the kids want to. You can *teach* children to be organized, however. If you walk children through the process of setting goals and working toward them, they'll learn a valuable skill that will be useful even when you're not around to scowl at them.

Saso offers an example: When one of her sons fell short of his academic goals, she asked him what he needed to do to earn the grades he wanted. He thought about it and came up with this solution: Turn in all of the homework and spend less time on computer games. Saso offered to help him manage his time. They agreed that from 4 p.m. to 6 p.m.—after school and before dinner—he would be free to play on the computer, but otherwise the games were off-limits. This was not punishment—it was her son's own solution to the problem. As the boy got older, he wanted more flexibility in his schedule. Saso agreed, but asked him to keep a record of all of the time he spent playing computer games so he would have a clear picture of how much time he was devoting to it.

College Kids: Out of Sight, Still on Your Mind

You might look forward to the college years as the time when the kids finally leave the house. Well, your children may leave, but the parental worries stay behind. Here are some clever tricks for this special brand of long-distance parenting.

Instant College Organizer

Does organizing personal affairs come naturally to your child? No. So she's going to need an easy-to-manage system for keeping track of all of the paperwork that goes hand in hand with college life. Elizabeth Hagen, author of *Organize with Confidence,* had four kids in college at the same time. For each child, she bought a plastic, lidded hanging-file box at an office supply store. She bought files in the corresponding school color and gave them the following labels:

- "Activities." (For keeping a record of clubs and service projects, to put on a resume upon graduation.)

- "Bookstore." (Book receipts are kept separate, because you can return a textbook for a full refund if you decide to drop a course in time. Also, for store coupons and fliers.)

- "College." (Administrative materials.)

- "Coupons and Menus." (From all of the businesses and restaurants that spring up around a university.)

- "Courses—History." (One file for each course subject.)

- "Dorm." (Rules, hours, and dining information.)

- "Employment." (She needs spending money, right?)

- "Financial." (Bills and banking papers.)

- "Fraternity" or "Sorority." (If the child decides to participate.)

- "Instruction Books." (Manuals for the iPod®, computer, cell phone, microwave, and refrigerator, with receipts.)

- "Receipts." (Except for those mentioned above.)

- "Take Home." (Fliers, programs, and other information to discuss with parents. When taking off for home, she just grabs the whole folder.)

- "Travel." (For e-tickets.)

Easy Laundry 101

Family therapist Pat Saso was quite proud to send her son Brian off to college fully trained to wash his own clothes. She didn't realize, however, that he also was armed with a clever, cheat-at-organizing streak.

Brian's roommate didn't know how to wash clothing—he routinely took his dirty clothes home, and his parents did the laundry for him. This was the source of much ribbing, but it also presented an intriguing opportunity. The roommate's dad was laundering the college wardrobe one day when he found himself thinking, *Hey, this shirt isn't familiar—and these pants are way too big for my boy.* You see, Brian had slipped his own clothing into his roommate's laundry for a little zero-effort (on his part) cleaning. The entire family still laughs about the corner-cutting stunt.

It's nice to see kids learning practical skills in college!

Get dorm gear delivered. You can cut corners on outfitting your child's college dorm room if you take advantage of a service that's typically offered by universities. Saso was delighted with the package of dorm supplies she bought when one of her kids started college. The package included sheets, bed pad, towels, a laundry basket, and more. Everything in the package was in the same color, but since the service offered a variety of colors, it was easy to keep these possessions separate from those of other students. Saso ran the numbers, too—buying the package was less expensive than buying each item individually. So it was convenient *and* less expensive.

Make bins the norm for the dorm. Stacking bins, the kind with doors or drawer-type access on the side, are doubly useful if you have a child attending college. Dorm rooms are notoriously cramped, offering little in the way of closet or dresser space. But stacked bins offer a ton of storage while only taking up a few square feet

of the floor. Let them take over the dorm closet—student clothing is casual and does nicely folded into bins anyway. Also, possessions that are kept in bins are easy to haul around without further packing—a blessing when it's time to make the annual pilgrimage to or from college.

Supply a bookmobile. A bookcase is a must for any student's dorm room. If one isn't supplied already, look for one that's on wheels, says organizing writer Gracia—or attach casters to a conventional bookcase. Your young scholar will be able to roll the books to a spot near his work area when needed. The top of the bookcase also can double as a writing area or worksurface.

A course in personal finances. At college, learning is not confined to the classroom. Parenting author Neujahr's son spent his senior year learning to live within a budget. Before the start of the academic year, parents and son sat down to plot out methods for managing his money. They created a budget that accounted for all living expenses while away at school—including sports, events, dances,

GREAT GEAR

Safeguard Those Valuables

Here's an extremely handy item for any college-bound kid: A small, portable safe, the kind available at office supply stores. Privacy and security can be casual concepts in many dormitories, and a heavy-duty, fireproof, locking box is ideal for keeping a passport, money, and traveler's checks, plus copies of the student's birth certificate and Social Security card. Coins for the laundry room have a particular habit of "walking off" in a dorm environment, so even pocket change should be kept under lock and key.

pizza, and nightlife. They took the money the student had earned during the summer, added a contribution from the parents, and then broke that total down into chunks that were spread over the school year. At the beginning of each month, the parents gave their son the monthly allotment, and that's what he had to work with. He had his own checking account to pay for his cell phone and any other bills. By the time he graduated, he knew how to write checks and manage a budget. He knew, for example, that if his money was running low, he should skip going out for pizza.

Manage their accounts online. The Internet will help you monitor your student's personal finances at college, says professional organizer Elizabeth Hagen, author of *Organize with Confidence.* She was the cosigner for each of her children's checking and savings accounts, so she had online access to their finances. Every week, she transferred a certain amount into each child's account. "They know they get so much a week extra, and when it's gone it's gone," she says.

She believes giving a credit card to a college student is "playing with fire." Her kids got debit cards, which drew straight out of their checking accounts. As each child graduates, Hagen removes her own name from the account and the child is free from Mom's oversight. "That's always a very fun thing to do," she says.

Kids and Their Stuff

Have you noticed that you never have to teach a kid how to want more things? Keeping all of their possessions in order—that's the part that doesn't come naturally to them. Here are tricks for making clutter control easy.

Conquering Toyland

Is your house wall-to-wall toys? A rippling carpet of brightly colored action figures, building sets, and games? You probably know instinctively that containers are the key to keeping toy clutter under control. Right you are—but you also need some crafty strategies to go along with the containers.

Get the right bin. One secret to controlling the clutter that comes with children's toys is to give each kind of toy its own storage bin— a bin that's no larger or smaller than necessary to contain every piece. This way, all of your daughter's Barbie® dolls and accessories stay in one place—simple to find at play time, and simple to stash away again at cleanup time. Buy all of your bins in the same brand so they can be stacked and the lids are compatible. Clear plastic is a good idea, so the child can see what toys are inside. Also, to help nonreaders, label the bin with a cutout picture that represents the contents. If the toy collection grows, buy a larger container to accommodate it. Don't worry, there will be plenty of uses for the old, smaller container. This approach works for virtually every kind

Provide "I'm Done with It" Bags

How many articles of clothing cycle through your laundry without actually getting worn? Here's how this typical, unproductive routine goes: A child pulls a T-shirt out of the dresser and tries it on. It no longer fits, so he throws it on the floor and finds another one. Mom or Dad comes along on wash day, finds that T-shirt on the floor, washes it, and returns it to the dresser. That's a waste of time, effort, and laundry products.

Michelle Neujahr, author of *The Family Plan: Keys to Building an Awesome Family*, has a simple solution: Give each child an "I'm Done with It" shopping bag to place on the floor of the bedroom closet. Anytime the child encounters clothing that doesn't fit or he no longer likes, he puts it into the bag. When it's time to make clothing donations to a charity, a parent collects the items from the "I'm Done with It" bags and gets them out of the house—and, thank goodness, out of the laundry cycle.

of kids' toy—action figures, cars, crafts, puzzles, building sets, and more. Open-style cubby storage is a good alternative for organizing toys without hiding them from the child's sight.

Cut toy clutter with the crate rule. Parenting author Neujahr hated finding her kids' toys strewn about the house all day, every day. So she put her foot down and established a clutter-busting rule that would serve any parent well. She placed a crate in the living room and told the kids that at any one time they could only have out the amount of toys that would fit into the crate—and the toys had to go back into the crate at the end of the day. This reduced the toy clutter during the day and made cleanup easy for the kids.

Limit the toys on "active duty." Neujahr has another clever solution to toy clutter. Give each child four plastic stacking storage bins to keep in the bedroom closet. Have the child use these bins to keep toys sorted—dolls in one bin and Lego® blocks in another, for example. These are the toys that are available for the child to play with day in and day out. Any toys that do not fit into the bins must be packed away in the basement. When the child gets bored with the toys that are on "active duty," he may swap them with toys that are in storage. This approach limits the number of toys that could be circulating throughout the living areas at any one time, and it makes toy cleanup at the end of the day easy and systematic for the child.

Invite millions to your yard sale. To control clutter, make sure there's a steady flow of unnecessary possessions out of the home. Yard sales and donations to charities are the traditional paths. However, the Internet age presents another easy option: selling your stuff by online auction. Among the millions of people browsing eBay[SM], somebody somewhere is willing to pay for your family's unwanted action figures, Legos, CDs, and books.

"I'm an eBay freak," says Neujahr, who lets her kids keep half of the money from toys sold on the auction site. The other half goes into the family vacation fund, which has paid for a cruise and a trip to the Cayman Islands, among other exotic jaunts. Elementary school kids are old enough to help with online selling. Neujahr's children chose the items to sell and took digital photos of them, while Neujahr handled the eBay arrangements.

In with the new, out with the old. The "one-in, one-out" rule will stem the tide of toys that's threatening to inundate your home, says professional organizer Hagen. If your child has a birthday party and gets eight toys as presents, she has to choose eight old toys to donate to charity. She has the option of donating any of the new toys if she prefers the old ones.

Bedlam in the Bedroom?

The easiest, cheating-est cure for a child's messy bedroom is this: Close the door and find something else to worry about. But if you want to get a child in the habit of imposing order on her personal space, here are some easy approaches.

Dream up a system—together. Help your children take responsibility for controlling the clutter in their own bedrooms. Toddlers can start out with basic concepts (returning toys to a bin), and by elementary school age, kids can handle a rudimentary organizing system (don't expect perfection). Your core strategy, says Scott: First, establish with your child what feature of the room you want to organize—say, the desk. Then identify all of the kinds of things that need to be contained by the desk—art supplies, projects, and homework materials, for instance. Then come to agreement on the specific places where each category of things will be kept. This might mean putting art supplies on a shelf above the desk, projects in the top right-hand drawer, and homework in the bottom drawer. On another day, follow the same procedure for the closet (specific places for shoes, sports equipment, and rain gear), shelves, night table, and any other storage.

When your child is actively involved in establishing the system, he will take more ownership of it and will be able to put his room in order with less supervision on your part. Your time invested in the system will pay off handsomely over the long haul.

Ten animals—that's enough of a circus. A child's bedroom can become so overwhelmed with toy stuffed animals that it's impossible to impose order. Establish a firm rule with your kids, advises Neujahr, a variation of the "one-in, one-out" concept mentioned earlier: 10 animals per child is the limit. If they get a new animal, they have to donate an old one to a family crisis shelter or some other charity.

Put "friends" in high places. Organizer Maria Gracia has a clever way to keep stuffed animals from cluttering the floor of a child's bedroom: Make a simple hammock for them. Take a stretch of cloth that's 4 or 5 feet long and about 2 feet wide. Cut two lengths of twine and tie each end to a corner of the cloth, so there's a loop of twine at each end of your "hammock." Stretch the hammock, high up, across one corner of the child's room, fastening it to each wall with hooks. The hammock will accommodate several stuffed animals, which will be well out of the way when it's time to dust.

An easy variation: drape a length of cloth across the top of a high dresser or bookshelf and arrange the stuffed animals on that. Once a month, launder the cloth to remove accumulated dust and then put it back.

Get flexible shelving. As your children grow, the books they want to keep on their shelves will vary in size—from oversize picture books down to conventional paperbacks. So when you install shelving or buy bookcases, make sure the shelves are adjustable, says Scott, the VP for California Closets. This allows you to make the best use of shelf space without buying new furniture every couple of years.

A cool accessory organizer. To keep a girl's zillion tiny accessories from sprawling across a dresser top, give her a set of inexpensive ice cube trays or muffin tins from a dollar store, says organizer Gracia. Those small bins are perfect for keeping tiny pieces organized. An over-the-door shoe bag also is ideal for bringing order to a girl's small possessions—particularly hair accessories.

Box up those memories. Let your children participate in the decision making about what childhood memorabilia gets saved for posterity, says Neujahr. After all, they're the ones who will ultimately own and store these items in adulthood. Buy one plastic storage box for each child, and use it to hold that child's arts and crafts projects, baby photos, baby clothes, and such. But stick to this important rule: Everything must fit in the bin. If the child decides to save a new item and the bin is full, something must come out to make room. This technique allows you to preserve the most important items without creating a heaping storage problem. Besides, your kids are likely to move several times in their adult lives, and a dozen boxes of memorabilia would become a burden.

Winning Strategies for Sports Gear

Sports equipment presents some special organizational challenges. There are a lot of different pieces to keep track of—cleats, helmets, pads, uniforms, sticks, balls—all of which should be easy to find when game time approaches. Afterward, these same items should be easy to stow as well. Here's how to cheat at the sports equipment game.

Give each kid a sports depot. Are your kids in the habit of showing up at their sporting events without all of their equipment? Then provide each child with a central depot where all of the equipment is stored together. Neujahr bought a large plastic bin for each youngster and parked them in the laundry room. When the kids are getting ready for a game, they pull their gear out of the bin. When they return home from the game, they go straight to the laundry room, put all of their gear into the bin, strip down, and throw the uniform in there, too. On washday, Mom pops the bins open and plucks out any uniforms that needed washing, returning them to the bin when they're clean. If Neujahr buys new sports gear—say, a pair of batting gloves—she just drops it into the appropriate bin, where the child will find it.

With this system, sports gear doesn't get spread all around the house and go missing—or forgotten—at critical times. The contents of the bins change season to season, depending on what sport is currently being played. Establish a deep-storage spot for keeping out-of-season sports gear in a remote closet, the basement, or the garage.

Keep the playing field outside. Sports equipment and dirt go together like a hand in a baseball glove. If sporty dirt tends to invade the interior of your house, establish a convenient drop-off point for such gear near a commonly used entrance—say, in the mudroom or the garage, says Scott. Inexpensive lockers, available at home improvement stores and discount stores, are great for storing hockey, golf, and baseball gear. For balls that may roll around on the floor (soccer balls, footballs, or basketballs), try a large lidded chest. Such chests also provide a convenient spot for sitting while you change into or out of cleats.

Give gear the brush-off. Keep a stiff-bristled brush in any sports equipment locker. When shoes, balls, or other gear comes back from the playing field caked with grime, have your kids grab the brush and give the muddy items a quick scouring out on the lawn.

The Family as a Group

One vital aspect of a family is that all of the members work together as a unit. This is not empty jargon. Experts say the families that function most smoothly have a couple of characteristics in common: They hold family meetings, and they set goals. These are easy habits to institute, and the payoff is enormous. Here are tricks for getting your family members to pull in the same direction.

Calling a Family Huddle

Parents usually don't have any trouble concentrating during a family meeting, but there are so many potential distractions around the home that a child can easily lose focus—snacks, the telephone, the computer, pets, books, and music are all contending for your child's attention.

Therapist Pat Saso has the solution: She often holds family meetings at a restaurant on Sunday evenings. It doesn't have to be fancy—any eatery will do. Sitting around a restaurant table, your children are a captive audience. They're also trained to control their behavior in such public places, so they'll participate politely in the family discussion. Their options are minimal, after all. "Where else are they going to go—to the bathroom?" says Saso.

Focus the family with goals. Goal setting sounds like something out of the management handbook at work. But it's actually a very practical way to keep family members focused on what really matters—academic performance, for instance. Setting goals—deciding specifically what you want to accomplish, how you're going to accomplish it, and over what period of time—helps to clarify what's important and what activities should take priority. It's a skill that separates productive people from unproductive people, Saso says.

A family meeting is the time to set goals for the whole group—saving for a vacation or cleaning out the garage, for instance. Each family member should have individual goals, too. Take your child aside periodically for a private goal-setting session, Saso says. A casual restaurant meal is ideal. Keep the conversation relaxed, emphasize the child's strengths, and help him identify specific desired accomplishments. For instance, what grades does he want to earn by the end of the next marking period? Did he meet his goals for the last marking period? If not, what can he change to succeed the next time?

Chart the chores. Make a simple chart listing the 10 or 20 chores around the house that need to be performed by some family member. At the weekly family meeting, discuss who will handle each item and write those names beside each duty. Make sure the duties rotate from week to week, and that each person gets a mixture of the most desired chores (playing with the dog) and the least desired (picking up the dog's poop). Don't worry about nagging or supervising the chores during the week. Just establish a firm consequence for failure to perform. In Neujahr's home, no child gets to go out on the weekend unless his chores for the week are done.

Audit the living areas. Walk through each room of the house and conduct a quick audit from the point of view of each member of the family. In each general living area, each family member deserves space for keeping his or her personal items, says Ginny Snook Scott of California Closets. If it's not available, then you will find possessions lying in annoying places—on the floor, coffee table, furniture, and counters.

Consider the entertainment center, for example: You and your spouse probably have ample room for your stereo and other electronic equipment. But is there good storage available for your teenage daughter's CD collection? How about your 9-year-old's game controllers and cartridges? Remember, possessions are more likely to be put away when their storage spaces are convenient to the place where they're used. In the garage, you could create a potting area for Mom, a workbench for Dad, and a models-and-rockets area for kids. Even in the kitchen, a youngster might want a place to store a pad of paper and crayons she can use while you're nearby making dinner.

At the end of your audit, write out a shopping list for the organizing items you need in order to give each family member a bit of personal real estate in every room.

After-dinner cleanup—for everyone. After-dinner cleanup is already an established work time—at least for the adult who has to rinse dishes, clean pots, and load the dishwasher. Why not make this a quick-and-easy work period for the entire family? Set the kitchen timer for 15 minutes, says motivational speaker Allyson Lewis, and assign each family member to straighten up a different part of the house. Once this practice is established, your house will never again descend into chaos. A variation: Put cookies into the oven, and stop cleaning when the timer goes off—time for dessert!

Your Spouse and Relatives

Simple communication does a lot to enhance your relationship with loved ones. So here are some easy ways to keep connected with relatives near and far.

Organize relatives by e-mail. E-mail seems like a terribly impersonal way to communicate, especially when it comes to keeping in touch with relatives. However, it can save you eons of time at such routine tasks as providing driving instructions to a get-together or trying to pick the date of a celebration. Saso's husband, who has eight brothers and sisters, finds e-mail a godsend in coordinating with loved ones. E-mailing software allows you to set up groups, so you can send the same e-mail to all group members with one mouse-click. To get several family members to participate in a group discussion, instruct them to respond by clicking on "Reply to All," which will send copies to everyone. Save the telephone or letter writing for more personal communication.

Find the right home for correspondence. Open up your filing cabinet and look inside. How many feet of filing space are devoted to personal cards and letters from loved ones? Personal memorabilia

Automate Those Thank-Yous

From a youngster's point of view, writing thank-you notes is the dark side of any gift-giving holiday. You'll be the hero of the family when you automate the process for children and adults alike. Michelle Neujahr, author of *The Family Plan: Keys to Building an Awesome Family,* keeps a computer file containing the names and addresses of all of the relatives who typically send gifts at the holidays. Using the label-printing feature of her word-processing software, she prints out several copies of the addresses. She parks these in the kitchen, along with pens, paper, envelopes, and stamps. Family members just go to the thank-you-note station, write their short letters, stick them into envelopes, and add the appropriate address labels and stamps.

She has an enforcement rule, too: No child may cash a gift check until the thank-you note is written.

will overwhelm your filing space in no time, so reserve the filing cabinet for information you need for the business of routine life, says Scott. Let's say you receive a letter from your mother. First, ask yourself whether the letter contains data you will need in the future for some practical reason—such as health care or inheritance information. If the answer is "yes," then file the letter under one of those topics. If not, then ask a second question: "Is this a letter that I will cherish several years from now?" If the answer is "yes," then put the letter into an airtight container that will protect the paper from bugs and mildew. Keep this container accessible in your home office, and when it's full, mark the date on it, put it into storage, and start on a new container. If the letter isn't a "keeper," share it with other family members and recycle the paper—secure in the knowledge that you're preserving a good number of more memorable missives.

Aunts and uncles to the rescue. If one of your children is having a hard time in life, it helps to have an adult they respect—besides Mom or Dad—provide some love and support. Contact a relative and suggest that he or she check in with your troubled youngster to provide an emotional boost. Ten minutes on the telephone will go a long way. "They need other adults in their lives," Saso says.

Treat yourselves to a treaty. No two adults have the same set of values about organizing a home. That's a common source of stress in relationships—you're a neatnik, and your spouse is happy to leave piles of chaotic junk all around the house. Or vice versa. A simple compromise will soothe this sore point, says Neujahr. Her husband agreed to only use certain spots as his cluttered "dumping grounds." These spots include a large in-box on his desk and certain drawers around the house. Within those specific spaces, he can create all of the clutter that he wants. However, over the years, he has actually come to appreciate the orderly look of the home. In his work, he sees the chaos inside many other houses. He comes home gushing to his wife, *"Thank you!"*

Get Your Photo Archive Clicking

It would be a shame if the photographic record of cherished family events—say, that special ski trip to Colorado—were forever buried under a mountain of unsorted photo envelopes. If your eyes are starting to cross, don't fret—I'm not going to turn you into a permanent snapshot librarian. The following cheats are not much harder than pushing the shutter release on your camera.

Photo box is a snap. Many families have a messy, ever-growing mound of photos waiting to be sorted. But parenting author Michelle Neujahr has a bare-minimum, nuts-and-bolts system that will keep them organized easily.

Find an empty shoebox, or go to an office supply store and buy a file box that will accommodate the size of photo prints you prefer. Mark index cards (or dividers, if you bought a file box that comes with them) with each family member's name and give another card the generic label "Family," for group snapshots. Whenever you get a new set of prints, take them out of the envelope, sort the best ones into the proper spot in the file box, throw away the bad photos, and toss what's left into a separate box marked "Extras." The filed photos are destined for the family album when you get time. Any family member may take the extras for any use—even cutting them up for a collage or a school poster.

Pitch those negatives. What's the best way to handle the negatives that come with your snapshots? The hard-core *How to Cheat at Organizing* approach is just to throw them away. You almost never use them, excellent copies can be made straight off prints, and you're just working with informal snapshots anyway—not presidential documents that need to be preserved for centuries to come.

HELP!

A Snapshot of Online Services

If you use an online photo service, you don't have to fret about owning and maintaining a photo-quality printer that's going to be obsolete in a few years. You just transfer digital photos to the service, and they'll send you prints to your specifications. On such sites you can typically change photo size, crop, enhance color, reduce red-eye, convert to black and white, add messages and captions, and even have your photos emblazoned on merchandise. If you prefer, use photo-editing software on your own computer and send the enhanced images to the service.

At this writing, popular services include www.kodakgallery.com (operated by guess-who), www.photoaccess.com, www.shutterfly.com, www.flickr.com, www.photobucket.com, and www.snapfish.com. Some discount stores and drugstores also offer online photo services. Online companies come and go, however, so conduct an Internet search on the term "online photo service" and browse through the current offerings.

If you can't bear to part with the negatives, mark the date on each negative sleeve and slap them into in a separate box in chronological order—so you can retrieve them when curators from the Smithsonian come knocking on your door.

Digital: Should you byte? The ultimate *How to Cheat at Organizing* technique for organizing family photos requires an investment: Convert to digital photography. Suddenly, every step of managing your photos gets extremely easy. You can delete the lousy photos with the push of a button. You can sort the good ones into folders on your computer. (As with hard prints, label a folder for each family member, plus a generic "Family" folder.) There are no negatives to deal with. If you want prints for some reason, some home printers can produce "photo quality" copies. However, it's easier just to pass your digital images to an online photo service and have it mail you the prints you select. If you want to share your photos with relatives, forget about mailing prints—use an online photo service that allows you to post "albums" that you control access to.

That annoying mountain of unsorted hard-copy snapshots will obviously stop growing once you convert to digital. If you can't find the time or energy to sort through the remaining prints cluttering up your house, dump them into a storage bin, mark the date on the outside, and carry them to the basement. The next time you have a bout of insomnia, pull out the bin and sort the photos.

As you start implementing the advice in this chapter, you will quickly discover that a family pulling together—using simple organizational principles—is astoundingly more powerful than its individuals working alone. Yes, these measures make your parenting life easier, but in one way or another every family member shares in the payoff. Don't forget that mission statement: You're turning your youngsters into happy, competent, and productive adults. That's definitely worth cheating for.

Chapter Ten

Collections

Preserve Your Treasures— and Your Sanity, Too

I WANT YOU TO BE HAPPY. Really. Do all of the things that nourish your soul—grow an herb garden, visit the Great Wall of China, and take up flamenco dancing. Collect rare, beautiful, or curious objects, too, if they "speak" to you in some spiritual way. But understand how treacherous an idea collecting is within the covers of a book about organizing shortcuts. Most of us can barely manage the possessions we need in order to survive. And you want to acquire *more* possessions and cram them into your living space—items that aren't even *necessary?*

So I hope you will forgive me, dear collectors, when I say that the certified, hard-core, *How to Cheat at Organizing* approach to collecting is . . . just not to do it. Collecting done right, in an orderly way, requires so much more than just buying stuff—it entails display, research, preservation, and even some paperwork. So save yourself the bother. Frequently visit museums and galleries, where they manage collections so much better than you could ever

hope to. And keep your home and your calendar blessedly free of the resulting clutter.

Gee, now you're mad at me. You have already filled the spare bedroom with 729 lunch boxes, or antique poison bottles, or Charlie Tuna mementos, or hat pins, or soft drink cans, or Three Stooges items—and the only advice I have for you is "Get rid of them"? You know me better than that. Of course I'm going to help you. Here's a chapter full of ways to simplify and manage the collecting process so it interferes minimally with the rest of your life and your living space. You nut case.

Set Up a Sane Process

I know of a woman who went so wild with her collecting that she had to rent an outside storage locker to accommodate the overflow of possessions from her three-story townhouse. And then there's the guy who had so many bicycles and old newspapers crammed into his home that there was no room for a bed—he slept on the front porch.

You probably don't go to these extremes, but they are examples of what can happen when you get way too emotionally engaged with your physical things. If you are determined to collect objects, set some rational limits and stick to them. And have the cheat-at-organizing wisdom to remove objects from your collection just as regularly as you acquire them. Ask yourself every month, *Is this collection adding to my life or detracting from it?*

Here are techniques for imposing control on any collection.

Fine-Tune Your Plan

Before you start collecting, decide first what you're willing to pay for your collection, how many pieces you can handle, and what the focus of your collection will be, says Linda Kruger, executive

ONCE UPON A TIME . . .

The Accidental Collector

Did you enter the collecting world by the "back door"? Professional organizer Misha Keefe recalls a client who had a drawer stuffed with name tags from every convention he had ever spoken at—an enormous mound of name cards, plastic sleeves, and lapel clips. The collection wasn't being managed. It was just piled up, with no thought to organizing, display, or cleaning.

So Keefe asked the crucial question: Why did he begin collecting the name tags in the first place? Early in his career, he replied, he was ecstatic the first time he was invited to speak at a convention. So he saved the name tag as a memento. He saved the tag from his next speaking engagement, too, and the next, and the next. Years later, speaking at conventions was old hat—just a facet of his work—but he kept socking away the name tags out of habit.

When you realize that the reason you started a collection is no longer valid, you can make a break from these items and do something more sensible. For instance: Throw away all but the oldest or most significant piece. Frame that one and hang it on the wall. This will satisfy the sentimental side of you without cluttering up your house. This is called the Keep One rule.

director of the Collector's Information Bureau, based in Grundy Center, Iowa. Of course, if you're in the midst of collecting and you haven't decided these issues, do so immediately.

Cost: Decide how much of a regular expenditure your personal budget can handle. Can you afford to buy a $300 item every month? Or is $50 a month more like it? You might start with less expensive items in a category (say, movie posters) and then start to specialize in pricier items as you can afford them later (perhaps vintage posters from popular '40s and '50s movies).

Quantity: How many items can you reasonably display in your home? Do you have the wall space for a poster collection? If you're collecting small items, will you need display cases—and how many?

Focus: How narrowly focused will your collection be? Toys from the '50s? Or perhaps a specific brand of toys from that era? If you're collecting Art Deco prints, will you specialize in a specific artist? With a focused strategy, your collection will have a pattern behind it—a mission you can fulfill. Choose a focus that's broad enough that you will be able to find new items at a reasonable cost, yet narrow enough that your pieces have a coherent theme. Otherwise, your collection will be more frustrating than joyful.

Make Wise Choices

Above all, make sure you're in love with the things that you are collecting, says Bobbie Zucker Bryson, coauthor of *Collectibles for the Kitchen, Bath & Beyond.* "Buy what you like the most, what you can't live without, and that's what you should put on display," she says.

There are both emotional reasons and practical reasons for this. If your collection is a labor of love, you are surrounding yourself with objects that you admire—you're enhancing your life. You will have the passion necessary to display, care for, and learn about your collection. If you decide to sell off your collection sometime in

4 Signs It's Time to Quit Collecting

It's a wise collector indeed who knows when to stop acquiring items, pare them down, or dispose of them altogether. This may sound like blasphemy to some collectors, but now and then that spark of passion does burn out. Here are the warning signs, says Bobbie Zucker Bryson, coauthor of *Collectibles for the Kitchen, Bath & Beyond:*

1. You stop caring about how your collection is displayed.

2. You don't enjoy seeing your collection daily.

3. You have started packing some of your collectibles into boxes because you don't want to look at them anymore.

4. You have no room for your collection or your other personal possessions.

"If you start to not enjoy something, get rid of it," says Bryson. "If you don't enjoy it, what are you keeping it for? You control your collections, or your collections will control you."

the future, even if you only break even, it won't matter—you got to experience those beautiful objects for the time that you had them.

If you're starting a collection because of a fad or because you want to make money, a little alarm should go off in your head. Fads inevitably fade, and you'll be left with a roomful of worthless objects you don't even like. And while collecting may bring happiness, it's not a road to riches.

Get the scale right. Make sure that anything you collect is appropriate for your living space, says Bryson. If you don't have a lot of room in your home, collect only small items and confine your collection to one tabletop, a small cabinet, or the compartment underneath a glass-topped coffee table that's designed for displays. "Can you collect carousel horses if you live in a loft in SoHo in New York?" asks Bryson. "It would have to be quite a big loft."

Buy better, not more. Dorothy Breininger, a professional organizer based in Canoga Park, California, and coauthor of *The Senior Organizer,* believes that the wisest approach to collecting is never to store any of your items. When you run out of space in which you can comfortably, pleasingly display your collection, it's time for discipline. Use the "one-in, one-out" rule. That is, if you buy a new item for your collection, you must sell one of your old items. Not only will this keep your collection to a manageable size, but it also will improve your collection. Why? Because you gain knowledge over time, and often your disposable income increases, too. This means you buy better pieces for your collection and get rid of the worst ones. Over time, your collection will increase in value and take on a sharper, more sophisticated focus.

Bryson, the collectibles author, follows this philosophy, too. She and her husband have numerous collections, including antique furniture, juice reamers, vintage gloves, plant waterers (decorative watering spikes), ribbon dolls, Depression glass, and green-handled kitchenware. The couple pared 100 of their least favorite items out of their reamer collection. When they gazed upon what was left, Bryson said, "Wow—now these look great!" So if your collection is out of control, roll up your sleeves and weed it aggressively.

Consider the kids. If you have kids in the house, trying to collect vintage toys could cause more heartache than it's worth. For instance, it's hard to explain to a 4-year-old that the antique doll collection on the display shelf in the den is only for looking, says Misha Keefe, a professional organizer in Washington, D.C. Those dolls then become "forbidden fruit," and sooner or later your child is going to find her way into that collection.

Chat up the dealers. One of the best ways to learn about the items that you collect is to strike up conversations with dealers at antique shows or shows that focus specifically on the items that you collect. Why? Because dealers are often collectors themselves, and they've turned their passion into a business, says Kruger, of the Collector's Information Bureau. Ask dealers what interesting trends they've noticed, what kinds of items are the most sought after, and where else you might be able to buy the items you collect. To find notices of upcoming shows and events, check collector publications and web sites. Before you buy from a dealer you don't know, at least make a couple of quick checks: Ask the dealer whether you can return the item if you're not satisfied. Also, find out whether your dealer has a good relationship with the other dealers at the show. As a whole, dealers will not be very chummy with a disreputable merchant.

Managing Your Collection

Okay, you have several like items that relate to each other themat-ically somehow. What you do next with them makes all the differ-ence—will they be mere clutter, or a collection you can be proud of?

Show Off Your Stuff

Sure, you may love hunting for your collectibles and researching their history, but a collection just isn't a collection until you've put it on display for all to see. There's more to displaying a collection than just plonking each item onto a shelf, however.

Make like a curator. If the size of your collection exceeds the dis-play space available, you have two choices: dispose of some items, or store the excess. Limiting your collection to the display space available is the easier, certified *How to Cheat at Organizing* tech-nique. Storing the excess items is a time-consuming hassle, and it's also a shame to have prized pieces that never see the light of day. However, if you insist on going the storage route, try this approach: Appoint yourself the curator of your own mini-museum. On the dis-play shelves, you have only select, prized pieces. The rest, carefully inventoried, are in protective storage. Now and then you rotate the items that are on display, so guests see something new the next time they visit. When you accept the curator role, you automati-cally focus yourself on pleasing displays, protection of your pieces, and an orderly system. Your collection will be lively and never fall into neglect.

Collections should be seen and not tripped over. Make sure your collection can be seen by admirers yet does not interfere with daily life. When collectibles author Bryson redesigned her kitchen, she included special shelving for her collectibles. Her sister went the kitchen route as well. She removed the doors from a couple of her cabinets, lined the shelves in vintage paper, and stationed her collections there, providing a funky look to her 1930s kitchen. Both treatments make the collected objects visible, central, part of the décor—and yet out of the way.

Close up your collection . . . Display cases with glass doors are ideal for showing off a collection of small, intricate objects, says Bryson. A closed case will keep dust off your pieces, so you won't have to clean them very often. Also, cases protect your objects from grabby little hands (if you have kids or if they visit now and then) and waggy little tails (if you have dogs or if *they* visit now and then).

. . . or think outside the cabinet. When you talk to collectors, you often hear mention of fancy airtight wooden cabinets with mirrored backing and tricky little doors. Well, you don't have to take out a mortgage just to house your collection. Creativity will take you a long way. "You have to be clever—there are no boundaries," says Bryson. "I have seen people take concrete blocks, paint them, take plain planks of wood, paint them, and build funky display configurations." Here are some other clever ideas:

- To display her wall pocket vases, Bryson filled a wall of her home with empty picture frames. When she acquired a new piece, she would mount it on the wall in the center of one of the frames. Some of the frames remained empty for a long time, but they never seemed out of place.

- In a modern house, use high-tech industrial shelving. Or cruise kitchen and bath stores for inexpensive cabinets or shelves.

- Bryson's husband had a quandary—how to display his collection of plant waterers. The carrot-shaped devices can't stand on their own, and they look ho-hum just lying on their sides. Finally, he hit on the solution: He propped them up in old pipe stands, which he picked up for pocket change at flea markets.

Get wrapped up in protective materials. For virtually every collectible item known to humankind, there are corresponding protective materials in the form of paper, boxes, and plastic sleeves—all made free of the acids that will degrade your prized items. You can find archival materials at art shops, and trade publications and collectors' price guides provide listings of companies that sell such materials by mail order, says Kruger. Also, conduct an Internet search on the term "archival supplies." While such amenities may sound finicky to newcomers to collecting, the peace of mind they provide is well worth the nominal cost. For instance, you can display your baseball cards in a binder of acid-free plastic sleeves. Just drop the binder on your coffee table, and you can rest assured that your 1957 Hank Aaron will remain fingerprint- and spatter-free.

Do Your Paperwork

You know I'm no fan of paper shuffling. But if you have chosen to manage a home collection, you have committed yourself to at least a little bureaucratic work in the background. (Hey, I warned you that collecting could get involved.)

Catalog your collection. This is going to sound persnickety: If you're going to collect, inventory your items, says Kruger, of the Collector's Information Bureau. It's part of the price of admission to the world of collecting. Your inventory doesn't have to be complex. In the simplest, cheat-at-organizing form, you could just take snapshots of each item and throw them into a folder along with your receipts (or store digital photos in a computer folder). A video of your collection also works (you can provide details with a narration). A little written data would be a good idea, too, however— a text file or spreadsheet recording a brief description of the item,

Snap Out of It: The Photo Solution

Even the most exquisite collection can become a burden under certain circumstances, says professional organizer Dorothy Breininger.

For instance, Breininger had a client who had a large collection of Civil War memorabilia and another client who had collected thousands of dolls. Both clients had to give up their collections because of personal circumstances, and both clients were wracked with guilt.

Their salvation lay in a compact little device called the camera. At Breininger's suggestion, the families photographed each item in their collections and then assembled the snapshots, along with inventory information, into an album. Thus, the sentimental part of the collection—the memory—was preserved and the families were able to sell off the actual collections without another thought.

This concept also works well with bulky, impractical furniture that gets handed down from relatives—grandma's piano, for instance, or an enormous dollhouse. Gather the family around the item, take the snapshot, and sell the furniture to the highest bidder.

"People are so relieved with that idea," Breininger says.

price paid, date purchased, from whom it was purchased, condition of the item, serial number, and any story behind the item. Add each item to your inventory the moment you make a purchase. Maintaining the system won't seem like much of a chore that way, and you'll be able to capture the relevant details about the item before they evaporate from your brain over the next few months. To make inventory easier, you can find personal computer software that will help you manage your collection, or go to a collector's web site such as www.smartcollector.com and store your data online.

Why bother with an inventory? It's handy in a number of ways. If your collection is ever damaged or stolen, you can document for your insurance company the extent and condition of your collection (the condition is a key part of establishing value). The images and data will come in handy when you decide to sell an item (particularly if you're working through an auction web site such as eBay or corresponding with potential buyers by e-mail). And when you do make a sale, you will have a record of profits made, for tax purposes.

Review your insurance needs. If the *How to Cheat at Organizing* gods are smiling on you, you may not have to bother with insuring your collection. Here's how to decide, says Kruger: Take a look at the inventory of your collection and estimate how much it would cost you to replace it. Then take a look at your personal finances—how much of a burden would that cost be? If it feels like pocket change, then consider your collection to be "self-insured." That is, you will pay to replace it yourself and forgo the cost of added insurance premiums. Congratulations: You have just saved yourself an organizational hassle.

If the cost of replacing your collection feels like a hardship, however, contact your insurance company. (Another way to think about it: A common rule of thumb recommends insuring a collection that's $2,500 in value or more.) Unless you have made special arrangements, your conventional homeowner's insurance probably does not fully cover the value of your collection. What to you is a shelf full of priceless figurines might be merely 5 pounds of porcelain in the eyes of your insurance company. You might have to ask your insurance company for a special rider, or you might even have to go to a separate company for a special policy.

Specific Collections

Here are some notes on organizing specific kinds of collections, from Misha Keefe, the professional organizer in Washington, D.C.

Figurines and glass: Don't choose an accessible spot for displaying delicate objects, especially if you have kids or kids visit your home frequently. A closed cabinet, a high shelf, or an out-of-the-way table-top is best.

Paintings: Experiment with layout. Small paintings work well as a grouping. If you have a large painting, you can create an interesting look just by standing it on the floor and leaning it against the wall. An inexpensive poster sandwiched between sheets of glass makes an unusual top for a coffee table.

Framed photos: Nobody will have the patience to peruse 20-plus photographs in your home. Choose a half-dozen that have the most impact and display them in one place. Or buy a frame that has multiple windows cut into the matting so you can slide several photos into the same display. They're available at discount stores, art supply stores, and home décor stores.

Stamps, coins, and cards: Discipline yourself—display only a few of your rarest or most interesting items. The rest are easy to stash away in an archival album. Stamps, coins, and cards are so popular with collectors that there are zillions of products for displaying them and protecting them at the same time. Check online or at hobby stores.

Dolls: If your dolls are "untouchable" antiques, display them on a high shelf in your living room or dining room. Position the shelf 12 to 18 inches below the ceiling and run it around the entire perimeter of the room.

So now you have the bare truth: Incorporating a collection into your lifestyle is almost as complex as adopting an Irish setter. Go into such an endeavor with both eyes open, and weigh the joys against the hassles. At least you don't have to feed your Hummel® figurines or follow them around with a scooper.

3-Step Program for Messy Collectors

Have your hunter-gatherer instincts gone berserk? Got first-edition detective novels spilling off overstuffed shelves? Ceramic figurines covering every conceivable surface in the den, living room, and dining room? A closet stacked floor to ceiling with comic books? Professional organizer Misha Keefe offers these three steps for bringing order and sanity to your living areas.

Step 1: Realize that you are collecting. A collection assembled unconsciously and without a plan is little more than clutter.

Step 2: Figure out why you are collecting. Make sure there's a rational connection between the reason you're collecting and the reality of the collection. Are you collecting out of sentimentality? (Your granny gave you a teapot decades ago, so now you buy teapots that are like it.) Your best or most interesting item, lovingly displayed, might provide all of the sentimentality you need. Get rid of the rest.

Is it aesthetics? (The stark beauty of black-and-white western landscape photography stirs your soul like nothing else.) Thoughtful display and preservation of your items will be crucial. Display some, clustered in the same place, and store some. Use a wall or shelving to create an organized, artistic display.

Or are you collecting for financial reasons? ("Hey, these G.I. Joe® dolls are gonna be worth a mint someday.") Hour for hour, a job flipping hamburgers would probably pay better. If you insist on collecting as a business, figure out how to inventory and store your items properly—and keep them out of your daily living space.

Step 3: Either become a purposeful collector or quit. Collecting is a commitment. Make a decision: Either you have the time and energy to display, care for, and learn about collecting your chosen items, or you are better off without these items in your life. Anything in between will generate frustration, guilt, and clutter.

Simple Steps to Health and Happiness

Y OU'RE GOING TO GET an odd feeling when you read this chapter. Many of us are concerned about health and fitness, so
there's a good chance that you're a veteran reader of articles or
books about weight loss, exercise, and wellness. As you read the
advice here, you'll say something like this to yourself: "Yes, this is
simple. Yes, I can do this. But where are the startling new scientific
discoveries? Where's the celebrity? Where's the exotic location?
Where's the miracle food of the month?"

Well, I have done a lot of work in the health publishing industry,
and here's a deep, dark secret: Health writers and health editors
are all bald. They've torn their hair out trying to dream up new
gimmicks, new sensational headlines, and new come-ons. The reason they're so frustrated is this: Year in and year out, there's very
little new in the science of weight loss, nutrition, and exercise. So

every day of their working lives, they have to spin the same old advice in new ways.

How to Cheat at Organizing is just the opposite. My goal is to save you enormous amounts of time and frustration by dispensing with the hype and the myths. We want to identify simple but highly effective steps that you can take to bring order to your life. In respect to your health, this means no-nonsense ways to supply your body with good nutrition, to lose weight, to exercise, to interact with doctors, and to bolster your emotional well-being. My hope is that you will use this chapter as a personal health checklist. Put these simple fundamentals into place, and you will be taking enormous strides toward longevity, feeling good, and happiness. You'll also be miles ahead of 95 percent of the population.

And by all means, talk to your doctor about the lifestyle changes you want to make and any medical issues you have. You will find no better ally in health matters than your own doc, and no book or magazine or web site can substitute.

The World's Simplest Weight-Loss Plan

Since you're reading one of my *How to Cheat* books, it's a given that you are no fan of complex systems and formulas for accomplishing what you want to do. Which is one major reason that the established, highly hyped diets fail you time and again. Once you get the slightest whiff of calorie counting, record keeping, club memberships, prepackaged foods to buy, public weigh-ins, and rigid recipes to follow, an internal alarm starts screaming, "Don't make me do that! Don't make me do that!" and you suddenly feel the urge to nosh.

Which is why I am going to introduce you to the world's easiest-to-follow diet, one that just about any doctor or nutritionist on the planet would approve of. It's easy because there's just one simple thing to do, yet it puts healthful food into your body, it keeps you from feeling deprived—and you lose weight.

But first, let's take a quick look at how weight loss works. Your body weight is a balancing act. You take calories into your body by

Weigh the Facts

A lot of myths swirl around the issue of weight loss. If you're trying to trim some pounds off your frame, here are some crucial facts that will help you focus your efforts intelligently, provided by fitness and nutrition experts:

- Trying to lose weight solely through exercise or solely through eating less is extremely difficult. You're much more likely to succeed through a combination of the two.

- You may drop pounds through a crash weight-loss program, but you're likely to put the weight back on again as you revert to your former habits. Instead, make more modest lifestyle changes that you can live with for the long haul. You will lose weight gradually, and you will have exercise and eating habits you can sustain.

- Every little bit helps. Look for small ways to burn energy and small ways to save calories. Diet and exercise are not an "all-or-nothing" concern.

eating food, and you get rid of calories by moving your body around, burning up the energy that comes from food. If you consume more calories than you burn, the excess calories are stored in your body as fat. If you consume fewer calories than you burn, your body uses stored fat to supply the energy for movement—meaning you lose weight. Now, don't panic here—I'm not going to make you count calories. But it helps to know that most weight-loss diets require women to consume 1,200 to 1,500 calories a day. For men, it's typically 1,500 to 1,800 calories a day.

By the way, there's an interesting thing about food and the human body: For just about any health concern—for instance, weight loss, blood pressure, preventing diabetes, or preventing heart disease—the nutrition-and-exercise prescription is the same. So if you're on a program for trimming inches off your waist while eating nutritious food, you're doing yourself a world of good in combating a broad range of serious diseases as well.

The SHOK Diet

Here's the simplest, anybody-can-do-it way to lose weight. First, as with any new diet or exercise regimen, talk to your doctor about your plans. Once you have his or her blessing, start every lunch and every dinner this way: Pile a dinner plate with a salad that is so large that people stare at you. Do not just spread a handful of spinach leaves about the plate. Mound up the salad fixings until the broccoli florets, cherry tomatoes, and bell pepper slices start rolling off the sides. Sprinkle some vinaigrette dressing over your salad, and eat it. Then proceed to whatever else you're going to have with the meal, but stop when you're not hungry anymore. That's it.

A few tricks will make this dieting approach go more smoothly:

- Buy your salad greens in those plastic bags available in your supermarket's produce section, prewashed and ready to eat. All you have to do is grab a handful out of the bag and drop it onto your plate.

- Chop up a week's worth of salad veggies on Sunday night and store them in plastic containers in the fridge. Just sprinkle them over your salad greens, add dressing, and you have instant salad.

- If you find that you can't leave Tin Roof Sundae ice cream alone, then quit torturing yourself by having it in the house. It's much easier to make this weight-loss decision in the supermarket aisle—by not buying tantalizing ice cream in the first place.

- Don't rush to the bathroom scale twice a day to see how your weight-loss program is coming along. This will just drive you nuts, because a body's weight naturally edges up and down during the course of a day. Check your progress with a once-a-week weigh-in, on the same day and at the same time every week.

I'm calling the world's simplest weight-loss program the SHOK Diet for a couple of reasons. First, I didn't think I could complete this chapter without an acronym, and this beauty stands for Salad Helping OverKill. More important, this eating approach was suggested to me by Jeff Novick, director of nutrition for the Pritikin Longevity Center^{SM} and Spa in Aventura, Florida. He calls megasalads the "shock and awe approach to weight loss" (parents are so stunned by the size of your salad that they grab their children and hurry out of the room). So SHOK is an acknowledgement of his input, too.

What makes this simple weight-loss plan work? With vegetables, it's almost impossible to overeat, Novick says. On average, veggies supply about 100 calories per pound, so you would have to eat 5 *pounds* of vegetables in a day just to get yourself up to 500 calories. Vegetables are bulky, too. With an enormo-salad in your belly, you're not going to see much need for a large cheese steak and an order of french fries. You'll happily settle for something smaller. The total volume of food you consume will go up, keeping you satisfied, while the calories you consume will go down.

Now, I promised you a simple diet, and the approach above will shrink your waistline if you stick to the plan over the weeks and months. But if you want to turbo-charge your weight loss, here are a couple of easy enhancements.

Soup up your meal. Follow your gigantic lunch or dinner salad with a large bowl of vegetable soup. That's even more nutritious, low-calorie food taking up real estate in your stomach. You might not even want anything else for lunch or dinner.

Be fruit-full, too. We don't usually think of salad as a breakfast food, but you can follow the same pattern with large servings of fruit, Novick says. Yes, fruit may be higher in calories because it naturally contains more sugar, but the calorie count is nothing compared to cheeseburgers, cookies, and ice cream. Fruit is chock-full of healthful nutrients, too. So feel free to pack in some fruit at your first meal of the day—or any other time, for that matter.

More Hassle-Free Nutrition

Okay, some of you are hankering for more. Not more food, but more weight-loss and healthy-eating advice. So if you're going for your master's degree in *How to Cheat at Organizing* nutrition logistics, here are some core strategies for buying, preparing, and eating food. If you have finicky eaters in your family, don't try to make all of these changes at once. Introduce one small change a week. Also, see Chapter 4 for many more shortcuts for buying and preparing food.

Buy powerful foods. Buy foods that give you the biggest health benefit for the least calories. This means buying foods made from whole grains, fresh fruits and vegetables, reduced-fat dairy products, and the leaner protein sources (fish, white poultry meat rather than dark, and red meat from the leg and loin).

Change with the seasons. Make seasonal produce a cornerstone of your menu. Not only will you be treating your family to fresh, unprocessed foods, but you also will keep your family entertained with an ever-changing lineup as the vegetables, fruits, and herbs go in and out of season.

Buy local. If produce had to be shipped thousands of miles to reach your supermarket, there's a good chance that the growers had

6-Point Test for Packaged Food

Many people mistakenly assume that big-time food companies care about your health. They don't—they care about selling, says Jeff Novick, director of nutrition for the Pritikin Longevity Center and Spa in Aventura, Florida. The large print that you find on food packaging—"Low in Carbohydrates!" or "Cholesterol Free!"—is so misleading that you might as well dismiss it out of hand. But there are two spots on packages where you can find good information that's useful for appraising any food—the Nutrition Facts box and the fine-print ingredients list, where the most plentiful ingredients are listed first. Here is Novick's six-point test for any packaged food. Not many foods pass muster on all accounts—but when you find one that does, "99 out of 100 times, that's a good product," he says.

On the Nutrition Facts box:

Calories from fat. If few of the food's calories come from fat, that's good.

Sodium. Also known as salt. You'll see a figure telling you what percentage of the Daily Value (government-recommended amount) of sodium this food provides. Most of us consume way too much sodium, so less is better.

Fiber. Look at the number of grams and the percentage of the Daily Value. Most of us get too little of this disease-fighting stuff, so more is better.

In the ingredients list:

Harmful fats. You want little in the way of saturated fats, hydrogenated fats, and tropical oils.

Added sugar. If sugar is high in the ingredients list, that means it's a significant component of this food—not good news.

Whole grains. A good sign, particularly if whole grains are high in the ingredients list.

to monkey around with it to help that food endure the long trek. Local produce is less likely to have been picked too early or treated for shipping.

Buy more plants. If your family eats in the old-time way—a huge slab of meat on the plate, surrounded by a few specks of vegetables—turn that pattern on its ear. Let fruits and vegetables dominate the plate, and demote meat to a secondary role. If this will throw meat-loving family members into shock, ease them into the new eating approach by scaling down the meat serving gradually over two months.

Choose leaner cooking methods. Heart-healthy cooking doesn't stop with picking low-fat ingredients. Use low-fat cooking techniques, too, such as roasting, broiling, grilling, and steaming. Use rubs and fat-free marinades instead of sauces. Grill with herbs instead of basting with butter. Cook your vegetables lightly, since overcooking destroys nutrients. Avoid frying altogether.

Moderate those yummy foods. If you have to totally eliminate your favorite high-calorie foods from the menu, you're going to get frustrated and feel deprived—which leads to giving up on nutritious eating. So entertain yourself with small touches of such foods rather than forgoing them altogether. Don't stir a lot of olive oil into your marinara sauce, just drizzle a little onto the sauce after cooking to give it that tantalizing aroma. Sprinkle slivered almonds onto your green beans rather than eating nuts by the handful.

Take it slow. Stop wolfing down your meals, rushing so you can get to the next urgent item on your daily to-do list. Take it easy, says Lisa Talamini, R.D., chief nutritionist and program director for Jenny Craig®, based in Carlsbad, California. When you're eating fast, it's easy to pack in too much food unintentionally. Spend 20 minutes to 30 minutes eating each meal, so your tummy's sensors have time to alert you that you've consumed enough. Remove distractions from the eating area so you can focus on the food and savor it, noticing the flavor and texture. After each bite, take a breath, sip some water, and ask yourself, "Am I satisfied—have I eaten enough?" Stop when you're no longer hungry.

Take out insurance. One aspect of a weight-loss program is that you're eliminating some amount of food consumption. Just to be sure you're not depriving your body of some of the essential stuff it needs, take a good multiple vitamin and mineral supplement, says Talamini. No mega-doses—simply follow the instructions on the bottle. Sure, the best source of nutrients is regular food. But think of your vitamin pill as insurance.

Exercise: Smart Moves

If you're not exercising these days, your reasons probably go something like this: First, you're way too busy earning a living and caring for your family. Second, all of that moving and sweating sounds so downright uncomfortable that it's hard to get enthusiastic about it. And third, it's all so complicated and expensive—club memberships, workout clothes, equipment, videos, and special drinks.

Now, bear with me for just a moment, because it's time to do a little *How to Cheat at Organizing* myth-busting. The truth is, the more fit you are, the more energy you have and the more effective

Fear No Fruit

It's funny how we can get our facts twisted and our priorities out of whack. Jeff Novick, a Pritikin nutrition guru, often hears his weight-loss clients fretting about fruit. It's true that fruits are generally sweeter than vegetables because they have higher sugar content. But it's almost impossible to make yourself fat by eating fruit. Their bulk will make you full before you can consume too many calories. Besides, they're also an awesome source of nutrients. If you're too wide, it's not because you've been eating apples, grapes, or watermelon.

you are at work and at home. So exercise is a crafty investment. I won't lie, though—exercise is work. But it should never be painful, and the people who do it regularly actually enjoy it. They like the act of working out, and they like how they look and feel afterward. So you have something to look forward to. As to the complexity and expense—that's a lot of hoo-ha. There's an enormous fitness-industry hype machine prodding you to spend money unnecessarily. But the truth is, you can get a full workout using nothing but your body and a pair of sneakers—although social conventions often encourage a shirt and pants, too. Wearing grubbies is fine, as long as they're loose and comfortable. And unless you're a professional athlete, tap water is the best fitness drink around.

Easing into Exercise

If you're a total novice at working out, here's a simple technique for moving you from the category of people who don't exercise into the category of people who do exercise. Once you get started, the idea is to gradually increase the duration and intensity of your exercise over the weeks and months. You're in charge—challenge yourself, but progress at your own pace. And don't forget to check in with your doctor to talk about what you have in mind.

Begin your exercise program "low and slow," says Ron Knaus, D.O., a sports medicine physician and productivity coach in Clearwater, Florida. That is, start with low goals and slow movements. For instance, on your first morning of exercise, put on some loose and comfortable walking clothes, walk half a block, and stop. Then return home and go to work. No kidding. The next day, walk for 3 to 5 minutes. On each subsequent day, add a couple of minutes.

If you already get some amount of exercise, your workouts probably lie somewhere between the simplest program just described and the ideal level of exercise recommended for good all-around fitness. As you add more activity to your workouts, what's your goal? Eventually, you want your exercise program to include a blend of

A Helpful Step: Buying a Pedometer

Taking the dog for a stroll, crisscrossing the office floor, and hoofing it between stores at the mall—the regular walking you do every day can make a big contribution to your fitness. But how do you know whether you're walking enough?

The recommended target is 10,000 to 12,000 steps a day, says Lisa Talamini, chief nutritionist and program director for Jenny Craig. However, if you work at a desk for a living, you probably don't reach that. So buy a pedometer, a simple device that clips to your waistband and counts each step you take. The device will inspire you to add extra steps to your routine life—parking your car at the far end of the lot, for instance, or taking the stairs instead of the elevator. You'll be able to check how many strides you have taken midday. If you're falling behind the target, you can look for ways to "step it up."

Pedometers are sold just about anywhere you can buy fitness products.

three kinds of activity, says Novick, the Pritikin nutritionist. Here's what a basic fitness regimen looks like:

AEROBIC EXERCISE: 30 minutes a day, 5 days per week. If you want an accelerated program to lose a serious amount of weight, exercise 60 to 90 minutes a day, 6 days a week. This kind of exercise includes walking, running, cycling, swimming, or rowing.

STRENGTH TRAINING: two or three times per week. This includes sit-ups, push-ups, squats, dumbbell exercises, other weight training, and stretch-band workouts.

FLEXIBILITY TRAINING: 10 to 15 minutes most days. Buy a video that takes you through stretching exercises. Or take up yoga. Stretching keeps you limber and maintains your range of motion—a particular asset as you age. Some people use stretching as a warm-up for other exercise.

Make a date for fitness. You loosely had it in mind that you would suit up for a 2-mile jog sometime during the day. But by the time you had waded through a hectic workday, fixed dinner, got little Lauren through a homework crisis, and then finished summarizing a report for your boss, the idea of exercise was nothing but a faint memory. Here's the simple way to make sure you get your regular exercise, says Dr. Knaus: Schedule it on your calendar, just like dental appointments and committee meetings. It will be hard for other matters to intrude on your workout time when you have committed to it on your desk calendar or in your scheduling software.

Watch your wallet. The moment you show an interest in fitness, Madison Avenue types will start lining up to sell you stuff—$150 pairs of sneakers, pricey gym memberships, heart-rate monitors, high-tech clothing, "sport" drinks, and enormous exercise machines reminiscent of medieval torture devices. Ignore these expensive distractions. If you're hankering to spend money, invest in a small set of dumbbells and an exercise stretch band.

If you're determined to buy bulky fitness equipment for your home, says Dr. Knaus, make sure it has plenty of places to hang clothes on it—because that's how most people end up using it. Only 5 percent of the people who buy such equipment exercise on it for more than 2 months. Here are Dr. Knaus's rules for purchasing workout gear:

- Never buy on impulse. As you develop your workout routine, carefully identify items you really need and will use, then research your options.

- Write down your commitment—how often you intend to use any new piece of gear.

- Never buy an enormous unit. Exercise gear that's an uncomfortable fit for your home will create more stress than wellness.

- Ignore that salesperson's offer of a "limited-time discount" or other come-ons.

- Only buy exercise equipment if you know an organization you can donate it to. You'll feel too guilty to throw it out.

Sneaking Exercise into Everyday Life

Think about it: Whether you're wearing workout sweats or a business suit, your body still benefits when you move it around. So a great way to meet the requirements of a fitness program is to sneak your exercise into your daily routine. Here are the official *How to Cheat at Organizing* ways to do that.

Build muscle at your desk. You can tone up your arm muscles while you're just sitting in your office chair, says Dr. Knaus. Here's an exercise that simulates a weight lifter's arm curl—except that you need no equipment. Sitting in your chair, place your left arm on top of your left leg and turn your palm up. Place your right hand over your left, pull your left hand up to your left shoulder, and then return it to the starting position. During this movement, provide resistance by pushing down with your right hand. Repeat six to 12 times, and then do the same exercise with your right arm. You can probably do this exercise and read a boring report at the same time.

Work out in your car. Here are exercises that Dr. Knaus uses when he gets stuck in a traffic jam. Give safety the top priority, however. For instance, put the car in park before you exercise. (The people in the surrounding cars will think you're nuts, but that's okay. When traffic starts moving again, they'll give you wide berth.)

- Practice deep breathing, inflating your lungs by pushing out and in again with your abdominal muscles.

- Store a rubber squeeze ball or hand grips in the glove compartment to strengthen your hands.

- To exercise your arms, position your hands on oppose sides of the steering wheel and press toward the center. ("Do not tear off the steering wheel," Dr. Knaus warns. "It becomes difficult to drive your car.")

- Do abbreviated sit-ups. Tighten your abdominal muscles and lean toward the steering wheel in a "mini-crunch."

- Strengthen your back and abdominal muscles by rotating your trunk. Tighten your abs, twist to the right, and then to the left.

Line up for exercise. If you want to exercise while you're standing in line at the supermarket or at a ticket window, first ask yourself how much attention you're willing to attract to yourself. (Some folks will assume you're "off your meds.") A fine person such as you, with plenty of self-esteem, should be able to get away with these little workouts:

- Adapt the arm exercise above (in "Build muscle at your desk") to the standing position.

- "Row" your way through the line. With your arms by your sides, tighten your abdominal muscles. Put your fists just above your belly button and slowly pull your arms back, as if you're trying to pull your shoulder blades together. Variation: Raise your elbows even with your shoulders and draw them back.

- Practice deep breathing while holding your chest, arm, and abdominal muscles tight. When you inhale, keep those muscles tight. When you exhale, relax your muscles and drop your shoulders.

- Stand on one leg. This builds leg and abdominal strength. You may need to start out by holding on to the checkout counter, a magazine rack, or the stranger in front of you. Each time you stand on one leg, try to extend the time that you can hold your balance. Give each leg equal time.

Make the extra effort. Talamini, the Jenny Craig nutritionist and program director, has further ways you can sneak some exercise into your daily life:

- When you need a break from your desk, instead of wandering over to the vending machines, go for a short walk.
- Rather than e-mailing a note to a coworker, walk across the building to convey your ideas in person.
- Instead of asking the kids to walk the dog, do it yourself.
- Instead of hiring a lawn service, mow your own grass and rake your own leaves.
- Become a kid again, and play tag with your children and join them on the playground equipment. In the winter, build snowmen and have snowball fights.

Dealing with Docs

One of the basics of managing your health is having a team of professionals backing you up. This typically means, at a minimum, visiting your doctor for a checkup once a year and your dentist twice a year. Having health experts give you a once-over periodically can help you catch and treat problems before they do serious damage to your body. That's how you cheat the reaper, as they say. Also, if you come down with a serious medical problem, it helps to have an established relationship with a pro who will jump on the case right away.

Keep in mind that the typical doctor-patient relationship has changed significantly in recent decades. Much of the responsibility for managing health has shifted to the patient. You can no longer be submissive. No one knows your body better than you—how you feel and what causes you discomfort or pain. Educate yourself about the health matters that pertain to you, ask your doctor questions about what's going on with your body—and ask again until the doc explains it in a way you can understand.

Here's a look at specific ways that you can take control of the management of your health.

Keep Your Own Records

Don't count on any medical professional to be your record keeper, says L. Jo Parrish, vice president of institutional advancement for the Society for Women's Health Research in Washington, D.C. There's a lot of potential for your records to fall through the cracks if you switch doctors or if your health insurance changes and you end up working within a new system. Label a file folder "Medical Records," park it in your filing cabinet, and drop into it the paperwork from your latest examination and any test results. Make sure the date is clearly marked on every record. Anytime you visit the doctor, take the folder with you.

Track your tests. Don't leave the monitoring of tests to your doctor alone, either. The tests that are appropriate for you will vary according to such factors as your age, your gender, and your risk factors for certain diseases. They may include screenings for cholesterol, blood pressure, weight, diabetes, colon and rectal cancer, prostate cancer, breast cancer, cervical cancer, osteoporosis, abdominal aortic aneurysm, eye health, and dental health. When you receive results of a test, pull the previous results out of your medical records folder and compare the scores. Ask your doctor whether the scores indicate any improvement or any cause for concern.

Explore your risks. During your medical checkups, ask questions related to your age, race, and gender. At this point in your life, what are your risks and what should you be doing to prevent problems? Are there any other medical tests you should have? Remember, preventing medical problems or catching them early is a thousand times easier than treating them at an advanced stage.

In case of emergency, take folder. Make sure your family knows where your medical records are kept. If you aren't in any shape to retrieve them—say, you're being rushed to the emergency room—they can do it for you. Having these records with you when you enter the emergency room is an enormous advantage. With reports on your last exam and the medications you are taking, the ER staff will have a big head start on caring for you.

Talking with Your Doctor

Before doctors can graduate from medical school, they're given a special operation that removes their ability to talk like normal folks. Poor dears, their $10 words stack up higher than their student loans. So you have to be assertive about improving communication between you and your doc. Here's how to go about it.

State your purpose. When you make an appointment with your doctor, be sure to tell the office staff why you are making the appointment, says Parrish. Just a routine exam? Do you want to discuss symptoms, too—headaches or other pain, for instance? Are you interested in taking a test? If you haven't alerted the doctor that she needs to reserve time for such considerations, she might end up telling you, "We don't do that kind of testing here" or "We didn't set aside time for that."

Take your doc a list. As questions occur to you between doctor appointments, write them down and slip them into your medical records folder. Then, as soon as the doctor comes into the examination room, tell her that you have some questions. This way, the doctor can pace himself and reserve time for the issues you want to raise.

Ask about alternatives. Whenever a medical issue comes up, explore all of the potential solutions before you make a decision about how to treat your problem. Keep in mind the point of view of the medical professional that you are consulting with. A surgeon, for instance, will often lean toward surgical solutions. So get a variety of opinions about significant decisions.

Press for clear answers. As smart as they are, doctors often have trouble translating their med-speak into common terms. Ask questions during your medical appointments—and keep asking until you get answers you can understand in clear, direct language.

Tell your doc what's up. You might fib to your friends and family about how many cigarettes you smoke a day or how many chocolate bars you eat, but one person you don't want to tell little white lies to is your doctor, says Parrish at the Society for Women's Health Research. What you tell your doctor is totally confidential. Your doctor has seen hundreds of examples of bodily abuse worse than yours, so she's not likely to be judgmental. And besides, your doctor is there to help—she can't do that if she doesn't have the right information. So be truthful about any tobacco, alcohol, or other drugs you use, plus any other risky behavior. Be up front about your eating habits and whether you're using herbs or other supplements, too. All of these factors can affect your health, and all of these factors can affect medications you take.

Ask the gender question. Many people don't realize this, but much of the information we have about the effectiveness of medications is based on research done solely on men. Many drugs affect women

differently because of hormones and other physical differences. So if your doctor is proposing a new treatment, ask the big question: "Has this drug been tested on women?"

Confronting Serious Health Problems

Most of us have little practice at dealing with serious health problems. When they do emerge, we're overwhelmed. That's why it helps to get others involved—to make sure we're thinking straight at such critical times.

Double-check a serious diagnosis. Any time you have a serious diagnosis or are facing major surgery, get a second opinion from another doctor, says Parrish. Don't be afraid of offending your original doctor—he knows that getting a second opinion is wise and done routinely. If your doctor does get huffy, then it's time to find a new doctor.

Take an advocate. If you are confronting a serious health issue, take a friend, your spouse, or another family member with you to the doctor's office. If you're getting or discussing bad news with the doctor, you will often be wrapped up in your emotions—which is understandable. But your sidekick will be more levelheaded, will be able to capture all of the information being conveyed, and can ask questions about the next steps.

Take an assistant. Studies show that you will get better care in a hospital if you have a companion with you. Such a helper can provide small comforts that an overburdened medical staff might not have time for, such as fetching ice chips or drinks and helping you to the bathroom. But this sidekick can also serve as an intelligent observer for you, making sure your medications are given on schedule, that your allergies are being considered, and that nurses know of new symptoms immediately. So when you schedule a hospital stay, ask in advance whether taking a friend along is allowed.

If you have a choice of which hospital you go to, this could be the decision maker.

Plan for a short stay. When you have to go into a hospital for treatment, make arrangements for the shortest stay possible. Research shows that hospitals are great places to pick up an infection, so a shorter stay means less exposure to that risk. A lot of recuperation after a medical procedure can easily be done at home.

Nurturing Your Emotional Health

At first blush, it might seem odd to treat your happiness and emotional health as an organizing issue. But your organizing skills can have a big impact on your mental state, particularly if you never pencil in some "me time" on your personal schedule.

For example, psychologist Raymond Crowel, Ph.D., vice president of mental health and substance abuse services at the National Mental Health Association, tells the story of one of his relatives. She had a suspected heart attack in early middle age. When Crowel went to visit her in the cardiac care unit of the hospital, he found her on the phone canceling a job interview for her teenage daughter. Crowel asked her why she was doing routine tasks like that from her hospital bed, for goodness sake. She replied that her daughter didn't know how. This was how Crowel's relative had been spending her life, constantly doing for others and not having time for herself. Wouldn't you know, it wasn't a heart attack that landed her in the hospital after all, but an extreme reaction to stress.

Now, untangling a lifelong habit like this is no easy task. But Crowel set her on the right path with the following exercise, and it could do wonders for you as well if you have trouble devoting time to yourself: Take a pad and pencil. Write a list of the things that you most want to accomplish *for yourself* in the coming year. Whenever you start writing about someone else, you have to scratch it out and start over. This list becomes a road map for your personal

News Flash: "Me" Time Works

When psychologist Raymond Crowel was in the throes of graduate school, he gave himself a little gift. As busy as his life was, he decided to carve out some inviolate personal time. For his own edification, he was going to watch the evening news on television for an hour and a half every night—no matter what. It was tough at first, fending off all of those interruptions and phone calls. But eventually, everyone around him learned of this habit and began to respect it. The intrusions evaporated.

"People learn what your boundaries are in time—but you have to retrain them a little bit," Crowel says.

happiness—maybe you want to start a flower garden, get an article published, or get specialized professional training. Break these accomplishments down into steps and enter those steps onto your calendar.

Many people have major-league guilt over doing things for themselves, but the truth is that when you take care of yourself, you're in a better position to take care of others, too.

7 Simple Steps to Happiness

Wow. So the way we organize our lives really does directly affect our happiness. In that light, I put the question to Crowel: If you could persuade all people to make a handful of basic changes in their lifestyles to ensure better emotional health, what would those changes be? Thus we have the *How to Cheat at Organizing* 7 Simple Steps to Happiness. (And you thought all you'd get out of this book was an orderly cupboard.)

1. **Make more time to play.** Cell phones, laptops, and Black-Berry® smartphones make it all too easy to pack every spare moment with work. Even if you enjoy the heck out of your work, you need regular breaks—joyful and fun activities that have nothing to do with your job.

2. **Find something to laugh at every day.** Crowel keeps a collection of Gary Larson's "The Far Side" comic strips at his desk and starts every day by reading a page. So read the comics, listen to your favorite humorous radio host, flip on the comedy channel, or sit down with a friend who likes to tell jokes. The earlier you do this in the day the better, especially if you have a tough day ahead.

3. **Get plenty of rest and exercise.** Way too many people short-change their bodies by not sleeping enough and not moving around enough. Rein in that nightlife, stick with an exercise program, and get up from your desk a few times a day for 10-minute walks. Here are ways to ensure you're getting high-quality sleep:

- Eat early enough in the evening that your system has a chance to digest dinner before you go to bed.

- Sleep in a quiet, darkened space. Eliminate distracting

SLEIGHT OF HAND

Shrug Off Stress

Feeling stressed out? Muscles tensed up like one of those old wind-up alarm clocks? Here's an old tai chi trick for letting the stress flow out of your body instantaneously, says Ron Knaus, D.O., a sports medicine physician and productivity coach: Just drop your shoulders. The tension will evaporate.

light. If you must watch TV in your bedroom, put it on a timer so it will turn off automatically. Then you don't get awakened by the tube in the middle of the night.

- Make sure the temperature in your bedroom is not too hot and not too cold, Goldilocks. An uncomfortable temperature could wake you repeatedly during the night.
- Don't exercise just before bed.

Blues Got You Down? Play a New Tune

We all slide into a funk now and then. But you needn't wallow there, says psychologist Raymond Crowel, Ph.D., of the National Mental Health Association. When you have a bout of sadness, here are some good ways to shrug off the blues.

Shake things up. Do something to change your immediate circumstances. Break your routine. If you haven't been to a movie in a while, go to one. If you've been listening to jazz lately, switch to R&B. Take a walk, spend time with a friend, or start up an impromptu poker or bridge game.

Understand the cause. Identify the thing that's making you sad. Keeping the issue in perspective puts you one step closer to getting past it.

Reconnect. If you're upset because of a conflict you have with a loved one—say, you've had a fight with your boyfriend—get back in touch and talk. You don't have to apologize, and you don't have to resolve the conflict. But resuming the connection will make you feel better.

Some common responses to sadness are counterproductive, Crowel says, including these:

- **Drinking or doing drugs.** Self-destructive behavior will only multiply your woes.
- **Shopping.** You'll get the blues all over again when your bills arrive.
- **Overeating.** You'll be even less happy with yourself when your waistline expands.

If your sadness is persistent, find someone you can talk to about it.

4. **Take up a sport you don't have to feel competitive in.** Find an activity you enjoy just for the beauty of doing it—where you don't feel the added stress of having to vanquish the other player. For you, this may mean hiking, golf, chess, or kite flying.

5. **Help somebody every day.** We're not talking about being helpful in your job—that's expected. And this doesn't have to be heavy-duty volunteer work, such as feeding the homeless. Just compliment someone's tie or earrings, buy someone coffee, or give a befuddled tourist good directions. You will feel good, and the other person will feel good.

6. **Spend more time with people you care about.** When you telephone, write to, or have lunch with family, friends, and loved ones, you come away feeling good.

7. **Spend some time in reflection.** Give yourself some quiet time every day in which you can block out immediate distractions ("I have to pay the electric bill") and think larger thoughts: "How's my life going?" "Am I happy?" "Are things going in the direction I want?" Quiet time can come in many forms, including meditation, a pleasant walk, reading, prayer, and listening to peaceful music.

Pull the Plug on Stress

There are more definitions of stress than there are varieties of coffee, but you know it when you see it. Unhealthy stress can grow out of overscheduling, pressure to perform, unresolved conflicts, disappointment, and bodily abuse. It leaves you feeling wound up, anxious, irritable, angry, overwhelmed, and helpless. You snap at the kids, you slam pots and pans around, you honk the car horn way too much, and you wonder why.

Stress will wreck your physical health, too. Here's an interesting tidbit from the National Mental Health Association: Between 75 percent and 90 percent of all visits to a doctor are stress related.

(Whoa, I'm gonna find my hammock and do my part to relieve the medical system!) The 7 Simple Steps to Happiness listed on pp. 241–243 are all stress-relieving measures. Here are more anti-stress tactics recommended by Crowel, the psychologist and VP at the National Mental Health Association.

Know what ails you. If you can identify the factors that are causing your stress, you're on the path toward fixing the problem. Tell yourself, "I'm stressed out right now because my project deadline is an hour away, and the coworker in the next cubicle has been humming the same song all morning."

Take a break. Temporarily get away from the thing that's causing your stress. Pause and regroup. If the kids are driving you crazy, ask the neighbor to watch them for half an hour while you take a walk.

Simplify. We are constantly barraged with too many choices, so when the variety of options is distressing, go the simplest route. If you're baffled by the 20 models of cell phones available, start with a simple one with the fewest features. You can always upgrade later if you want to.

Learn to meditate. Take a class in yoga or meditation. Learn to relieve stress with proper breathing. Breathing techniques vary, but meditation instructors typically say to breathe by expanding the abdomen, rather than doing shallower breathing from the chest.

5 Helpful Facts about Addiction

If you have an addiction–to smoking, to alcohol, to painkillers, or to cheese-cake–you probably already know it. I'm not going to get judgmental with you. But I have a handful of statements of fact that will help you–take 'em or leave 'em. I asked psychologist Raymond Crowel, Ph.D., vice president of mental health and substance abuse services at the National Mental Health Association, what thoughts he would like to instill in anyone who was struggling with an addiction. Here's what he said:

1. Physical, biological mechanisms are causing your addiction.
2. Your addiction may be tenacious, but you have the ability to pause and recognize the triggers for your addictive behavior.
3. You have alternatives to indulging in your addiction.
4. If you have other mental health issues–perhaps depression or an anxiety disorder–you can tackle these without substance abuse.
5. Addiction is nothing to be ashamed of. It's not a matter of weakness of character.

Eat right. Sometimes it's hard to tell the difference between hunger and stress. Your "stress" problem could be just a case of low blood sugar. Eat nutritious foods to keep your energy level up and drink plenty of water.

Exercise. Crowel's favorite stress-relieving exercise is going to the golf course and hitting balls on the driving range. "By the 10th ball, I tend to forget about what was stressing me out," he says. If not, he puts names and faces on the golf balls before he whacks them.

Read poetry. Crowel's favorite: *The Rubaiyat of Omar Kayyam,* edited by Edward Fitzgerald. You may prefer Frost or Dickinson.

Keep a reasonable to-do list. We stack ourselves up with too many tasks—long hours at work, soccer games to attend, a garden to weed, and a dinner party to plan. Here's how to free yourself of guilt and lower those unreasonable expectations, says Crowel: At the start of every day and every weekend, list five things you hope to accomplish, in order of priority. But draw a line under the third item. If you accomplish the top three, "that's 100 percent," he says. Anything else you accomplish is pure bonus.

Give Your Medicine Cabinet a Checkup

That mirrored door in your bathroom, the one above the sink—is that a medicine chest, or a time capsule? If it's a medicine chest, you want to be sure that all of your pills, ointments, sprays, and such are fresh and current. If they aren't, they're probably weak or totally ineffective by now—and that's the best-case scenario. Some medications are actually harmful in their old age.

So we're going to conduct a quick-and-easy audit of your medicine chest (and you should include any "honorary" medicine cabinets as well—such as that bathroom drawer or the shoebox you parked in the linen closet). To get started, follow the good ol' S4 technique to sift through every item in the chest. (By now, the terms *Strip, Scrap, Sort,* and *Store* come to you in your dreams. If they don't, take a quick peek back at Chapter 1.) The discarded packaging goes into the trash. Rather than putting your old medicines directly in the trash, where small children could find them, or flushing them down the toilet—an environmental hazard—ask your pharmacy if they will take them back for disposal (that's common practice in some communities). If they won't, pour some kitty litter into a plastic bag and pour any old liquids over the litter. Crush your old pills and pour the remains into the plastic bag, too. Seal all of that in a second plastic bag, and drop it into the trash.

One factor that makes this audit easy is the small size—a medicine chest is teensy compared to a closet or pantry shelf. One factor that makes this audit tricky is knowing whether to toss out an old bottle of pills or a tube of ointment. So here are guidelines from Lisa Chavis and Paul Reyes, pharmacists for Medco Health

Solutions, which processes more than half a billion prescriptions a year. Throw away:

- nearly empty bottles of medicine (they're just taking up space, and you probably don't have a complete dose in there anyway)
- medicines that are past their expiration dates
- medicines that were improperly stored—in open containers that allowed evaporation, for instance, in a spot with extreme heat, or in a spot with temperature fluctuations
- old or partially used prescriptions (call your doctor's office if you're not sure)

HELP!

The Best Health Reference Info

Want to know how to treat a twisted ankle? Wondering whether you have the flu or just a cold? Savvy consumers want basic, reliable health information at their fingertips any time of day or night. In many cases, calling the doctor seems like overkill. Nevertheless, you want authoritative advice even when you're treating little bumps and scrapes. So where are you going to turn?

Start by buying a big, fat family health encyclopedia—one published by an authoritative institution, says L. Jo Parrish, a vice president at the Society for Women's Health Research. Her own organization publishes *The Savvy Female Patient*. You also will find health encyclopedias published by such groups as the Mayo Clinic, Harvard Medical School, Johns Hopkins, the American Medical Association, and Merck. These books need updating as medical knowledge advances, so count on replacing your health reference every 4 to 5 years.

The Internet also is a ready source of health information. However, it's often hard for consumers to distinguish the sound health advice from the scams and quackery. Parrish recommends starting with the U.S. government's health web sites. Go to the National Institutes of Health site—www.nih.gov—click on "Health Information," and you will find a vast array of helpful health text broken down by specialty. This stuff is as authoritative as you can get.

Aside from packaging expiration dates, what are other signs that a medication is past its prime?

- Any antibiotic pills or over-the-counter pain relievers that have been exposed to heat are suspect, because they deteriorate easily. Besides, antibiotics aren't a medicine you hang on to long term anyway. You take the amount your doctor tells you to, and if there are leftovers for some reason, throw them away.

- Flush any tablets that have changed in size, shape, or color.

- Lots of powder or particles in the bottom of a container are a sign that pills are deteriorating.

CHECK THIS OUT

Medicine Cabinet Must-Haves

Here's a checklist of items always to have on hand in your medicine cabinet.

- aspirin and any other pain relievers you use
- antibiotic cream, to prevent infection of small cuts and scrapes
- antacid, to relieve indigestion
- bandages, gauze, and first-aid tape
- calamine lotion, to relieve sunburn, rashes, and insect stings
- other insect-bite relief and insect repellant
- cough and cold medicine
- eyewash, to clear specks or chemicals out of the eyes
- sunscreen, to prevent sunburn
- aloe vera, to treat burns
- ipecac syrup, to induce vomiting for some poisonings
- thermometer, for detecting fevers
- heating and cooling packs, to treat sprains

How to Cheat at Organizing

- Inspect pills for cracks, chips, or the development of crystals on the surface—all signs of spoilage.

- Inspect ointments for a change in consistency or the separation of active ingredients.

- Make sure clear liquids *remain* clear—contact lens solutions, eye drops, and ear drops, for instance. If they're discolored, they've gone bad.

Store your meds in their original packaging, so you don't lose track of what they are and you always have the directions for their use at your fingertips. Check the package for any special storage instructions—some meds require refrigeration, for instance. If your bathroom isn't ventilated, find another spot to store your medications, because the humidity could harm them. Also, don't store more than one kind of pill in the same container—they could chemically react with one another, and you also could get confused and take the wrong pill.

So we have taken your cheat-at-organizing skills into places where you never thought possible—your fitness, your doctor's office, and your mental well-being. Don't underestimate the gift you've been handed here: Instructions to read the comics and play golf often. Who are you to ignore doctor's orders?

Put Your Car on Easy Street

ONSIDERING HOW MUCH money cars cost, how many choices there are to make, and how many times a day we're all assaulted with obnoxious car ads, buying a car can be one of the scariest moments of your life. We'll simplify your decision making drastically, and then give you a pared-down step-by-step process for getting the right car at the best possible price.

And then, let's talk about how to cheat at the day-in, day-out use of your car. How to control that tide of possessions rolling around on the floor and in your trunk. How to use cutting-edge technology to get you where you want to go without getting lost. And how to stock your car with the little accoutrements that will make your driving life easy and comfortable.

Buying and Maintaining Your Wheels

By now, you expect me to make a really crazy recommendation once in a while. And upon further reading, I hope, you discover that the "crazy" idea actually makes a lot of sense once you set aside some myths and preconceptions. So here's the simple, stripped-down-to-the-essence, *How to Cheat at Organizing* way to choose your next $15,000 or $25,000 automobile: Find one that has a cup holder that you really, really like.

Once you have picked yourself up off the floor and stopped laughing, let me explain. You're probably thinking, *Surely mechanical reliability of the car is more important than whether I like the cup holder.* In a way, you're right. However, here's an interesting observation from Philip Reed, senior consumer advice editor for the car information company Edmunds.com[SM]: Modern carmakers have gotten so good at what they do that almost every model is considered reliable—any edge that one has over the other is just splitting hairs. So that means that issues like convenience and personal comfort leap to the forefront. And cup holders are king among these considerations. Even journalists give cup holders so much attention that "some say auto journalists are just cup holder reviewers," says Reed.

So finding a cup holder that's convenient, deep, sturdy, and secure could well be your deciding factor between one car model and another. In that light, you'll want to know that auto writers

DVD Player? Press "Skip"

Any parent who has driven more than half an hour with toddlers in the backseat understands the allure of a built-in DVD player in the car. It's awfully tempting to mesmerize the little pumpkin-heads with a Disney flick. But resist the temptation, says Philip Reed, senior consumer advice editor at Edmunds.com. A built-in DVD player adds an outrageous $1,000 to the price of your car. Nice home DVD players—and even portable players, which you could use in the car if you really needed to—cost a fraction of that. Besides, driving is a good time to focus on family togetherness. Car games or singing will still get you from point A to point Z with your nerves intact.

tend to test out a cup holder by placing a 1-liter bottle of water in it to check its convenience and stability—so you might as well do the same. Another handy feature: Some cup holders have a little rubber mat in the bottom that you can remove for easy cleaning.

Finding a Fabulous Fit

Now, it must be said that not every driver is crazy for cup holders. For instance, Europeans—and Germans in particular—take driving very seriously and tend to frown on cup holders as a frivolous distraction. What if you don't care about cup holders? There are other comfort and convenience items to weigh: Is there a handy spot to stash your sunglasses? (Reed is a big fan of Honda's® solution, a compartment right above the rearview mirror.) Is there a spot to store coins for tolls, parking meters, and roadside lemonade stands? How about a pocket on the front of the driver's seat where you can stash your wallet—handy, yet out of sight? Or a clip

SLEIGHT OF HAND

Catch Those Ideas Before They Evaporate

You never know when a brilliant idea might dawn on you—an astounding product innovation, a gift idea for your aunt, or a clever phrase for that letter you want to write. If you have this revelation while you're running errands in the car, it will be wiped clean from your memory by the time you get back home. So everyone needs a system for recording ideas in the car, says professional organizer Ali Kaufman. She always drives with a notepad open on the seat beside her. She also likes to use a tiny digital recorder. When she gets home, she just hooks her recorder up to the PC, and her Dragon NaturallySpeaking software converts all of the audio into a text file. No more misplaced million-dollar ideas!

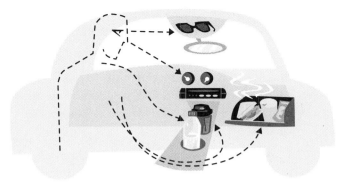

built into the top of the dashboard that will grasp parking receipts or park admission slips so they don't blow around? Plenty of bins and cubbies to hold the miscellaneous gear you like to have within arm's reach? Any spot to stick CDs you're not listening to at the moment? (Beware the CD holders sold in stores that affix to the visor—sun exposure could damage your disks.)

Just to be sure you're happy with the design of the cockpit of any car you're thinking of buying, run this little test: Toss your sunglasses, note pad, water bottle, maps, cell phone, and any other car paraphernalia into a gym bag and go to the dealership. Sit in the driver's seat of "your" car, and slide all of your stuff into place. Practice retrieving it from the driver's seat—how's it feel? Some designs will feel good to you and some will feel awkward, so make sure that this new car you're going to own for several years is a good "fit."

"I often say that choosing your car is a lot like trying on clothes," Reed says.

Cup holders and cubbies aside, here are a few more very helpful gadgets you might want inside your new car:

- A compass. When you're driving in unfamiliar territory, just knowing east from west can be a big help.

- A "distance to empty" fuel indicator. This tells you how far you can drive before refilling the tank—particularly good to know if you're uneasy about the neighborhood you're driving through.

- A refrigerated glove box, for stashing that sandwich and yogurt you want to eat later.

- A thermometer showing outside temperature. This is handy, for instance, if you're driving up mountain roads in the summer. If you see it's hot outside, you'll know to turn down the air conditioner to put less strain on the engine so it won't overheat.

10 Easy Steps to a New Car

Everybody knows that buying a new car is a mind-boggling process. Dealers are actually happy about that, since it means that you'll be off balance and less able to work the system for a good deal. Auto advice editor Philip Reed has whittled car buying down to 10 simple steps that will help you keep your focus, however. This process becomes an absolute breeze when you incorporate some valuable tools that are available on his company's web site, www.edmunds.com. Print out all research and keep it in a folder as you work through the steps.

1. Make sure you have thoroughly researched the car market. Identify the kind of car that best fits your needs and also the options that you want on that car.

2. Research all of the incentives offered on the car that you want to buy. These may be in the form of low-interest loans or "cash back." Advertisements are a good place to start. Edmunds.com tracks all such deals, including hidden cash that carmakers slip to the dealer—which you'll want to know about when you negotiate.

3. Most cars actually sell well below the sticker price you'll see on the showroom floor. On Edmunds.com, you'll find the average price that people in your area are *actually paying* for the car you want. Take this price and deduct any rebates to arrive at a reasonable target price.

4. Call or e-mail the dealers in your area to get price quotes for the specific car that you want. If you're flexible about some of the fine points—say, the car's color—then you will find more cars, and you will be in a better position to negotiate. Wouldn't you know, Edmunds.com has an easy

Trunk Essentials

If automobile emergencies only happened in the driveway, there would be no problem—you'd just saunter over to the tool shed and grab the implement that would remedy the situation. But life doesn't happen like that. In road emergencies, you're dependent on the stuff you brought along. What's the ideal just-in-case gear for your trunk? Here's a checklist from auto and organizational experts:

- spare tire *that works*
- lug wrench
- first-aid kit
- quart of oil
- blanket
- reflectors or flares
- jumper cables
- salt (if your region gets ice and snow)
- tire pressure gauge
- simple tool set
- flashlight
- water

It's also nice to have

- glass cleaner
- paper towels
- squeegee
- reusable cloth shopping bags

tool that will allow you to request e-mail quotes from multiple dealers near you, and other Internet services will provide similar help. Keep specific notes about what cars are available at which dealerships.

5. While you're collecting quotes from dealers, also be on the lookout for a salesperson you are comfortable with. Are you getting straight answers to your questions, or sneaky and evasive ones? Is the salesperson pushy or easygoing? Does the salesperson focus on your needs—or on the dealership's need to sell certain cars? When you find a salesperson you're comfortable with, set up a time for a test drive (avoid busy times, such as weekends, if possible). Take your car-buying file folder with you.

6. If you're reading a book called *How to Cheat at Organizing*, it's assumed that you would rather trade in your car to the dealer when you buy a new one than tear your hair out as you deal with classified ads and potential buyers. There's a trick to getting a dealer to give you the top price for your old wheels. Tell the salesperson that closing the deal hinges

Repair or Replace?

When's the right time to buy a new car? Well, driving your car for years and years is one of the best ways to save money. On the other hand, nobody wants a car that breaks down every other week. So here's a good rule of thumb: When the monthly repair bill for your old car is more than the monthly payment you would have to make on a *new* car, get the new car, says Philip Reed, senior consumer advice editor at Edmunds.com. There are other considerations, though. Convenience and safety may be a stronger motivation to buy a new car—if, for instance, one of your kids has to drive through a bad part of town regularly and you don't want to risk having the car break down.

not only on the price of the new car but also on the trade-in allowance. Make it clear that you're visiting several dealers—and do so, because you could save hundreds of dollars this way.

7. If your research and negotiating instincts indicate you can work the new car's price down somewhat, get three quotes from local dealers. Take the lowest price to the other two dealers and ask them to do better. You can't play this game forever, but a few rounds of price shaving won't hurt. Just keep your eyes on the entire deal—some car dealers will juggle their numbers and make up for a lowered base price elsewhere in the paperwork.

8. When you're happy with your buying price, review all of the fees of the deal. Taxes and other expenses will vary depending upon where you live, but Edmonds.com offers a calculator that will get you a figure that should match pretty closely with the dealer's paperwork. A lot of these fees will be nonnegotiable, but do watch out for bogus add-ons.

9. At actual purchase time, the dealer will have you sign a truckload of paperwork. Take your time with this. Make sure you read and understand every document, and ask all questions that occur to you. Make sure no one has slipped extra fees into the deal. Just say "no" to any last-minute pitches for further spending (fabric protection, for instance). The possible exception: For some, an extended warranty is worth the peace of mind.

10. Inspect your new car before final acceptance. Look closely for scratches or dents, and make sure all equipment and accessories you're paying for are there. If you have to bring the car back later for any fix-ups, get the work specified in a "due bill."

A Little Paperwork, Lots of Mileage

Whenever you visit the dentist, the receptionist will inevitably invite you to schedule your next appointment then and there at the counter. When you get your next date and time for dental work, you obediently enter that into your main planning calendar, be it electronic or hard copy. Well, to keep on schedule with maintaining your car, all you have to do is follow that same practice. When you have your car serviced, look in the owner's manual to figure out when the *next* scheduled maintenance should be. Do some simple math to estimate the next date for service. For instance, if your car needs service after you drive 6,000 more miles, and you drive roughly 1,000 miles a month, then write "service car" on your calendar for 6 months from now. If you follow this procedure, you'll never forget to change the oil or swap out the timing belt.

Copy the maintenance schedule. You want to keep your owner's manual in your car, so when you're trying to figure out how to operate the trip meter, the information is at your fingertips. However, there's a crucial page in that manual that you often need elsewhere—the maintenance schedule. Photocopy this page, says automobile editor Reed, and put it in a file folder along with your maintenance records. "This is your bible," he says. You'll be able to schedule a service appointment from your home office without having to trudge outside and paw through the glove box.

Go by the book. In the world of car maintenance, Reed says garages and dealers will often recommend maintenance on your car well before the manufacturer recommends it. Oh, it's probably pure coincidence, but if you follow the garage's recommendations, you end up paying them more money. For instance, many garages will tell you to change your oil every 3,000 miles. Check your owner's manual: For many cars, the manufacturer recommends an oil change every 5,000 to 7,000 miles. So go with the manufacturer's guidelines—you'll save yourself tons of money, time, and hassle.

Introduce Your Car to SAM

You can check your bank balance or pick up cash at an ATM on just about any corner in any town. So why shouldn't you be able to pull your car up to a kiosk and get a full mechanical analysis of your jalopy, too?

Imagine how comforting that would be when your vague-but-alarming "Check Engine" light flashes red on your dashboard. There are *thousands* of things that could trigger that warning light. It might be a niggley little you-can-almost-forget-about-it issue, or it might be a monstrous car-ruining issue.

How nice it would be to drive to a machine at your gas station, hook the machine up to a wire under your dash, and get a specific rundown of your car's ailment—in layman's terms. For, say, a $15 fee you would know whether the problem is urgent or could wait a few weeks, as well as how to talk to your mechanic intelligently about the repair—a refreshing feeling for any of us.

This is the thinking that led to Smart Auto Management (SAM)ˢᴹ. As this book went to press, SAM was being introduced across North America, and rollouts in Europe and Japan weren't far behind. The kiosks are being posted at gas stations, garages, emissions-testing facilities, and other locations.

When it comes to your neighborhood, jump on it. SAM has the potential to turn automobile maintenance on its ear. SAM's inventor, Art Jacobsen of Environmental Systems Products Holdings, likens his product to the consumer empowerment that happened in the health care field when health information became easy to find on the Internet. (Suddenly, patients became fluent in the language of diseases, treatments, and prescriptions.)

Initially, SAM will analyze four critical automobile systems: engine, transmission, antilock brakes, and safety restraints. To do this, it taps into your car's On-Board Diagnostic System—the same technology that mechanics use. Eventually, it will analyze entertainment systems and climate control as well. The service will only work on cars manufactured in 1996 or later, and it won't be able to address car features that require hands-on inspection by a mechanic, such as brake wear or tire tread depth. The SAM folks also will post a web site offering free warranty recall information and subscriptions to technical service bulletins.

SAM is likely to build trust between consumers and mechanics, since it provides an impartial analysis of the car's troubles. It also will revolutionize the used-car market. Savvy sellers will pop for a SAM report and provide copies to potential buyers.

I'm hoping they offer a discount program for repeat users called "Play It Again, SAM."

Monitor your gas mileage. You don't have to be a mechanical genius to monitor your car's performance. All you need is a small notebook and a pen you can leave in the car. Here's how Reed does it: When you fill your tank with gasoline, write down two numbers: the mileage on the odometer and the number of gallons of gas you pumped. Then the next time you fill the tank, record the same numbers. Do the subtraction to find out how many miles you have driven since the last refill. Then divide that mileage figure by the number of gallons you just pumped. (Use the calculator function on your cell phone if that helps.) This figure will tell you how many miles per gallon you just got in your car.

What do you do with this number? Compare it to the miles per gallon promised by the manufacturer. If your mileage is on the mark, that's a good indication that your car is healthy. If you're seriously under the mark, then your car isn't running efficiently— talk to a mechanic. Monitoring your miles per gallon also will inspire you to drive more moderately (avoiding rapid accelerations, for instance), which saves gas.

If you have children, turn this system into a game. Involve them in the record keeping and the math. It will be a good lesson in budgeting and fuel economy.

How to Cheat at Organizing

Join the club. Look at roadside assistance membership as an insurance policy. For a modest fee, you get peace of mind—if your car breaks down, help will be close at hand. Many new cars come with roadside assistance for a set time, so make sure you're aware of what this service covers and when it expires. Then sign up for a travel club such as AAA (the oldest such club—very reliable and highly recommended). Put this protection in the "just do it" category, along with fastening your shoulder harness and eating your vegetables.

Using and Stocking Your Car

If you read *How to Cheat at Cleaning,* then your car is a now a gleaming showpiece inside and out—accomplished with minimal effort. Either that, or your car falls a notch short of a gleaming showpiece, but you're no longer guilt-stricken. The cleanliness of your car and the order of the possessions found inside of it go hand in hand. So let's look at sneaky ways to think about, manage, and use your car.

The Inside Job

If you think about the interior of your car at all, you probably think of it as The Place Where I Operate the Controls. Or perhaps The Place Where I Listen to CDs, or The Place Where I Shout at Bad Drivers. For just 2 minutes, however, think of the interior of your car as The Place Where Things Collect. Think of all of the things that come into your car, says Ali Kaufman, a professional organizer in Boca Raton, Florida. This would include deposit slips from the bank, customer loyalty punch cards, dry cleaner receipts, coupons, car maintenance reports, maps, and even little bits of trash. Assign each item an easily accessible home in your car, decide how you are going to process that item, and decide on a schedule for processing.

Keep this system simple and convenient. For instance, you might say, "I will keep all coupons in an envelope that I store in the driver's side door pocket. After every shopping run, I will discard all of the unused coupons."

If you assign an easily accessible spot to put all of these items, they won't mount up into an unholy heap (you know it's a mess, but you don't dare throw it all out).

Assign homes to the permanent items, too. Just as you assign homes to the incoming items you stash away in your car, you should also assign homes to the handy gear that you stow in the car permanently. This applies to the extra pens, the wipes, your change, the stain stick, the lip balm, and your sunglasses. CD organizers that clip to your visor are a great way to protect your disks and keep them handy (just make sure the design doesn't expose your CDs to direct sunlight). This way, none of these items will be rolling around loose in your car, adding to the detritus. And you'll never waste a second wondering where they are when you need them.

Get the grab-it habit. Five percent of the time that you get out of your car, your hands are totally burdened with the stuff you need to carry

Put an Office in Your Trunk

Barb Friedman, a professional organizer in Milwaukee, Wisconsin, puts together traveling file-drawer kits for real estate agents, and this approach will work swimmingly for anyone who conducts a lot of business while on the road. Go to your office supply store and buy a plastic container, the kind with ridges inside that accommodate hanging file folders. Put the container in your car's trunk, stock it with folders, and slide into those folders every bit of paperwork you need to efficiently conduct your business away from the office—for instance, brochures, blank contracts, and disclosure forms. Also, make a file for each client. Now you don't have to run back to the office for crucial bits of paperwork (or make promises about mailing them), your business arrangements will move along more smoothly, and you'll impress clients with your efficiency. Your container probably will have enough room to hold a few office supplies, too, such as pens and paper clips.

How to Handle Killer Shopping Bags

The handles of heavy shopping bags can feel like they're about to slice right through your skin sometimes. A cushioned grip made to carry several items at once—plastic supermarket bags, other shopping bags, or hanging clothes from the dry cleaners—will remove significant pain from your next errand run. EZcarry™ handles are designed to carry six bags, or 50 pounds, per grip. These ouchless devices are available in supermarkets, drugstores, or over the Internet.

inside—shopping bags, briefcase, gym bag, and a novel. But the other 95 percent of the time, you have at least one hand free, which means you can grab something that doesn't belong in your car and put it in the right place. So develop the "Okay, what can I grab?" habit. When you stop at the gas station, snatch up trash and throw it into the bin. At home, grab up the sweatshirt, tennis balls, and drinking cups that the kids left in the back seat. If you do this routinely, your car will never become an embarrassing rolling trash heap.

Get a handle on paraphernalia. Find a container for your trunk that will keep all of your safety equipment, tools, cleaning stuff, and extra map books from spreading about in a confused mess. Trunk organizers with tons of handy storage compartments are easy to find at auto supply stores, organizer stores, and online. You also can improvise, less expensively, with a heavy plastic crate, a retired gym bag, or some other sturdy container (cardboard won't hold up long term). No matter what kind of trunk organizer you use, make sure it won't slip around on the floor of your trunk. A rubberized bottom will prevent this, or you can affix a couple strips of hook-and-loop fastener material (use the hook side) to the bottom of your organizer so it will grip the trunk's mat.

Put bins in the boot. Put at least three collapsible bins in your trunk to organize all of the items that fly into and out of your automobile daily, says Kaufman. One bin would hold the stuff that you're taking to the office, another is for items you need to take into the house, and yet another contains errand-related items. These bins need to collapse so you can get them out of the way when you want to load groceries or large items into the trunk. You can find a couple of options at The Container Store, such as fabric cylinders called Crunch Cans or Folding Mesh Cubes.

Space-Age Guidance

If you've never driven with a GPS® navigation system, you have at least seen one on television. These are the gizmos that display a small map of where you are going and give you voice directions about where and when to turn. And if you take a wrong turn, it senses that immediately and gives you directions to get back on track. Are such systems worth it? The answer depends on the kind of travel you do, says consumer advice editor Philip Reed. If you drive through unfamiliar territory a lot or if you're directionally challenged, a navigation system will reduce your stress. It also will give you the most expedient routes, saving you time and money.

"It's a different way of thinking about driving," says Reed.

The systems that you buy with a new car, installed by the manufacturer, are pricey—adding about $2,000 to the cost of your chariot. However, they have the advantage of larger map screens, and they're wired directly into your car's sound system.

On the other hand, the portable navigation systems are lightweight and easy to transfer from one car to another. They're less expensive, too—as little as $400. The high-end portables still cost several hundred dollars less than the factory-installed systems. When choosing a portable system, focus on how easy it is to use for its core function—plotting out a route and providing directions. Ignore add-on features, such as the ability to play digital music files.

There's a trick built into navigation systems. For reasons of safety and liability, manufacturers have designed navigation systems so you can't order up directions unless the car is stopped. (If only cell phone makers would follow suit.) However, certain functions are allowed while your car is moving, so there are a couple of ways to request navigation help without pulling over to the side. (But the old rule still applies: Safety first. Let a passenger fiddle with the navigation system while you keep an eye on the road. You don't want to run over somebody's poodle while you're trying to find an intersection on the map.)

Even while the car is moving:

- If your passenger can identify where you want to go on the map screen, he can enter a "place marker" on the map in lieu of entering a specific address. The system will give you directions to that spot.

- Or, let's say you're driving around in unfamiliar territory and you want to know how to get back to the office. Your navigation system probably has several of your most recent locations logged in a "Previous Locations" menu. Have your passenger punch up the right one, and you're on your way.

Call ahead anyway. Navigation systems are wonderful features, but they aren't foolproof. No matter what kind of onboard assistance you have in your car, do your basic research before any trip—get directions and track the route on a map. Call your destination and ask whether Internet services such as MapQuest^{SM} offer reliable directions. If there are any such problems, the people at your destination probably will have heard about it from other travelers.

Add maps to your organizing software. Professional organizer Kaufman swears by a free download that incorporates automatic maps and directions into her PC's Outlook software when she enters meeting destinations. The download, available on the Microsoft® web site, allows you to send maps and directions to other people attending your meeting and to receive traffic updates for the route to your meeting so you'll be sure to arrive on time. To find the program, go to www.microsoft.com and look for Windows® Live Local among the downloads. If getting add-on software for Outlook sounds like a lot of high-tech bother, try this instead: Get your driving directions from MapQuest, e-mail them to yourself, and then cut-and-paste them into your meeting notice on Outlook, Kaufman says.

Miniatures: A Little Goes a Long Way

When you're at home, the everyday products you use—wipes, ketchup, conditioner, snacks, aspirin—come in large packages that sit on the shelf. Perfect: That's economical, and your home can afford the space. In a car, all of that changes. You still have everyday needs to tend to, but your car would be stacked to the ceiling with product packaging if you tried to haul along all of the personal-care products that you want to have available. As with other

ONCE UPON A TIME . . .

Sticky Space Problem Solved

Nobody knows more about packing lightly and tightly than space travelers. To entertain the taste buds of astronauts on the International Space Station, NASA went to the miniature products company Minimus.biz for a variety of condiments. What's in the space station's high-flying pantry? Teensy packets of horseradish sauce, barbeque sauce, cranberry sauce, cocktail sauce, Dijon mustard, orange marmalade, and honey.

Oddly enough, NASA can be finicky about what brands it launches into space. They recently ordered a shipment of Sue Bee® honey packets, but Minimus was out of that brand in its warehouse. The company offered another brand, but NASA said no way. As it turns out, all food products have to be tested for suitability first in NASA's laboratory, and Sue Bee honey was certified as space worthy. So Minimus got a case shipped from the manufacturer overnight.

How to Cheat at Organizing

types of travel, the secret lies in miniatures. Become a big fan of your favorite products in teensy bottles, envelopes, and squeeze tubes. They're often packaged in single-use amounts so there's no spoilage. They save space, they're lightweight, and they're easy to use.

Drugstores have special racks of miniature products, and you can find them sporadically in discount stores and supermarkets. You can snatch them up in hotel rooms (although you'll rarely find your favorite brand). On the Internet, you can find them all clustered in one place, a traveler's wonderland called www.minimus.biz.

The miniatures you stock your car with fall into two categories:

- The items you want at your fingertips while you're driving. Collect these in a small box or zippered pouch you can stash under the seat.

- Emergency items, or other important stuff that you would only use once in a long while. First-aid materials, for instance, and snack food for those times when you're dashing from one meeting to another and have no time for a meal. Store this stuff in the trunk.

Paul Shrater, vice president and cofounder of Minimus, says these are some of his favorite miniature products that work especially well in a car:

Tissues in a cup. Fifty WeGo® facial tissues pop up out of one cup—which is designed, of course, to fit into your cup holder. This makes them particularly handy for nose-blowing and mopping up spills.

Handy hand sanitizer. Shrater keeps a 1-ounce bottle of Purell® hand sanitizer in the armrest console of his car. Smear a few drops of this stuff over your hands just before lunch, and those germs are goners.

No-melt trail mix. The mini-packages of Kar's® unsalted trail mix offer nuts and dried fruit—but no chocolate chips, which will melt in a car's heat and make a mess.

Stain saver. When you dribble barbeque sauce onto your skirt, an individually wrapped Shout® wipe will get you office-presentable again.

Minimus also sells various car travel kits that will outfit you with such micro-products as hot-pepper sauce, snacks, toilet paper, wipes, paper towels, disinfectant, a light stick, an emergency blanket, first-aid gear, over-the-counter medicines, a poncho, duct tape, a sewing kit, coffee, antiperspirant, a toothbrush, and a disposable camera.

Now you're armed with the cheatingest car advice to be found. Implement these measures a little at a time, and your auto anxieties will melt away. Remember, organizing your car is not about alphabetizing the paperwork in your glove box. Instead, you'll measure your success by how you feel in your heart as your car becomes a place of ease and driving comfort.

Chapter Thirteen

Special Events

Travel, Entertaining, and Holidays

U P TO NOW, we've been discussing ways to cheat at organizing your everyday life—rooms of the house, your family, food preparation, finances, your desk, storage, and your car. The special events in our lives, such as vacations and celebrations, are fraught with complexities and frustrations as well, particularly when we fall victim to the mantra "We've always done it this way." Here are fresh ways of looking at these special times—how to organize the things that are important as simply as possible, and how to dispense with the things that aren't important. All 100 percent guilt-free, of course.

5 Steps to a Hassle-Free Trip

Travel ought to be fun and carefree, says New Yorker Pauline Frommer. She's had a little time to think about this, having grown up as the daughter of renowned travel guru Arthur Frommer. She's also the creator of her own line of budget-oriented travel guides.

The key to making your travel carefree lies in a handful of easy preparations you can take care of well in advance.

Check your insurance. Many travelers either buy insurance that's not necessary or ignore the kind of insurance that's a good idea. First, find out what coverage you already have—for instance, what your car and homeowner's policies already cover and what protections are offered by your credit card. You might discover that your homeowner's policy covers loss of luggage or other possessions, and that your car policy or credit card covers rental cars, so you don't need to pay that add-on fee. Find out whether your health insurance covers you in exotic locales, and explore whether you should have a medical evacuation policy for such destinations. (If you're traveling in Africa and meet with a health disaster, evacuating you could cost $40,000 to $50,000, for example.) Go to www.insuremy trip.com for a good primer on travel-related insurance. One kind of insurance you surely don't need, says Frommer, is flight insurance. The odds against your flight crashing are so great that such policies are of little value.

Buy a guidebook or two. Okay, this is not very surprising coming from a guidebook maven, but the advice is wise nevertheless: Investigate the geography of your intended destination and make sure your travel schedule is reasonable. Many enthusiastic travelers map out an overly ambitious itinerary. Thus they spend too much time in transit and too little time enjoying the location.

List everything you want to take before you pack. When you study a packing list, it's easier to limit the amount of stuff you take with you. And packing lightly translates directly into flexibility and freedom, Frommer says.

Read books set in your destination. Don't limit your travel research to guidebooks. Read history, art history, and even historical novels set in your vacation spot. "You'll have a stake in what you're seeing," Frommer says. This advice applies to children as well as adults. For instance, she read Irish myths to her children before a trip to Ireland.

Explore booking options. Frommer is a fan of Internet sites that comparison shop for you. They search the web for the best deals in transportation and lodging and present the information in one place. Unlike other travel web sites, these "aggregator" sites or "travel search engines," as they are called, do not charge users a fee—although they do typically get kickbacks from the hotels and airlines. Browse www.sidestep.com, www.kayak.com, www.mobissimo.com, and www.cheapflights.com.

Reading Up and Reserving

I know you're rarin' to go, but we have just a tiny bit more homework that will make your travels smooth sailing.

Cruising? Book your own side trips. Many of us think the price of a cruise includes all activities. However, the off-the-boat excursions usually cost extra, and the cruise lines charge hefty fees for them. There are a couple of ways to have fun onshore and also keep a lot of money in your pocket. Before the cruise, contact the tourist boards for the destinations where you will be docking. When you make arrangements for your own adventures, you can be sure that you won't find yourself shoulder-to-shoulder with hundreds of folks from your ship. You also can just take the ship's shuttle to the dock, where you will inevitably find people offering excursions for far less than your shipmates just paid. Another alternative: Hire a cab for a day to drive you around. These approaches will easily save you 50 percent or more over the cruise line's prices.

One caution: Keep an eye on your watch. If a group from the official cruise excursion gets held up, the ship will wait. If you're on your own and you get held up, you've missed the boat, as they say.

Find government web sites. If you are researching your next vacation on the Internet, make sure that you find the official, government-run web site for the location you're interested in. Government sites are reliable and often give extensive listings. Many other web sites make a great effort to appear "official" but may actually have commercial backing—which means they offer skewed content, says Laurie Borman, the Chicago-based editorial director for Rand McNally®. Always click on the "About" section of any travel web site so you are clear about who's behind the information you're reading. Another clue: An abundance of ads is an indication that you're looking at a commercial site.

For reservations, make a direct check. You may be a veteran of the online travel sites, but whenever you are making a transportation or hotel reservation, also check directly with the web site of the airline or hotel you want to book. These businesses have become determined not to be undercut, says Borman, and you might be surprised by how much money you can save with a direct reservation. So make your hunt a two-pronged effort: travel web sites *and* a direct check.

Look beyond the road maps. You probably think of the road atlas in your car as a handy book of maps—which is true as far as it goes. However, if you flip through the front and back pages of your atlas you will discover some resources that could help you out of a jam the next time you drive long distance. The listing of toll-free numbers for hotel chains and car rental companies is an example. Imagine rolling into a city at 11 p.m., dead tired and hoping to find a hotel room—only to discover that a Shriners convention has snapped up every bed. With a call or two on your cell phone, you will quickly be able to locate the nearest available room and reserve it. So open up your road atlas now and review the handy information it offers besides maps.

What the Professionals Pack

Now let's take a look at the handy items that veteran travelers add to their suitcases. (I know *you* have already committed Chapter 3 to memory, but for casual browsers, I'll mention that you'll find super tips for packing clothing there.)

Be ready for repair jobs. Stuff a few small, versatile items into a zip-closing plastic bag to rescue you from the myriad emergencies that travelers confront. Rand McNally's Laurie Borman recommends taking along rubber bands, safety pins, twisty-ties, and tape. Use them to fix falling hems, to hold business cards together, to secure clothing that you have rolled up, and to repair eyeglasses.

Corral those receipts. Keeping a business traveler's receipts organized during an extended trip is always an organizational challenge. Little bits of paper wind up everywhere, stuffed into various pockets and compartments, and by the end of the trip, recalling what they were all for is next to impossible.

Here is Borman's simple solution: Find an oversize envelope (she uses a 5- by 11-inch manila envelope). Go to your computer and use your word-processing program or your spreadsheet program to create a grid that's the same size as the envelope. Write the days of the week across the top and the categories of your common travel expenses down the side (meals, lodging, cabs, and incidentals, for

GREAT GEAR

This Vase Takes No Space

If you have more than one night's stay in the same hotel room, a handful of fresh flowers from a street vendor will really brighten up your temporary digs. The problem is finding a vase. A folding travel vase will save the day. This device starts out looking like a plastic envelope. Pour warm water into it to make it pliable, shape it into vase form, pour cold water into it, and drop your flowers in. When it's time to pack up, you rinse the vase out and fold it flat again. Buy travel vases where travel accessories are sold, or search the Internet.

How to Address Writer's Cramp

When you're traveling, you find yourself writing out your address again and again—on luggage tags, on liability forms, and on hotel registration cards. Sidestep that case of writer's cramp by taking along preprinted name-and-address stickers, says Laurie Borman, editorial director at Rand McNally. You can either use those labels that come in the mail from organizations that seek donations, or you can have your own printed up. While you're at it, go to your computer and print out a sheet of address labels for all of the people you will want to write to while you're on the road. Those labels will turn a time-burning chore into a peel-and-stick pleasure.

instance). Print this out and paste it to your envelope. (If you're really handy with the computer, you might figure out how to print directly onto the face of the envelope.) While you're traveling, slip your receipts into the envelope each night and jot your expenses for the day in each category on the grid. When the trip is over, your expense report will already be done and the receipts will all be in one place.

Cord control made easy. Being a modern traveler means you have a certain number of electrical cords in tow—detachable wires for your laptop, your camera, your cell phone, and a number of other devices. Like so many other travel accessories, your cords are probably black and therefore hard to find in the bottom of a backpack. Borman's solution: Find a drawstring bag in a high-visibility color (hers is pink) to contain all of your cords. They'll all be in one place and easy to find.

Take a little light. No traveler should be without a mini-flashlight. It's handy for reading in bed, for finding your way to the bathroom in the dark, and for finding small items that are eluding you in the dark bottom of a backpack. If you have high self-esteem and don't mind looking a tad dorky, take the kind of light that straps to your forehead on an elastic band (available at camping stores). It leaves both of your hands free for such tasks as holding a book, carrying gear, and looking for lost objects.

Downsize your bottles. Visit a camping store or a travel supply store and pick up several tiny bottles for all of the personal care products you take on the road with you, says Misha Keefe, a professional organizer in Washington, D.C. Transfer your skin lotion, shampoo, conditioner, and other liquids to these little bottles and collect them all in a small toilet kit. Leaving the original product bottles at home will reduce the volume of stuff in your suitcase and lighten the load.

Keep fit with stretch bands. If you're traveling for more than a day or two, you're going to feel like a slug—and look like one, for that matter—if you don't keep up with your exercise program. One of

Take a Snapshot of Your Suitcase

With increased security in our transportation systems, it's more likely that your checked luggage will be opened and inspected. It's nice to know your airplane is safer—but it's also reasonable to worry that your personal possessions might disappear when your suitcase is opened and closed multiple times by strangers. Dali Wiederhoft, a public relations executive in Reno, Nevada, has the solution.

When she has finished packing for a trip, she lays her suitcase open and takes a photo of it with her digital camera. She makes sure to include in the photo any expensive electronic gear that's in the suitcase. She makes a large color printout of the snapshot and lays that across the top of the packed items, tapes her business card inside, and adds a note: "Suitcase and contents inventoried before departure." No one opening *that* luggage will get a case of "sticky fingers."

Space Squeeze?
Get a Compression Bag

If you've ever had to sit on a suitcase to get it closed, you need a compression bag. Here's how they work: Put your clothes inside the plastic bag, roll them up firmly, and all of the air inside is forced out a one-way valve. The bag and your clothes stay squashed flat, creating extra elbow room inside your suitcase. Oddly enough, compression bags also reduce wrinkling.

Laurie Borman, editorial director at Rand McNally, likes to pack an empty compression bag when she starts a trip. When she's on her way home again, she packs her dirty clothes into the compression bag. This way, the dirty clothes are separated from her clean ones, and there's extra space in the suitcase for any souvenirs or other items she has bought.

Look for these gizmos where you buy travel accessories. Make sure that what you're getting is a plastic "air compression travel bag," not one of those fabric bags meant for compressing a sleeping bag.

the best ways to exercise on the road: Take along a set of rubber exercising bands, says Rand McNally's Laurie Borman. They're lightweight, compact, and great for strength training. Here are some more fitness-on-the-road tips:

- Check out your hotel's fitness facilities the moment you arrive. You might be surprised at how inviting they are. Knowing a great gym is available will inspire you to stick to your exercise routine.

- Ask the concierge to recommend a safe running or walking route. Sometimes they have maps. At the very least, they will be able to give you directions.

- If you exercise in the evening, just leave your workout clothes on and wear them as your pajamas. You get fewer garments dirty that way. Quick-drying garments work best for this, naturally.

- No matter where you're traveling to, always take a swimsuit. Even in the winter, you never know when you'll encounter a hot tub or indoor pool.

Once You Get There

Enough about trip preparation. Now we get to what travel is all about—enjoying yourself once you arrive at your destination. There are plenty of ways to cut corners here, too.

Get lost. It sounds odd coming from a travel author, but Pauline Frommer is a big fan of getting lost. By getting lost, she doesn't mean wandering about the wilderness without food or water; rather, she means exploring your travel destination without an agenda. You may have booked tickets for a museum exhibit, for instance, but leave the rest of the day open to walk the streets and discover a street fair or a café that's jammed with engaging locals. Pick up the local free paper and scan its event listings—dance performances and poetry slams, for instance. Stroll the neighborhoods around a nearby university, where there are bound to be a host of unusual shops, restaurants, clubs, and galleries.

Start your day at a good clip. A small, magnetized, spring-loaded paper clasp will help you organize your daily comings and goings while you're traveling, says Rand McNally editorial director Laurie Borman. Go to your office supply store and pick up the kind of clasp that has a magnetic base, made for holding slips of paper against a filing cabinet or a refrigerator. If your hotel room's door is metal, affix the clasp to it. Before you go to bed each night, write yourself reminders about what you need to take with you the next day.

(This is a particular help if you're walking out the door without your morning dose of caffeine.) Also clip to it any tickets you'll need and any relevant pages you have ripped out of a guidebook.

Grab lunch at the grocery. You don't need an organizing book to tell you to visit museums, galleries, and historic sites when you travel. However, one of the sneakiest ways to experience the local culture is to buy your lunch every day at a grocery store. Why? The supermarket is where the local folks buy their food, so you will have a vast array of unusual delectables at your fingertips. Besides, both your taste buds and your wallet quickly tire of three meals a day at restaurants. To make this trick work smoothly, always carry a plastic fork and spoon in your backpack or purse. One of Borman's fondest travel memories involves buying lunch at a grocery store in Ireland and taking it to a park for a perfect day of eating and people watching. So drop into a grocery store during your travels if you really want to experience some of the local, uh . . . flavor.

SLEIGHT OF HAND

Snap Up That Shower Cap

Get in the habit of picking up those free shower caps you find in hotel rooms and slipping them into your carry-on bag. They're lightweight, they take up little space, and they are extremely handy. When your shoes get dirty, put them inside a shower cap so they don't get the rest of your clothes dirty in the suitcase, says Laurie Borman, editorial director at Rand McNally. On an airplane, take off your shoes and pull a shower cap over each foot—instant slippers! (Secure with a rubber band, if necessary.) When you're taking photos in the rain, wrap a shower cap around the body of your camera, with the lens extending through the opening. When you're packing but your bathing suit is still wet, wrap it up in a shower cap. Oh, yeah—they'll also keep your hair dry in the shower.

Don't leave "home" without the hotel's card. When you register at a hotel, pick up one of the establishment's business cards at the counter and slide it into your wallet. With that thin little slip of cardboard in your possession, you will never be lost while you're out and about, says Borman. If a cab driver doesn't understand your pronunciation of the hotel's name, just show the card, and you're on your way. Furthermore, if you're switching locations every day or two, there's a good chance that you'll forget the name of your current hotel.

Dump your photos daily. If you're taking lots of digital photos every day during your travels, upload your snapshots nightly to an online photo service (www.kodakgallery.com, www.photoaccess. com, www.shutterfly.com, or www.snapfish.com, for instance). This way, you will start each day with a clean memory card and will have no fear of maxing out its capacity, says Borman, the editorial director at Rand McNally. What's more, should your camera get lost or damaged, most of your travel photos will still be secure.

Take your money swimming. Canoe enthusiasts have long known the wisdom of "dry packs," waterproof tote bags that keep your possessions dry in inherently wet situations. Mini versions of the dry pack are a great travel accessory anytime you're going to be near open water, says Borman. When she swims on the beach, Borman likes to wear a belted dry pack that holds her hotel key and money—thus solving that old security quandary when you have to leave valuables on the sand. Other models will protect your camera, iPod, sandwich, and paperback novel. Visit an outdoor provisioner to find a wide variety of dry packs.

Carry a "peace" offering. When you're traveling, you never know when you might need to make friends with a little person—or at least keep a fussy one occupied long enough that you can catch a nap. So Borman keeps a couple of lightweight and compact items handy in a pocket of her travel backpack: a foldable fabric Frisbee® and a container of Silly Putty®. If you get seated next to a rambunctious youngster on an airplane and the kid's parents haven't brought enough gear to keep him entertained, whip out the Silly Putty and close your eyes. You've bought yourself 25 minutes of peace.

With kids, pick one central spot. Some vacations involve traveling to a different location every day. That requires a lot of packing and unpacking—which is no problem as long as every traveler can manage his or her own possessions. However, if you're traveling with small children, an aggressive itinerary will drive the adults crazy because the youngsters can't do their own packing and hauling, says professional organizer Misha Keefe. If you're taking little kids on vacation, give yourself a break—choose one great place to stay and satisfy your family with short day trips.

At Your Best with Guests

You're home from your travels. You're rested. And now it's time for a different kind of adventure—right under your own roof. The success or failure of a party in your home depends on subtleties that your guests are probably never aware of. It doesn't matter whether you left a speck of dust on a picture frame or whether you slaved in the kitchen for 7 hours making the appetizers. What does matter is how comfortable your guests feel in the space devoted to the party—whether they can circulate freely and have easy access to food, drink, and conversation. If you master these elements, nobody will care that your appetizers really came from the frozen food aisle of the supermarket.

Creating a Comfort Zone

Most people are clueless about arranging space and traffic flow at a party, says Melody Davidson, cofounder of Design Yourself Interiors in Prairie Village, Kansas. These factors may sound like subtle-

ties, but they're crucial considerations for making your guests feel comfortable.

- Leave at least 3 feet of space between any two major pieces of furniture—42 inches is better.

- In the dining room, leave at least 3 feet between the edge of the dining table and the wall or the nearest piece of furniture.

- Arrange your sofa, loveseat, and a couple of chairs in a circle. You need 5 to 7 feet of space between the front edges of the furniture. This way, when people sit they will be able to talk with the people sitting across from them. The "let's all face the TV" daily living arrangement won't do for a party.

- Pull the chairs away from the dining table and place them elsewhere for guests to use. Don't just line them up against the wall, however. Work them into furniture groupings around the house in a way that encourages conversation.

- Never put a chair alone in the corner. The person who sits there will immediately be cut off from party conversation. You might as well toss that poor soul into solitary confinement.

Expand your party space. When you're entertaining a crowd, don't forget about the "extensions" of your house—the garage, porch, patio, deck, gazebo, or pool area. Depending upon the weather, any of these spots can be easily converted into additional party space. For example, we know of one homeowner who turned his garage into a mini-casino, which became the most popular spot of the party. Another homeowner erected a tent above his back deck, stationed a DJ at one end, and positioned tables on the surrounding lawn, nightclub-style.

Decentralize the food. If you have only one food spread at your party, people will cluster near it and will be reluctant to circulate. Instead, place food trays in multiple locations in your home so people won't feel compelled to linger in one spot, says Laura Leist, an organization and productivity consultant in Mill Creek, Washington. Make sure each tray has a sampling of all of the food that's available.

Let glasses show your class. Interior designer Davidson likes to have special-occasion dishware and accessories do double duty as a decorative touch in the home—even when there's no party on the calendar. For example, she had a client put a beautiful silver tray on the coffee table. On the tray, she arranged martini glasses. When she has guests, they can just pick up one of the glasses and get it filled at the bar. When she's not entertaining, she can leave the martini glass arrangement on display—and she doesn't have to find cabinet storage for them.

Split up the entertaining gear. Don't try to store in the same place every single piece of equipment you use for entertaining. Instead, split these materials up according to event, says Ali Kaufman, a professional organizer in Boca Raton, Florida. For instance, you might have all of your formal stuff together—the beautiful serving trays and nice wineglasses—in a hutch in the dining room. However, the informal ware you use for the kids in the backyard—plastic plates and paper cups—can go in an outdoor storage locker, the shed, or the pool house. "Keep like occasions with like occasions," she says.

Instant Accommodations for Overnight Guests

Got more overnight visitors than you have beds? Ever find yourself less than pleased with the sleeping accommodations when you're away from home? For just these emergencies, the astute cheater-at-organizing stocks one or two of the modern inflatable beds in a hallway closet. Just plug one of these beds into an outlet (or use the battery option), and it unrolls itself and inflates in 45 seconds to 3 minutes, depending on the model. These are not the thin little camping pads that leave you achy and creaky in the morning. You get a full-size bed with support much like a conventional mattress.

Inflatable beds have a broad range of uses, says Kurt Owen, the senior director of marketing for AeroBeds®:

- when kids have a sleepover

- when the house is crammed full of guests for Thanksgiving

- when you're staying with friends who have dismal accommodations

- when you want to save space in a dorm room, deflating your bed in the morning and inflating it again at night

- when you have a lake house, a beach house, or a vacation cabin that attracts swarms of visitors

Owen offers these tips for using air beds:

Soften up, if you want. If the feel of your inflatable bed isn't just right, you can push a button to soften it a tad or turn the pump on again to firm it up.

Store it with the sheets. The typical AeroBed collapses down to a package about the size of a sleeping bag in its drawstring container. The carry bag that comes with it is oversize, which means there's enough room left over for sheets in there, too, when you're putting the bed away. You'll have everything together the next time you need it.

Yes, Happy Holidays *Are* Achievable

No wonder so many people get depressed around the holidays. Culturally, we expect a season of festivity and good cheer. In reality, we pack just a few weeks with so much mind-numbing drudge work (gift buying, feast making, cookie baking, card writing, and light stringing) that we all feel like Grinches. Except that the Grinch, that lucky devil, wasn't burdened with guilt about not feeling jolly.

Surveys support this. Half of the population lists gift buying as the top stressor around the holidays, says San Diego's Marcia Ramsland, a.k.a. "The Organizing Pro." Decorating the home and sending holiday cards are tied for the number two position.

So for the next holiday season, give yourself a gift. Lighten the workload and deep-six the guilt. Make some fundamental changes in how you celebrate. Don't worry: You can observe traditions and preserve your sanity at the same time. Here's how.

Just a Little Prep Work

Americans typically view Thanksgiving as a big signpost on the calendar, indicating that it's time to get serious about preparing for December's festivities. But that's a trap, notes Ramsland. Sometimes Thanksgiving occurs $3\frac{1}{2}$ weeks before Christmas; sometimes it's $4\frac{1}{2}$ weeks before Christmas. That 1-week difference is enormous, and if you're not aware of the tight schedule in such years, you're going to feel like you've been smacked in the head with a Yule log. Instead, start laying out your holiday plans right after Halloween—you'll get a reliable 8 weeks every time.

Get a big leap on decorating. It's a shame to invest money and effort into holiday decorations that are only on display for 2 weeks before they're taken down again. Here's an approach that will ease the pressure on your holiday planning and help you get more mileage out of your favorite decorations. Identify what one or two features lie at the core of your holiday decorating—perhaps it's a Christmas tree, or perhaps yard lights turn you on (sorry). Whatever this central item is, get it out and installed 4 weeks in advance of the big day. This removes a significant chore from the hectic week or two before Christmas. It also gives you the sense that only the decorating chores remain. (And if you skip them completely, who cares?) If it feels too early to be turning on Christmas lights, just leave them off for a while.

Yard lights? Cool it. Christmas light mania turns many a jolly ol' homeowner into a Scrooge. Quit trying to compete with the neighbors' light displays, and show your independent streak. From an artistic standpoint, an "elegant minimum" is all you really need, says professional organizer Misha Keefe—a simple strand of lights in a small tree, for instance. If you do display masses of lights in your yard, use nothing but the newer net style of light strings. They cover a lot of area and are easy to install and take down.

Try hands-off holiday cards. Have an online photo service print up your holiday cards for you. All you have to do is supply a family snapshot from summer vacation and select one of the easy

SLEIGHT OF HAND

Your Helpers Will See the Light

Marcia Ramsland, a professional organizer in San Diego, California, has figured out how to get her outdoor holiday lights put up without lifting a finger. On the day after Thanksgiving, she pulls together the males in her family, points out the storage boxes of lights, and gives them a choice: They may string up the lights, or they may go shopping with her—on the busiest day known to American merchandisers. So inevitably the lights get put up, even though she doesn't actually turn them on until the first or second week of December. A little mild extortion now and then works wonders!

templates provided by the service, says Keefe. Even better: Select a service that will mail the cards for you, so you never struggle with addressing, stamps, and running to the post office. You just supply the names and addresses of the recipients.

Make the mailing manageable. If you're a traditionalist and feel a strong need to send out holiday cards, at the very least make the project easier, says San Diego professional organizer Marcia Ramsland. For instance, whittle the list down every year so you're only sending cards to people who most appreciate them. Cross off anyone on your mailing list who hasn't reciprocated in the last 3 years. Also, quit handwriting those addresses. Machine-printed labels are now perfectly acceptable, so manage your mailing list on the home computer and print out the address labels each year.

A Gift to Yourself: Easy Shopping

Even if you're the "born to shop" type of person, give yourself a break leading up to the holidays—you have enough going on in your life. Try these angst-free ways of giving gifts.

Look for clutter-free gifts. Not many of us actually need more objects in our lives, which makes gift giving a terrible quandary. How did the holidays become a time when I shovel clutter into your home while you shovel different clutter into mine? Keefe's solution is to give gifts that take up zero space. For instance, buy a friend a gift certificate for a manicure or tickets to a sporting event.

Recycle that gift idea. Quit racking your brain and running from store to store, searching for the "perfect" gift for each of the 15 friends and neighbors you shop for. Relax and buy them all the same tasteful thing, says Keefe. "Nothing beats a bottle of wine or a box of truffles," she says. Besides, what are you afraid of—that all of your friends and neighbors will get together and compare gifts? Doesn't happen.

Stick to online shopping. Do as much of your gift giving as possible through online businesses that will wrap a holiday gift for you and ship it directly to the recipient, says Keefe. Yes, it costs a little extra, and yes, shipments can go afoul now and then. However, by shopping and shipping your gifts online, you don't have to wonder where the cellophane tape has gotten to, there's no need to wrestle with those rolls of wrapping paper, and you don't have to stand in the post office line with 27 other people who are hefting stacks of boxes to be mailed. Amazon.com^{SM}, for instance, allows you to combine books, toys, tools, CDs, and clothing all into one shipment. If picking gifts off the Internet feels impersonal to you, get over it. We're cheating, remember?

In the end, the surest measure of a successful trip—or party, or holiday celebration—is whether you were able to bask in the experience with an unburdened mind. If you prepared for what was important and shrugged off the rest, congratulations! You can honestly say that you have cheated your way to the good life.

Index

managing college budgets, 192–93
monitoring spending, 133, 134–36
paying bills on line and on time,
137–40
retirement strategies with, 145–49
teaching kids basics of, 188–89
Fish, 63
Flashlights, 274–75
Flexibility/stretch training, 230
Food:
building meal menus, 66
children assisting with shopping, 58
chopping and cutting of, 80–81
delivery option for, 64
eat first, then shopping for, 60–61
essential pantry items of, 78–79
good nutrition with, 221–28
list for shopping, 56–58
for parties, 282
shopping/buying, 55–67
speed "scratch cooking" of, 59–64
storing and preparing, 67–86
Formal dining rooms, converting
function of, 11
Fruits, 225, 228
Furniture, measuring and best use of,
13–16, 19

G

Garages:
core uses of, 96, 97–100
mapping out storage in, 94–100
Garden tools, 97–98
Gifts:
holiday ideas for, 286–87
unwanted, 96
"Go somewhere basket," 19
GPS navigation systems, 264–66
Grocery shopping, 55–67
Guests, overnight, 283

H

Happiness, steps to, 240–43
Headphones, wireless, 26
Health:

confronting serious medical
problems, 238–39
exercise options in, 228–34
good nutrition with, 221–28
keeping own medical records,
235–37
list of questions for MD, 236–37
managing/reducing stress, 243–46
mental/emotional well being in,
239–46
resources and references on, 247
routine screenings for, 235
SHOK (Salad Helping OverKill) diet
in, 223–25
simplifying steps to, 220–49
using vitamins, 228
weight-loss plans for, 221–28
working with doctors for, 234–39
See also Nutrition
Herbs, cold storage of, 76–77
HIRE principle, 9, 100, 151
Holidays:
decorations, storage of, 98
planning/preparing for, 284–87
Home equity line of credit, 144
Home offices:
banking/business accounts in, 144
computerized contact lists, 130–32
controlling paper clutter, 119–23
defining/scheduling productive
times, 117
efficient arrangement of, 118–119
filing systems in, 119–23
managing e-mails, telephone calls
and messages, 109–116
reducing distractions in, 116–17
Homework, 188
Housecleaning, 175

I

Ideas, writing down, 252
"In box," clearing and organizing,
165–66
Infants, managing gear and clothing for,
182–86

Insurance:
    reviewing and assessing needs for,
        149–150
    travel-related, 270
Internet, 131, 132, 167, 193, 247, 267
Investments:
    advisors for, 148
    401K programs in, 147–49

J

Jeans, 37
Junk mail, 7, 10, 18, 21

K

Keep One rule, 9, 209
    401K investment, 147–49
Kitchens:
    counter space in, 68
    storing food in, 55–86
    tools for, 67–73
    See also Food, storing and preparing;
        Pantry, organizing and stocking of
Knits, storage of, 44

L

Labels, 27
Laptop computers, 167, 275
Laundry, 191
Licenses, renewing, 52
License to Cheat at Organizing, 8
Life, long-term goals in, 166
Life insurance, 150–151
List(s):
    food shopping with, 56–58
    for suitcase packing, 270–71
    of to-do and tasks, 157–58, 245–46
Living spaces, best use of, 11–19
Loans, strategies for, 145–49, 187

M

Magazines, 19–22
Materials On a Program (MOP), 13–14
Meat, cold storage of, 75
Meat thermometers, 86
Media, organizing and storing, 19–27

Medicine cabinets, updating and
    organizing, 246–49
Meditation, 244
Meetings, organizing, 124, 200–202
Mental/emotional health, 239–46
"Me time," steps to, 239–46
Milk, cold storage of, 75
Mise en place, 80–81
Moving and storage services, 103–107

N

Nutrition:
    dining with awareness, 227–28
    low-fat cooking in, 227
    managing stress with, 245
    quality and seasonal items in,
        225–28
    reading labels and, 226
    using unprocessed foods, 225–28

O

"One-in, one-out" rule, 196, 212
Online photo services, 205
Organizational skills, importance of, 123
Organizing:
    mental challenges of, 4
    simplicity in, 4
    S4 technique of, 6
Organizing software, 112
Outdoor grilling, 84–86

P

Packing envelopes for travel, 49
Pantry, organizing and stocking of,
    77–80
Paper, clutter control systems for,
    119–23
Parties, planning/preparing for, 280–82
Pedometers, 230
Personal calendars, 171–72
Personal digital assistants (PDAs), 114,
    158–62
Photographs:
    archival storage of, 204–206
    collecting, 218